OCCASIONAL PUBLICATION no. 7

Hodson's
Booksellers, Publishers and Stationers
Directory
1855

A FACSIMILE OF THE COPY IN THE

BODLEIAN LIBRARY, OXFORD

With an Introduction
by
GRAHAM POLLARD

Oxford Bibliographical Society
Bodleian Library
Oxford
1972

SBN 901420 06 9

printed by SCOLAR PRESS LTD.
MENSTON, YORKSHIRE, U.K.

INTRODUCTION

OTHER BOOK TRADE DIRECTORIES

In 1872 Kelly & Co. published the first edition of *The Post Office Directory of Stationers, Printers, Booksellers, Publishers, and Paper Makers of England, Scotland, Wales, and the Principal Towns in Ireland*; and they kept it up to date with new editions at three or four year intervals until 1939. This substantial series provides a satisfactory means for checking the existence and approximate dates of even the smallest firms in the book trade over the years from 1872 to 1939.

But this sort of information is notably less accessible for the years before 1872. There are only three earlier national directories of the book trade:

(i)   *The London and Country Printers, Booksellers and Stationers Vade Mecum*, 1785. This was compiled by John Pendred; and the only copy known was acquired by the Bodleian Library in 1895 (pressmark: Vet. A.5.g.5). It was reprinted by the Bibliographical Society in 1955.

(ii) *Hodson's Booksellers Publishers and Stationers' Directory for London and Country*, 1855. Here reprinted from the Bodleian copy (pressmark: Dir. 2581.e.23). The only other copy known is in the British Museum. (pressmark: P.P.2495.aka).

(iii) *A Directory of Manufacturing, Wholesale, and Retail Publishers, Booksellers, Papermakers, Stationers, Printers, Bookbinders, Music-Sellers, Photographers, Perfumers, and all Dealers in Fancy Goods, Toys, &c. Presented to the Subscribers of 'The Stationer and Fancy Trades Register'*. Vol I. England. London, Dean & Son, 65 Ludgate Hill. E.C. This title-page occurs with the advertisements in the issue for 1 November 1866, and is followed by six pages of names for Manchester, arranged alphabetically from A to J. The December issue continues the Manchester names from J to T (on two leaves paginated 7-10); and the remainder of the Manchester section is included in the issue for January 1867. The directory is continued for twelve years until July 1878, when it comes to an end in Ireland with County Sligo. It is arranged roughly by counties in alphabetical order. London is not included. Each monthly part usually contains only two pages. A directory of paper mills (with the mill numbers) begins in August 1878.

This directory, though not at all convenient to consult, gives much information about the smaller firms in associated trades such as music selling and photography, and fills in the years immediately preceding Kelly's first edition of 1872.

The five volumes of the Bibliographical Society dictionaries of booksellers, chiefly edited by H.R. Plomer, end at 1775; and it is 97 years before the Kelly series begins. Pendred was printed in 1785, and no other directory of the book trade appeared until this directory by W.H. Hodson seventy years later. These gaps can to some extent be filled by reference to lists of particular sections within the book trade, to general trade directories, and to local directories. The trade lists and the relevant general trade directories covering this period were set out in the Appendix to the reprint of Pendred. The London directories from 1677 to 1855 were listed by C.W.F. Goss (Denis Archer, 1932); and those outside London by Miss J.E. Norton, *Guide to the National and Provincial Directories of England and Wales,* Royal Historical Society, 1950.

THE BOOKSELLERS' COMMUNICATION AGENCY

The Booksellers' Communication Agency which published the directory here reprinted does not seem to have lasted long. In the preliminary address dated July 1855 the manager, William Henry Hodson, says that 'upwards of twelve months have been expended in compiling the book.' So that work on it would have started early in the summer of 1854. The only other information about the firm comes from the annual editions of Kelly's *Post Office London Directory.* Each year consists of three parts, arranged by streets, by trades, and by names in alphabetical order. There were usually two issues each year, the first with the preface dated the previous November, the second normally dated the following March. For the period which concerns us, the March issue consisted of the November sheets: the preliminary pages are changed, but the main text is unaltered. We may therefore infer that the text pages of both issues went to press shortly before November, and that the appearance of a name at an address in (say) the 1855 edition of Kelly means that the person named was there shortly before November 1854. The editions of Kelly's *Post Office London Directory* give:

1854 [Nov. 1853] No relevant names in any section.

1855 [Nov. 1854] Booksellers' Registration Society, 20 Paternoster Row. Wm. Henry Hodson, manager. Matthew Orr, secretary. In all three sections.

1855 [March 1855] has the same information as [Nov. 1854]

1856 [Nov. 1855] Booksellers' Communication Agency, 20 Paternoster Row. Wm. Henry Hodson, manager. In all three sections.

1857 [Nov. 1856] Booksellers' Communication Agency, 20 Paternoster Row. Wm. Henry Hodson, manager. In the alphabetical section, but no entries in the Street or Trade sections.

1857 [delayed until 26 May 1857] has the same information as in [Nov. 1856].

1858 [Nov. 1857] No relevant names in any section.

Thus it appears that the firm was founded as The Booksellers' Registration Society in the summer of 1854 with William Henry Hodson as manager and Matthew Orr as secretary. The name of the firm was changed to The Booksellers' Communication Agency, and Matthew Orr the secretary dropped out before July, 1855, when the Directory was published. The second edition of the Directory which, in his preface to the first edition, W.H. Hodson had promised for January 1856, probably never materialised; and the firm itself came to an end before November 1856.

The firm, then, was short-lived: without substantial resources; and probably occupying no more than a small office on the premises of Messrs Remnant, Edmond, and Remnants, the edition binders, who occupied 9-12 Lovell's Court over the years 1854-58. Nothing is known about either W.H. Hodson or Matthew Orr except their connexion with the Booksellers' Registration Society. Its only interest is the Directory, which provokes three questions:

(i)   How did W.H. Hodson obtain the information for it?

(ii) What was his object in printing it? and

(iii) What sort of business was the Booksellers' Registration Society formed to carry on?

THE SOURCES OF HODSON'S DIRECTORY

The business was started under the title The Booksellers' Registration Society, which implies that a register of booksellers was maintained; and such a register may have been the nucleus of the material from which the Directory was later printed. William Henry Hodson clearly knew the booktrade, and was known to the trade. He had probably been a traveller or a clerk for one of the London wholesale houses. In his preface he thanks not only influential members of the Trade for their assistance, but the Postmasters of Great Britain 'for their promptitude in replying to my enquiries.' We may thus suppose that Hodson sorted out on a local basis the names he had already, added any further names which he could obtain from his acquaintance in the publishing world, and circulated these lists to the local postmasters with a request that they would check them and add any omissions. It is a considerable and surprising achievement to have gathered over six thousand names in this way. Pendred in 1785 contains about 1500 names: Kelly in 1872 more than 15,000.

THE MARKET FOR IT

The preface to the Directory is called 'ADDRESS TO THE TRADE,' and its first sentence begins: 'In submitting the first edition to the Trade . . .' Hodson thus makes it quite clear that he intended the Directory to be of use to the book trade rather than to the reading public. It was in fact an essential tool for any publisher or wholesaler who wished to circularise the trade. But in the 1850s there were not so many publishers in London (or elsewhere) in a large enough way of business to advertise their books by the extensive despatch of circulars. There may have been two, perhaps even three dozen, wholesale houses, and fifty — even a hundred — publishers in a position to make use of this directory. But it was not really of use to small local booksellers, or 98% of the names it contained. A list of their correspondents was a closely guarded secret for the large London houses; but there were not so many of them. The sale of perhaps 150 copies of the Directory at five shillings a time might cover Hodson's printing and paper bills, but it could never have recompensed him for the labour of compilation.

In his account of the functions of the Booksellers' Communication Agency Hodson emphasises the inadequacy of the information about forthcoming books available to booksellers in the country; and propounds a scheme whereby his firm might remedy this. In a footnote he says that he is willing to act as the London agent for country booksellers, which suggests that his real ambition may have been to found a London wholesale house.

Any brief account of the changes in the means of communication within the book trade over the hundred years or so before this directory was published is bound to be dangerously over-simplified; but something needs to be said in order to set Hodson's schemes in perspective.

THE LONDON SHARE BOOK SYSTEM

About 1760 the leading firms in the London book trade were at the same time publishers, wholesalers, and retailers; and all three functions were under the same management. When one of these firms published a successful book, it was customary to divide the copyright into a number of shares; perhaps only a dozen to begin with, but 128 shares was not unusual later on. Some of these shares would be offered at auctions restricted to the London trade a year or two before the statutory copyright elapsed[1]. The object was to spread the interest in the copyright, and thereby forestall any rival editions when the statutory copyright expired. The same sort of subdivision was used for older books: Shakespeare, Milton, the Delphin classics, and much else. A shareholder paid his share of the costs of paper and print for each new reprint of the book, and received the number of copies in unbound sheets to which his share entitled him. It was these share-books, obtained at net cost, that the London publisher-wholesalers supplied to their country correspondents at wholesale rates.

1 By 'statutory' copyright I mean that given by the Act of Queen Anne, which was fourteen years plus a second fourteen if the author was still alive. In 1774 the House of Lords decided that there was no copyright at Common Law, and thus no perpetual copyright and no legal copyright outside the Act of Queen Anne. But this did not prevent the London trade from maintaining their copyrights by means of the share book system for another three quarters of a century.

THE COUNTRY TRADE

The country bookseller normally corresponded with only one London house, to which he might be linked by a former apprenticeship or some distant family connection. The country bookseller expected of his London supplier:

(i) established credit in London;

(ii) news of forthcoming books;

(iii) some saleable books; and

(iv) the books which his customers ordered.

About 1760 there were some forty London wholesalers[2]: In 1785 Pendred names between 500 and 600 country booksellers. So we arrive at a very rough average of fifteen country correspondents to each London publisher-wholesaler. Obviously some would have more than others; but this correspondence was not too large to be carried on by the head of the London house, knowing each country bookseller personally and the sort of books he could sell. By the beginning of the nineteenth century the number of country booksellers was much larger; some of the leading London publishers were giving up wholesaling; and the wholesale houses had increased in size, but not in number. It was no longer feasible for the London houses to give their country correspondents the personal and detailed attention of the previous generation.

PUBLISHING SEPARATED FROM WHOLESALING

There was criticism of the way in which the London publisher-wholesalers supplied the orders of their country correspondents for books which the London house did not publish or have shares in. "Thousands of books" wrote James Lackington in 1791[3] "are yearly written for to London that are never sent; and in these cases plausible reasons are assigned for such omissions — As, 'the book is "too dear" ' or 'it is out of print,' 'the book is not worth your purchasing; such a one wrote better on the subject.' " Lackington does not suggest that the London supplier may have had shares in the book by 'such a one,' but not in the book ordered, though this must often have been the case. The London publisher-wholesalers did not like supplying books which they did not have in stock; it meant a special errand to the publisher, and the margin of profit between the net cost and the wholesale selling price had to be divided. 'Country orders' wrote John Murray in 1803 'are a branch of business which I have ever totally declined as incompatible with my more serious

2 In 1759 John Whiston, a minor London wholesaler, described 'a general meeting of all the considerable booksellers, and indeed almost the whole trade.' He mentions 33 wholesalers by name. (*Some Thoughts on the state of Literary Property*, 1764, pp.13-15).

3 *Memoirs*, 1791, (1st edition, end of letter xxxv. The passage is abbreviated and finally omitted in later editions).

plans as a publisher.'[4] T.A. Cadell of Cadell and Davies wrote the article on copyright in the third edition of the *Encyclopaedia Britannica,* and in the course of it observed: 'We have at present in one house (the house so well known as the publishers of Hume and Robertson [i.e. Cadell and Davies]) the example of an establishment avoiding all business, even wholesale, except what relates to books printed for their own account.'[5] This means that Cadell and Davies would supply their publications (or publications in which they had a share in the copyright) to country booksellers at wholesale rates; but they would not supply books published by other firms. The country bookseller therefore had to get his supplies from several London publishers or from a wholesaler on whom he could no longer rely for advance information or personal advice.

THE LARGE LONDON WHOLESALE HOUSES

'Before the year 1780' says John Nichols[6] 'George Robinson had the largest wholesale trade that was ever carried on by an individual.' But when he died in 1801 the firm collapsed. Some of its trade went to Longman's who in the 1820s had 'four departments of the country line,' one of which was conducted by Edward Moxon, then aged about 22. More of the George Robinson business fell to Benjamin Crosby who had been one of Robinson's apprentices. When Crosby retired in 1814 he turned over the business to his two managers and former apprentices: the London connection to Richard Marshall, who founded the firm of Simpkin and Marshall (Simpkin was a hosier who supplied the capital); and the country connection to Baldwin, Cradock, and Joy, who failed in 1837 and were taken over by Simpkin and Marshall. By 1889 this firm had absorbed all the other wholesale houses in the London trade.

TRAVELLERS IN THE BOOK TRADE

It is plain that the wholesale houses of the early nineteenth century were too large to maintain the personal relationship with their country correspondents which had been one of their principal assets in earlier days; and that this inadequacy of communication was a barrier to the further expansion of their trade. They sought to remedy this by employing commercial travellers, who had long been used in other trades. Benjamin Crosby is said to have been the first to use travelling in the

4 S. Smiles, *A Publisher and his Friends,* 1891, i, p.61.

5 *Encyclopaedia Britannica,* 3rd ed. Supplement, vol ii, p.336. The part in which this article appears was published in February 1818. Compare also: *Memoirs of Sir Richard Phillips,* 1808, p.104: 'He sells only his own publications.' Thus John Murray, Sir Richard Phillips, and Cadell and Davies led the way in giving up wholesaling, and were followed by the newcomers, Colburn, Bentley, and Moxon. But Longmans, the two Rivingtons and others continued to combine publishing and wholesaling into the second half of the nineteenth century.

6 *Literary Anecdotes,* iii, pp.445-6.

book trade; and he was his own traveller. G.B. Whitaker & Co., who were one of the larger wholesale houses in the 1830s, at that time employed 'two travellers who take the leading towns in England and Wales, and the great towns in Ireland and Scotland only, twice a year.'[7] Longman's must have considered this method of selling of great importance when they took their chief traveller, Thomas Roberts, into partnership in 1856.

The introduction of the Penny Post in 1840 encouraged the development of the older method of circularisation. The old method was to include bundles of prospectuses in the parcels of books despatched to the country booksellers by the London carriers, as described on p.vii of this reprint. The Penny Post made it for the first time economically feasible to maintain a rapid, regular, and comprehensive service to the country booksellers. But whether such a service could ever be as effective as a traveller has been much debated. The great merit of selling books by a traveller is that the local bookseller can see and handle *before he buys* the books in which he is expected to invest his money and salesmanship. On the other hand the employment of travellers is more costly than circularisation. In the third quarter of the nineteenth century it must have seemed clear both to W.H. Hodson and to Kelly & Co. that a regular system of circularisation was the coming method, and that a directory of the trade was an essential tool in that technique. 'These trade directories' wrote Kelly & Co. in the preface to their first book trade volume of 1872 'furnish a direct clientage [sic] to very many — addressed promptly and cheaply — far preferable to the old system of appeals by travellers.'

This brief sketch of the background to Hodson's Directory is probably too simplified; and we can never know quite how much Hodson understood about the situation of the book trade in which he worked. His financial resources were not adequate, and his commercial schemes were miscalculated. But I do not think he was exaggerating when he claimed: 'that the Trade at large will find in this work such a List of Names as has never before been in the possession of any firm.'

7 *First Report from the Select Committee [of the House of Commons] on Postage*, (Session 1837-38, vol. xiv, pt i) Minutes of Evidence, Questions 3701-3708, p.262.

GRAHAM POLLARD

HODSON'S
BOOKSELLERS
PUBLISHERS AND STATIONERS'
D I R E C T O R Y
FOR

London and Country:

CONTAINING

UPWARDS OF 6000 NAMES,

ARRANGED ALPHABETICALLY ACCORDING TO COUNTIES;

THE DISTANCE FROM THE RAILWAY STATION IN LONDON:

AND

THE POPULATION OF EACH PLACE

TAKEN FROM THE LAST CENSUS.

PRICE 5s. ENTERED AT STATIONERS' HALL.

LONDON:
W. H. HODSON,
Booksellers' Communication Agency,
11 LOVELL'S COURT, 20 PATERNOSTER ROW.
1855.

DOBBS, KIDD, AND CO.,

𝕴𝖆𝖍𝖔𝖑𝖊𝖘𝖆𝖑𝖊, 𝕲𝖊𝖓𝖊𝖗𝖆𝖑, 𝕺𝖗𝖓𝖆𝖒𝖊𝖓𝖙𝖆𝖑, & 𝕰𝖝𝖕𝖔𝖗𝖙

STATIONERS, AND MANUFACTURERS OF

EMBOSSED SCREENS in great variety.

EMBOSSED DRAWING BOARDS, White and Tinted.

EMBOSSED LETTER and NOTE PAPERS, Plain and Cameo.

EMBOSSED CARDS in every size, Plain, Cameo, and with Perforated Centres.

EMBOSSED TOMB CARDS and BOARDS, Plain, Cameo, or Black-bordered.

ENCHASED LETTER and NOTE PAPERS in all sizes.

ENCHASED ENVELOPES, Single or Double.

ENCHASED DRAWING BOARDS.

ENCHASED CARDS with Plain or Perforated Centres.

ENCHASED WEDDING CARDS.

ENCHASED PAPERS, for Drawing or Painting.

PERFORATED CARDS, Round, Oval, and Square.

PERFORATED BOARDS, for Silk or Wool-work.

SUPERFINE LONDON DRAWING BOARDS in all sizes and thicknesses.

SUPERFINE BRISTOL DRAWING BOARDS, ditto ditto.

SUPERFINE CRAYON BOARDS, ditto ditto.

SUPERFINE MOUNTING BOARDS, ditto ditto.

TRACING PAPERS of every sort.

PREPARED CUMBERLAND DRAWING PENCILS.

OFFICE AND CASE PENCILS of all descriptions.

SKETCH BOOKS of all sizes,—stiff Embossed Covers, or Whole-Bound.

SOLID SKETCH BLOCKS and Books —all sizes.

PORTFOLIOS, for Music or Drawings.

ENVELOPES, Concentric-shape, Machine and Hand-made, Double Thick, or Satined.

OFFICIAL ENVELOPES.

PAPER-CLOTH ENVELOPES.

BLACK-BORDERED ENVELOPES and NOTE PAPERS.

WEDDING ENVELOPES, CARDS, FASTENERS, PAPERS, and "AT HOME" NOTES.

NOTE PAPERS, in 5-quire packets,—all sizes and sorts.

PORCELAIN-ENAMELLED CARDS, Thin and Thick, White or Tinted,

THICK and THIN IVORY CARDS.

BLACK-BORDERED and GILT-EDGED CARDS.

PRINTERS' SUPERFINE CARDS.

SEALING-WAX, PENCIL POINTS, and QUILL-NIBS.

ENAMELLED PAPERS, White and Tinted.

MUSIC PAPERS and BOOKS.

CHIT PAPERS, Plain and Adhesive.

ACCOUNT BOOKS, CIPHERING BOOKS, MEMORANDUM BOOKS, and COPY BOOKS.

LOCK BOOKS and LEDGERS.

WEST END or LIMP BOOKS.

ALBUMS and SCRAP BOOKS.

BLOTTING BOOKS and PADS.

CARD CASES and WALLETS.

BLOTTING CASES.

READERS' COMPANIONS and PEN-WIPERS.

VALENTINES in great variety.

LUGGAGE LABELS and NEWS BANDS.

Dobbs, Kidd, and Co., 134, Fleet Street, London.

LIBRARY EDITION.

Size 12 *in. by* 8½.

In parts, each containing six plates and descriptive letter-press, at 3s. 6d.
Part I, June 15, to be continued fortnightly,

ROBERTS'S SKETCHES

IN

𝕿𝖍𝖊 𝕳𝖔𝖑𝖞 𝕷𝖆𝖓𝖉, 𝕴𝖉𝖚𝖒𝖊𝖆, 𝕬𝖗𝖆𝖇𝖎𝖆, 𝕰𝖌𝖞𝖕𝖙, 𝖆𝖓𝖉 𝕹𝖚𝖇𝖎𝖆.

Reduced from the lithographs by Louis Haghe; with Historical and Descriptive Notices, and an Introductory View of Jewish History, by the Rev. George Croly, LL.D. Part I, as a specimen of the work, will be sent to any address, carriage free, on receipt of 3s. 6d. in postage stamps. Messrs. Day and Son are preparing for publication, in double tinted lithography (facsimiles of the original issue), an edition of the above magnificent work, which will alike be suitable for the library or the drawing-room table. To ensure positive identity between this and the original edition, the whole of the plates have been reduced to the required size by means of photography, thus ensuring the reproduction of all the beauties of the originals, both of effect and artistic touch. A prospectus may be had on application, containing the names of the 250 prints of which the work consists :—" The Holy Land, Syria, Idumea, Arabia, Egypt, and Nubia. Following in the footsteps of our Lord, or in those of his Disciples, every spot treated by the artist is consecrated ground, hallowed by associations so deeply interesting, as very largely indeed to enhance the value of these views, beautiful as they are, considerad merely as works of art. The series is a rich and full volume of enjoyment and instruction, teaching while giving pleasure, and aiding to confirm that faith which is the surest basis of human happiness." Agents required for the sale of the work in every town and district.

London: 1855. Day and Son, Lithographers to the Queen, Gate-street, Lincoln's-inn-fields.

NOTICE TO BOOKSELLERS AND OTHERS.

G. WILLIS,

Great Piazza, Covent Garden, London,

Has constantly on Sale one of the Largest and most Attractive Stocks of

NEW AND SECOND-HAND BOOKS,

A Catalogue of which is published Monthly, and forwarded on the day of Publication; post free price 3*d.*, or for one year upon pre-payment of *three shillings* in postage stamps.

These Catalogues contain from time to time some of the Finest Works offered for Sale, and will be found of great service to Country Booksellers, to lend their Customers.

G. W. allows a per centage to the Trade upon all Orders obtained.

N.B.—A Catalogue of **G. W.'s** Remainders sent free by post.

POPULAR WORKS PUBLISHING BY WILLOUGHBY & CO.,
26, SMITHFIELD, & 22, WARWICK LANE.
Publishing in Parts.

Phelps's Edition of the Complete Works of Shakespeare; Revised from the original Text. Each Play accompanied by copious Notes, critical, general, and explanatory. Produced under the immediate and personal supervision of SAMUEL PHELPS, ESQ., of the Theatre Royal, Sadler's Wells. With Beautiful Engravings, designed by T. H. NICHOLSON. TWO HANDSOME VOLUMES, large royal 8vo. cloth, gilt back, price 25s.

Valentine Vox, the Ventriloquist; By Henry Cockton, Esq. Illustrated by Onwhyn. Boards, price 3s. 6d.—Cloth, 4s.

Christopher Tadpole at Home and Abroad; By Albert Smith, Esq. Illustrated by John Leech. Boards, price 3s. 6d. Cloth, price 4s.

Gulliver's Travels; By Jonathan Swift, Dean of St. Patrick's. Beautifully Illustrated with numerous Engravings from designs by Grandville. With a Biographical Sketch. In this edition of the celebrated Travels care has been taken to follow minutely the Text of the original. Demy 8vo. cloth back, 5s.

The Vicar of Wakefield; By Oliver Goldsmith, M.B. With a Portrait and Life of the Author, by G. Moir Bussey. Embellished with Two Hundred Engravings. Demy 8vo. cloth, gilt back (252 pp.) price 5s.

Mythology of the Ancients; With nearly Two Hundred Engravings, by first-rate Artists. Demy 8vo, cloth, gilt back, price 5s.

Adventures of Telemachus; Translated by Dr. Hawkesworth. Embellished with nearly Two Hundred Engravings. Demy 8vo, cloth, gilt back (402 pp.) price 6s.

The Adventures of Robinson Crusoe; By Daniel De Foe. Embellished with 300 Engravings, after designs by J. J. Grandville. Demy 8vo, cloth, gilt back (508 pp.) price 6s.

The Last of the Fairies; By G. P. R. James. Illustrated by John Gilbert. Foolscap 8vo. cloth, gilt edges, price 3s.

The Inundation; or Pardon and Peace; By Mrs. Gore. Illustrated with Steel Engravings by George Cruikshank. Foolscap 8vo. cloth, gilt edges, price 3s.

The Snow Storm; By Mrs. Gore. Illustrated with Steel Engravings by George Cruikshank. Foolscap 8vo. cloth, gilt edges, price 3s.

The Lamplighter; By Miss Cumming. with Illustrations on Steel by Nicholson, Ashley, &c. In Ornamental Paper covers, price 2s. 6d.; cloth, full gilt back, price 3s. 6d.

NEW BOOK POST.—SPEED AND CHEAPNESS.

MESSRS. WARD & CO., 27, Paternoster Row, London,

Will send any of Mr. Curwen's Publications, post-free, to any part of Great Britain or Ireland, the proper amount being sent, in postage stamps or otherwise, with the order on the following terms.

The Child's Own Hymn Book; full price One Penny. Nearly 80,000 a year are sold. A new edition greatly enlarged, post free. 4, 5, 6 or 7 copies at 1d., a parcel of 8 copies for 7d. The same in cloth, price 2d.; 2, 3, 4, or 5 at 2d., a parcel of 6 for 10d.

The School Songs, price 3d.; 2, 3, 4, or 5 at 3d., a parcel of 6 for 1s. 3d. The same, price 6d., 1 at 6d., a parcel of 2 for 10d. **The School Music,** price 1s.; 1 for 10d., 3 for 2s. 5d. **The Children's School Music,** Air and Second only, price 4d.; 1, 2, 3, or 4 at 4d., a parcel of 5 for 1s. 4d.

The Child's Own Tune Book, price 6d.; 1, 2, or 3 at 6d,, a parcel of 4 for 1s. 7d. **The Little Tune Book,** price 2d.; 2 to 9 for 4d., a parcel of 10 for 1s. 4d.

The People's Service of Song, Pianoforte edition, price 7s. 6d.; 1 for 6s. 2d., 2 for 12s 2d. The same in paper covers, price 5s.; 1 for 4s. 1d. The same, Organ and Shortscore edition, price 3s.; 1 for 2s. 7d., 2 for 5s. The same, Women's Part, Air and Second Treble, price 1s. 6d.; 1 for 1s. 4d. The same, Men's Part, Tenor and Bass, price 1s 6d.; 1 for 1s. 4d.

The Tonic Sol-fa Reporter, Nos. 1 and 25, 26, &c., price 1d.; 4, 5, 6, or 7 copies, at 1d., a parcel of 8 for 7d. Nos. 2 to 24 inclusive, 4, 5, 6, or 7 at 1d., parcels of 8 for 7d., of 12 for 10d., and of 16 for 1s. 1d. Vol. 1, in cloth, price 2s.; 1 to 7 copies at 1s. 8d., a parcel of 8 for 13s. 2d.

Grammar of Vocal Music, price 2s. 6d.; 1 for 2s. 3d., 2 for 4s. 4d. **The Modulator,** price 1s. 4d.; 1 for 1s. 1d. The same on rollers, price 4s. 6d.; 1 for 3s. 9d. **The Sol-fa People's Service,** price 1s. 6d.; 1, 2, or 3 at 1s. 4d., a parcel of 4 for 5s. **The Sol-fa Women's part** of ditto, price 6d.; 1 for 6d., a parcel of 2 for 10d., 22 for 9s. 1d. **The Pupil's Manual,** price 1s.; 1 for 10d. **The School Course,** price 4d.; 1 or 2 at 4d., parcels of 3 for 1s. 3d., and of 14 for 3s. 10d. **Sol-fa Music Paper,** price 6d. the section of 8 sheets; 1, 2, 3, or 4 sections at 6d., a parcel of 5 sections for 2s. 3d. **An Account of the Tonic Sol-fa Method,** 16 pages, 4 for 1d.; 7 for 3d.

N.B. Purchasers of these books should cut out this Advertisement and keep it in their pocket-book.

THE RECORD NEWSPAPER,

Conducted on Protestant Religious Principles, is published three times a week, on Monday, Wednesday, and Friday afternoons, and contains all the News up to the time of Publication, Foreign, Domestic, and Parliamentary, together with the Morning Markets, Prices of Stocks, Railway Shares, &c. &c.

Price, each Paper, stamped 4d., unstamped 3d.; or Annually, paid in advance, stamped £2. 12s., unstamped £1. 19s.

The wide and respectable circulation of the RECORD renders it a desirable channel for Advertisements.

Orders received at the Office, 169, Fleet Street, London; or by any Bookseller or Newsman in Town or Country.

THE RUN AND READ LIBRARY.

Consisting of Tales uniting Taste, Humour, and Sound Principles. " Your plan is a highly interesting one, and I wish it success. Giving support to National Morality and Religion, is the best service that a man can render to his country; and peculiarly so to a country like ours, whose prosperity, I fully believe, depends upon its principle."—*Rev. Dr. G. Croly to the Publishers.* The following volumes are ready :

Beatrice, by Miss Sinclair .	. 2s. 0d.	To Love and to be Loved .	. 1s. 6d.
Zenon, by Rev. R. Cobbold .	. 1s. 6d.	The Mysterious Marriage .	. 1s. 6d.
Julamerk, by Mrs. Webb .	. 2s. 0d.	Jane Rutherford	. 1s. 6d.
Modern Flirtations . .	. 1s. 6d.	The Confessor . .	. 1s. 6d.
The Lamplighter . .	. 1s. 6d.	The Five-pound Note	. 1s. 6d.
Mary Anne Wellington .	. 1s. 6d.	I've Been Thinking .	. 1s. 6d.

Shortly will be ready, "A Long Look Ahead; or, the First Stroke and the Last." By the Author of " I've Been Thinking."

London : Simpkin, Marshall and Co.   Ipswich : J. M. Burton and Co.

IMPORTANT TO COUNTRY PRINTERS.

COUNTRY PRINTERS, about to establish a LOCAL NEWSPAPER, may arrange for a Portion being Printed in London with FIRST CLASS ILLUSTRATIONS.

For Terms and Specimens enclose two Stamps to Mr. DORRINGTON, 4, Ampton Street, Gray's Inn Road, London.

BELMONT HOUSE ACADEMY, PITVILLE, CHELTENHAM.

MR. FURSEY respectfully announces that in his Establishment, in addition to the usual branches of a sound Classical, Mathematical, Commercial, and Scriptural Education, French is taught by a Parisian ; Drawing, Music, Phonography, Practical Land Surveying, Drilling, &c., by eminent Masters. Prospectuses, with Terms, and view of premises, sent on application. Domestic comfort is particularly attended to by Mrs. F.

N.B. Mr. Fursey would be willing to treat with a respectable Printer and Bookseller for the Exchange of a youth to be Boarded, Educated, &c., and his Son, about 14, well educated, to be taught the business of a Printer, &c., thus affording mutual advantages. References given and required.

THE STATIONERS'

AND

PAPER MANUFACTURERS'

PROVIDENT SOCIETY.

Established 1839.

OFFICE, 3, CHARLOTTE ROW, MANSION HOUSE.

President.—JOHN DICKINSON, ESQ. | Treasurer.—GEORGE CHATER, ESQ.

Vice-Presidents.

WILLIAM BATTY, ESQ.	WILLIAM GAUSSEN, ESQ.	HENRY POUNCY, ESQ.
JOSEPH BONSOR, ESQ.	WILLIAM JOYNSON, ESQ.	JAS. SMITH, ESQ., Watford.
WILLIAM COOPER, ESQ.	WILLIAM M'MURRAY, ESQ.	GEORGE VENABLES, ESQ.
H. T. CURTIS, ESQ.	J. M. MORGAN, ESQ.	EDWARD WIGGINS, ESQ.
THOMAS GARDINER, ESQ.		

Trustees.

H. G. BROWN, ESQ. | HANANIAH TEAPE, ESQ.
THOS. HOLLINGWORTH, ESQ. | ALFRED WILSON, ESQ.

Auditors.—W. BURNSIDE, ESQ. H. SPICER, ESQ. W. TYLER, ESQ.

Committee.

MESSRS.

ATKINSON.	FITCH.	HOWELL.	PATRICK.
BECK.	C. GRIMWADE.	W. KEY.	PEEBLES.
CLEMENTS.	S. GROSVENOR.	MARTIN.	POLLOCK.
J. COLLINS.	HODGKINSON.	MASTERS.	RAGG.
S. COLLINS.	HOBBS.	NEWALL.	J. WILLIAMS.

A. WILLIS.

Bankers.—MESSRS. PRESCOTT, GROTE, & Co.

Honorary Secretary.—MR. FREDERICK WEST, 3, Charlotte Row, Mansion House.

Collector.—MR. BENJAMIN BUTLER, 262, Oxford Street.

The objects of the Society are to raise funds, to be applied for the benefit of Stationers, Stationers' Assistants, Paper Manufacturers, their Clerks and Foremen, Stationers and Booksellers, Stationers and Printers, Stationers and Binders, and such other persons connected with the Stationery trade as the Committee shall think eligible to become Members; and their Widows and Orphans when in necessitous circumstances.

A person having been a Member seven years, and attained the age of 60, will receive, if his circumstances require it, an annuity of not exceeding 25 Guineas for the remainder of his life; and in case of his death, leaving a Widow unprovided for, she will be entitled to a similar annuity after the age of 55. After he has been a Member for three years, temporary assistance will be granted to him, his widow, or orphans, in case of casual sickness or distress, to the extent of 20s. per week for three months, and half that sum for a further period of three months. A sum not exceeding £10 can be allowed on the death of a Member, for funeral expenses; £6 on the death of a wife or widow of a Member; and £3 on the death of an orphan child, for the same purpose.

The Relief provided for Members by the Rules of the Society will be administered, without the trouble and expense of any canvass or election, by a Committee consisting of twenty-one Members—six wholesale traders, six retail, and nine assistants, elected by the Members at large.

Persons properly qualified may become Members, if approved by the Committee, *on payment of a Subscription of Two Guineas annually*, or by one payment of *Twenty Guineas, or two payments of* TEN GUINEAS EACH IN TWO SUCCESSIVE YEARS, or three payments of Seven Guineas each in three successive years.

The Committee meet on the third Tuesday in each Month, at No. 3, Charlotte Row, City, for the purpose of transacting the general business of the Society, and electing New Members.

The Rules of the Society, the last Annual Report, with the names of the Members, and any other information, may be obtained at the Secretary's Offices; and Donations will be received by FRED. WEST, Hon. Sec., 3, Charlotte Row, Mansion House.

NATURAL HISTORY.

MAY FLOWERS: being a Sequel of Notes and Notions on Created Things. By the Author of 'March Winds and April Showers.' With numerous Wood Engravings. 5s.

MARCH WINDS and APRIL SHOWERS: being Notes and Notions on a few Created Things. By the Author of 'Episodes of Insect Life.' With numerous Wood Engravings. 5s.

LITERARY PAPERS, by the late Professor EDWARD FORBES, F.R.S. Selected from his Writings in 'The Literary Gazette.' With a Portrait and Memoir. 6s.

FLORA of NEW ZEALAND. By JOSEPH DALTON HOOKER, M.D., F.R.S., &c. In 2 vols. With 130 Plates. Royal 4to, price £12 12s. coloured; £8 15s. plain.

PHYCOLOGIA BRITANNICA; or, History of the British Seaweeds: containing coloured Figures and Descriptions of all the Species of Algæ inhabiting the Shores of the British Islands. By WILLIAM HENRY HARVEY, M.D., M.R.I.A. With 360 Plates. Price £7 12s. 6d.

CONCHOLOGIA ICONICA; or, Figures and Descriptions of the Shells of Molluscous Animals. By LOVELL REEVE, F.L.S. In Monthly Parts, 10s. Any Genus may be had separately.   Part 146 on the 30th.

CONCHOLOGIA SYSTEMATICA; or, Complete System of Conchology. By LOVELL REEVE, F.L.S. Illustrated with 300 Plates of 1500 Figures of Shells. Two vols. 4to. £10, coloured; £6, plain.

TRAVELS on the AMAZON and RIO NEGRO, with an Account of the Native Tribes, and Observations on the Climate, Geology, and Natural History of the Amazon Valley. By ALFRED R. WALLACE, Esq. With Plates and Maps. 18s.

CIRCUMNAVIGATION of the GLOBE; being the Narrative of the Voyage of H.M.S. 'Herald,' under the command of Captain Kellett, R.N., C.B., during the Years 1845-51. By BERTHOLD SEEMANN, F.L.S. With Tinted Lithographs, and a Map by Petermann. 2 vols., price 21s.

WESTERN HIMALAYA and TIBET; the Narrative of a Journey through the Mountains of Northern India, during the Years 1847 and 1848. By THOMAS THOMSON, M.D. With Tinted Lithographs and a Map by Arrowsmith. Price 15s.

BRITISH ENTOMOLOGY: being Illustrations and Descriptions of the Genera of Insects found in Great Britain and Ireland. By JOHN CURTIS, F.L.S. 16 vols. 770 coloured Plates. Price £21.

POPULAR ECONOMIC BOTANY; or Description of the Botanical and Commercial Characters of the principal Articles of Vegetable Origin used for Food, Clothing, Tanning, Dyeing, Building, Medicine, Perfumery, &c. By T. C. ARCHER. 20 coloured Plates. 10s. 6d.

TALPA; or, Chronicles of a Clay Farm. An Agricultural Fragment. By C. W. H. With Frontispiece by George Cruikshank. Cheap Edition. 3s. 6d.

POPULAR BRITISH CONCHOLOGY: the Molluses and Shells inhabiting the British Isles. By G. B. SOWERBY, F.L.S. With 20 coloured Plates. 10s. 6d.

POPUPAR BRITISH MOSSES: their Structure, Fructification, &c. By R. M. STARK, Esq. With 20 coloured Plates. 10s. 6d.

POPULAR PHYSICAL GEOLOGY. By J. BEETE JUKES, Esq., M.A., F.R.S. With 20 double-tinted Geological Landscapes. 10s. 6d.

RHODODENDRONS of SIKKIM HIMALAYA: being an Account, Botanical and Geographical, of the Rhododendrons recently discovered in the Mountains of Eastern Himalaya. By J. D. HOOKER, M.D., F.R.S. With 30 Plates. Imperial folio, price £3 16s.

POPULAR BRITISH FERNS, comprising Figures of all the Species. By THOMAS MOORE, F.L.S. With 20 coloured Plates. 10s. 6d.

POPULAR BRITISH ZOOPHYTES. By the Rev. Dr. LANDSBOROUGH, A.L.S., M.W.S. With 20 coloured Plates. 10s. 6d.

POPULAR BRITISH SEAWEEDS. By the Rev. Dr. LANDSBOROUGH. Second Edition. With 22 coloured Plates by Fitch. 10s. 6d.

POPULAR FIELD BOTANY, a Familiar History of British Field Plants. By AGNES CATLOW. Third Edition. With 20 coloured Plates, 10s. 6d.

POPULAR MINERALOGY, a Familiar Account of Minerals and their Uses. By HENRY SOWERBY. 20 coloured Plates. 10s. 6d.

POPULAR SCRIPTURE ZOOLOGY; or History of the Animals mentioned in the Bible. By MARIA CATLOW. 16 coloured Plates. 10s. 6d.

PARKS and PLEASURE GROUNDS; or, Practical Notes on Country Residences, Villas, Public Parks, and Gardens. By C.H. SMITH, Landscape Gardener. Price 6s.

POPULAR MOLLUSCA; or, Shells and their Animal Inhabitants. With 18 coloured Plates by Wing. 10s. 6d.

POPULAR MAMMALIA. By A. WHITE, F.L.S. With 16 coloured Plates by B. Waterhouse Hawkins, F.L.S. 10s. 6d.

POPULAR BRITISH ENTOMOLOGY, a Familiar History of Insects. By MARIA E. CATLOW. With 16 coloured Plates by Wing. Second Edition. 10s. 6d.

POPULAR BRITISH ORNITHOLOGY, comprising all the Birds. Second Edition. By P. H. GOSSE. With 20 coloured Plates. 10s. 6d.

DROPS of WATER. Their marvellous and beautiful Inhabitants displayed by the Microscope. By AGNES CATLOW. Coloured Plates. 7s 6d.

LOVELL REEVE, HENRIETTA STREET, COVENT GARDEN.

HODSON'S
BOOKSELLERS

PUBLISHERS AND STATIONERS'

DIRECTORY

FOR

London and Country:

CONTAINING

UPWARDS OF 6000 NAMES,

ARRANGED ALPHABETICALLY ACCORDING TO COUNTIES;

THE DISTANCE FROM THE RAILWAY STATION IN LONDON:

AND

THE POPULATION OF EACH PLACE

TAKEN FROM THE LAST CENSUS.

PRICE 5s. ENTERED AT STATIONERS' HALL.

LONDON:

W. H. HODSON,

Booksellers' Communication Agency,

11 LOVELL'S COURT, 20 PATERNOSTER ROW.

1855.

BANK OF DEPOSIT,

National Assurance and Investment

ASSOCIATION,

3, PALL MALL EAST, LONDON.

ESTABLISHED A.D. 1844.

Empowered by Special Act of Parliament.

CAPITAL STOCK, £500,000.

This Association is composed of two distinct and separate branches: the one comprising the buisness of a BANK OF DEPOSIT for the Investment of Capital; the other the ordinary transactions of Life Assurance.

BANKING DEPARTMENT.

The object of this Department is to afford a safe and easy mode of Investment, and to effect important improvements in the present system of Monetary economy, both as regards the security afforded to the Public and the rate of interest realised.

The plan of the BANK OF DEPOSIT differs materially from that of ordinary Banks, or Savings' Banks, in the mode of investing Capital:—a Ultimate profit and security being the main objects regarded, the Board of Management principally employ their Funds in Loans upon vested Life Interests and other similar securities, and in the purchase of well-secured Reversions: a class of securities which, although not immediately convertible, it is well known yields the greatest amount of profit, combined with the most perfect safety.

RATE OF INTEREST.

The present rate of Interest is five per cent. per annum, payable half-yearly; and the Board of Management confidently anticipate that a careful and judicious selection from securities of the above description will enable them to continue this rate to the Depositors.

INVESTMENT ACCOUNTS.

Money is received daily between the hours of TEN and FOUR o'clock. Investment Accounts may be opened with capital of any amount, and increased from time to time, at the convenience of Depositors.

A Stock Voucher, signed by two Directors, is given for each sum deposited.

INTEREST.

The INTEREST is payable in JANUARY and JULY, and for the convenience of parties residing at a distance, may be received at the Branch Offices, or through Country Bankers, without expense.

PETER MORRISON, *Managing Director.*

Prospectuses and forms for opening accounts sent free on application.

ADDRESS TO THE TRADE.

IN submitting the first edition to the Trade, I have endeavoured to collect, in a concise and intelligible form, a list of all parties interested in the BOOK and PAPER TRADES, together with such other information as I thought might prove useful.

It is not to be presumed that a mass of names, thrown over so large a surface as is comprised in the limits assigned for this work, can in the first edition be complete or correct; and when it is affirmed that upwards of twelve months have been expended in compiling the book, and making such corrections as have fallen in my way, it is hoped that any error or omission will be kindly forgiven, and supplied to the Proprietor for correction in the next edition.

It will be observed that at the end of the work there is an extensive Miscellaneous List; in apologizing for this, I have only to state that many of the names arrived too late for insertion in their proper places, and the others relate to Ireland and Scotland, as far as I have been able at present to collect. I have therefore placed them together in this list, believing that, although they are not properly arranged, they cannot fail to be useful.

It is particularly requested that any errors of description or omissions will be forwarded to the Compiler, who will take care they shall meet with due attention in the next edition, which it is intended to publish early in *January* next, in which edition the list of names will also be arranged in alphabetical order; indeed, no exertion will be spared to make the DIRECTORY a welcome and useful Annual to the Trade.

I cannot close this short address without thanking many influential members of the Trade for the assistance they have rendered; and to the Postmasters of Great Britain I feel deeply indebted for their promptitude in replying to my inquiries: believing as I do that the Trade at large will find in this work such a List of Names as has never before been in the possession of any firm; and sincerely trusting what it has been my desire to make it will be realised, and that the price it has been published at will place it within the reach of the whole Trade.

W. H. HODSON.

20, Paternoster Row,
    July, 1855.

TABLE

SHOWING THE QUANTITY OF PAPER TO BE GIVEN OUT FOR ANY JOB, FROM 25 TO 5000

No. on Sheet.	2		4		6		8		9		12		15		16		18		20		24		32		36	
No. required.	q.	s.	q.	s.	q.	s.	q.	s.	q.	s.	q.	s.	q.	s.	q.	s.	q.	s.	q.	s.	q.	s.	q.	s.	q.	s.
25		15		8		5		4		3		2½		2		2		2		1½		1¼		1		1
50	1	4		14		9		7		6		5		4		3½		3		3		2¼		2		1½
75	1	16		20		14		10		9		7		5½		5		4½		4		3½		2½		2¼
100	2	4	1	2		18		13		12		9		7		7		6		5½		4½		3½		3
150	3	4	1	14	1	1		19		18		13		11		10		9		8		7		5		4½
200	4	4	2	2	1	10	1	1	1	0		18		14		13		12		10½		9		6½		6
250	5	4	2	14	1	18	1	7	1	5		22		18		17		15		13		11		8½		7½
300	6	4	3	2	2	2	1	14	1	10	1	1		21		20		17		15½		13		10		8½
350	7	4	3	14	2	11	1	20	1	15	1	5	1	0		23		20		18		15		11½		10
400	8	4	4	2	2	19	2	1	1	21	1	9	1	3	1	1		23		20½		17		12½		12
450	9	4	4	15	3	2	2	7	2	1	1	13	1	6	1	4	1	1		23		19		14		13
500	10	5	5	3	3	11	2	14	2	7	1	18	1	9	1	7	1	4	1	1		21½		16		14
1000	20	6	10	4	6	19	5	2	4	13	3	10	2	18	2	14	2	6½	2	1	1	17¼	1	7	1	4
2000	40	6	20	4	13	11	10	2	9	0	6	18	5	9	5	1	4	12	4	0½	3	9	2	12	2	6
3000	60	6	30	5	20	3	15	2	13	10	10	1	8	1	7	13	6	17½	6	0¾	5	1	3	18	3	9
4000	80	7	40	5	26	19	20	2	17	22	13	11	10	18	10	1	8	23	8	1	6	7½	5	0	4	12
5000	100	7	50	5	33	12	25	3	22	8	16	20	13	10	12	14	11	4	10	1	8	9	6	7	5	14

The First Column states the Number to be given out (25 Sheets to the Quire), allowing for Waste. The Figures at Top specify the Number on a Sheet. q. and s. stand for Quires and Sheets.

A Table Showing the equivalent Weights of Writing and Printing Papers.

Foolscap 16½ by 13¼			Post 18¾ by 15¼			Large Post. 20¾ by 16½			Demy 17¾ by 22½	Dbl. Fcap. 17 by 27			Royal 20 by 25			Sup. Royal 20 by 28			Dbl. Crown 20 by 30			Imperial 22 by 30		
lbs.	oz.	dwt.	lbs.	oz.	dwt.	lbs.	oz.	dwt.	lbs.	lbs.	oz.	dwt.	lbs.	oz.	dwt.	lbs.	oz.	dwt.	lbs.	oz.	dwt.	lbs.	oz.	dwt.
6	9	2	8	9	9	10	4	11	12	13	12	10	15	0	6	16	13	3	18	0	7	19	13	4
7	10	12	10	0	7	12	0	0	14	16	1	6	17	8	7	19	10	1	21	0	8	23	2	2
8	12	2	11	7	5	13	11	9	16	18	6	3	20	0	8	22	6	15	24	0	9	26	7	0
9	13	13	12	14	3	15	6	17	18	20	10	15	22	8	9	25	3	13	27	0	10	29	11	15
10	15	3	14	5	2	17	2	6	20	22	15	12	25	0	10	28	0	11	30	0	12	33	0	13
13	2	4	17	2	18	20	9	3	24	27	9	5	30	0	12	33	10	7	36	0	14	39	10	9
15	5	4	20	0	15	24	0	1	28	32	2	13	35	0	14	39	4	2	42	1	0	46	4	5
17	8	5	22	14	11	27	6	18	32	36	12	7	40	1	0	44	13	14	48	1	2	52	14	1
19	11	6	25	12	7	30	13	15	36	41	5	15	45	1	2	50	7	10	54	1	5	59	7	14
21	14	3	28	10	4	34	4	12	40	45	15	8	50	1	4	56	1	6	60	1	7	66	1	10
24	10	2	32	3	8	38	8	14	45	51	11	7	56	5	6	63	1	9	67	9	11	74	5	13
27	5	18	35	12	15	42	13	16	50	57	7	6	62	9	9	70	1	12	75	1	14	82	10	1

By the above Table it will be seen that Double Foolscap is about one-eighth, Royal about one-fourth, and Double Crown one-half larger than Demy.

ACCOUNT BOOK SIZES.

	Folio.				Quarto.				Octavo.			
	Broad.		Long.		Broad.		Long.		Broad.		Long.	
	Length	Width	Length	Width	Length	Width	Length	Width	Length	Width	Length	Width
	Ins.	Ins.	Ins.	Ins.	Ins.	Ins.	Ins.	Ins.	Ins.	Ins.	Ins.	Ins.
Foolscap	12½	8	15½	6¼	7½	6¼	12½	4	6	3 15/16	7¾	3
Demy	14¼	9½	18½	7⅜	9	7⅜	14½	4½	7	4½	9¼	3⅝
Medium	16¼	10¼	20½	8¼	10¼	8¼	16¼	5⅛	8	5	10¼	4
Royal	18½	11½	23	9	11½	9	18½	5½	9	5½	11½	4½
Super Royal . .	18½	13	26	9¼	13	9¼	18½	6½	9	6½	13	4½
Imperial	20½	14½	29	10¼	14¼	10¼	20½	7½	10	7¼	14¼	5

PRINTING PAPERS.

	Inches.		
Demy	22½	by	17¾
Royal	25	—	20
Super royal (about) . .	28	—	20
Imperial	30	—	22
Double foolscap . . .	27	—	17
Double crown . . .	30	—	20
Double demy . . .	35½	—	22½

SUGAR PAPERS, &c.

Double two pound . .	24	by	16
Large ditto . . .	27	—	17
Double small hand . .	30	—	19
Royal hand . . .	25	—	20
Lumber hand . . .	23½	—	18
Middle hand . . .	22	—	16
Purple copy leaf . . .	21½	—	16½
Ditto double ditto . .	23	—	16½
Ditto Powder ditto . .	26	—	18½
Ditto single ditto . .	28	—	22
Ditto large ditto ditto . .	29	—	23
Purple lump leaf . .	34	—	23
Ditto large ditto ditto . .	35	—	28

BROWN PAPERS.

Casing	46	by	36
Double imperial . . .	44	—	29
Double four pound . .	31	—	21
Imperial cap . . .	29	—	22
Haven cap	26	—	21
Bag cap	24	—	19½
Kent cap	21	—	18

MILLED BOARDS.

	Mark.	Size.		
Pott	P	17¼	—	14¼
Foolscap	FC	18½	—	14½
Crown	C	20	—	16¼
Small half royal .	SHR	20¼	—	13
Large half royal . .	LHR	21	—	14
Short	S	21	—	17
Half imperial . .	HI	23½	—	16½
Small half ditto .	—	22¼	—	15
Middle or small demy .	M	22½	—	18½
Large middle or large demy	LM	23¾	—	18½
Large or medium . .	L	24	—	19
Small whole royal .	SR	25½	—	19
Large whole royal . .	R	26¾	—	20¾
Whole imperial .	I	32	—	22½
Long thin	LT	30	—	21
Atlas	A	30	—	26
Long royal . . .	LR	34	—	21
Colombier . . .	Col	36	—	24
Portfolio	PF	34	—	27
Great eagle or dbl. elephant	GE	40	—	28
Emperor	E	44	—	30
Double royal . . .	DR	46	—	21
Long colombier . .	LC	49	—	21
Long double clephant	LDE	50	—	27½
Antiquarian	ANT	54	—	30½
Extra antiquarian .	Ex Ant	54	—	34

GLAZED PRESSING BOARDS.

	Inches.		
Foolscap	17½	by	13½
Demy	22	—	18
Royal	24	—	19
Royal extra	25½	—	20
Double foolscap . . .	29	—	18
Super royal	29	—	21½
Imperial	31	—	23
Large size for dyers .	36	—	24

WRITING AND DRAWING PAPERS.

	Dimensions. Inches.			Usual weight per ream.
Emperor . .	66	by	47	lbs.
Antiquarian .	53	—	31	240 „
Double elephant .	40	—	26¾	130 „
Atlas . .	34	—	26	98 „
Colombier . .	34½	—	23½	102 „
Imperial . .	30	—	22	72 „
Elephant . .	28	—	23	72 „
Super royal .	27	—	19	54 „
Royal . . .	24	—	19	44 „
Medium . .	22	—	17½	34 „
Demy . . .	20	—	15½	25 „
Large post .	20¾	—	16½	23 „
Post . . .	18¾	—	15¼	20 „
Foolscap . .	17	—	13½	15 „
Pott . . .	15	—	12½	10 „
Copy . .	20	—	16	17 „

LETTER, NOTE PAPER, &c., &c.

Medium	4to	10¾	by	8⅜
„	8vo	8⅜	—	5⅜
Demy	4to	7⅜	—	9⅜
„	8vo	4¾	—	7¼
„	16mo . . .	3⅝	—	4⅝
Large	4to	8	—	10
„	8vo	5	—	8
Post	4to	7⅜	—	9
„	8vo	4½	—	7⅛
„	16mo	3⅝	—	4⅜
Copy	4to	7¾	—	9⅝
„	8vo	4⅝	—	7¼
Fcap.	4to	8	—	6⅜
Albert	. . . . .	3⅞	—	6
Queen	. . . . . .	3½	—	5⅜
Prince of Wales	. . . .	3	—	4½
Foolscap	. . . . .	8	—	12¾

CARTRIDGE PAPERS.

Copy	20	—	16½
Demy	22½	—	17¾
Royal	25	—	20
Cartridge	26	—	21½
Elephant	28	—	23
Double crown	30	—	20
Double demy	35½	—	22½
Imperial	30	—	22

𝕭𝖔𝖔𝖐𝖘𝖊𝖑𝖑𝖊𝖗𝖘' 𝕮𝖔𝖒𝖒𝖚𝖓𝖎𝖈𝖆𝖙𝖎𝖔𝖓 𝕬𝖌𝖊𝖓𝖈𝖞,

11, LOVELL'S COURT,

AND

20, *PATERNOSTER ROW, LONDON.*

IN compliance with the wishes of many of the Country Trade, I have opened the above Central Office with the view of more effectually carrying out the objects of the Agency. The main object is to place Publishers, Booksellers, &c., residing in any part of the United Kingdom, on an equal footing with the trade of the City and Suburbs of London.

The Country Trade generally have long complained of the uncertain transmission from their London Agents of Bills, Catalogues, or Specimens of New Works, &c., of whose existence they have often remained in ignorance a considerable time after the announcement of publication, the excuse of the Town Agent being, that the difficulty of collecting Orders left them no time for collecting Bills, &c. It has also occurred that when numbers of Bills or Show Cards were entrusted to the Agents, some have had sent to them considerably more than they could turn to profitable use, whilst others who should have received their share have been entirely forgotten.

To counteract these evils, I shall devote a great portion of my time to the collecting of Bills, Show Cards, Manufacturers' Price Lists, &c., and distribute them in equal proportions to all my Subscribers, monthly or oftener, as the case may require; the parcels will be addressed individually, and delivered to their Town Agent for enclosure. (*Bookage paid by me.*)

For collecting Bills, Show Cards, Specimens, &c., receiving parcels for *enclosure,* packing and forwarding to Agent, &c., it is proposed to charge the sum of *Ten Shillings per annum,* or *Five Shillings* the half year; One Shilling to be paid at the *time of entrance,* which it is hoped will be considered moderate in comparison with the labours I undertake and the advantages I offer.

In addition, any inquiries my Subscribers may require to be made in Town will be promptly attended to, *without any extra charge,* but in each instance two postage stamps must be sent for my reply.

Respectfully soliciting your patronage,

I remain,

Your Obedient Servant,

W. H. HODSON.

***⁎** I am also willing, on the most equitable terms, to undertake the Town Agency of any Country Booksellers wishing their interests to be looked after in London, and regularly forward parcels, weekly or monthly, as may be required.

SOVEREIGN
LIFE ASSURANCE COMPANY,
49 ST. JAMES'S STREET, LONDON.

ESTABLISHED 1845.

THIS OFFICE PRESENTS THE FOLLOWING ADVANTAGES:

The security of a large paid-up Capital.

Very moderate rates for all ages, especially Young Lives.

No charges whatever, except the Premium.

All Policies Indisputable.

By the recent Bonus, four-fifths of the Premium paid was in many instances returned to the Policy-holders. Thus:—on a Policy for £1000 effected in 1846, Premiums amounting to

£153 8s. 4d. had been paid,

while

£123 7s. was the Bonus added in 1853.

A WEEKLY SAVING OF FOURTEEN PENCE (£3 0s. 8d. yearly) will secure to a person 25 years of age, the sum of £100 on his attaining the age of 55, or AT DEATH, should it occur previously.

Rates are calculated for all ages, climates, and circumstances connected with Life Assurance.

Prospectuses, Forms, and every information, can be obtained at the Office, 49, St. James's Street, London, or of the Agents.

HENRY D. DAVENPORT, *Secretary.*

HODSON'S
BOOKSELLERS' AND PUBLISHERS'
DIRECTORY,

&c. &c.

BEDFORDSHIRE.

AMPTHILL.
From Euston-square 57 *miles.* *Pop.* 1961
Cook, George, Church-street
Shaw, Ann, Market-place

BEDFORD.
From Euston-sq. 63 *miles.* *Pop.* 11,693
Grey, William C., St. Mary-street
Hill, Rowland, High-street
Hill, Samuel W., High-street
Lawrence, Thomas (publisher) High-street
Merry, C. B., Wells-street
Perfect, W., Conduit-street
Skene, George R., Mill-street
Smith, M., Silver-street
Thompson, Frederick, High-street
Timaeus, C. F., High-street
Musicsellers.
Bithrey, Charles, Tavistock-street
Nunn, John, Crescent
Rose, Robert, High-street

BIGGLESWADE.
From King's-cross 41 *miles.* *Pop.* 3976
Gardner, Elias, High-street
Spong, T. W. (library) High-street
Twelvetrees, William, Shortmead-street

DUNSTABLE.
From Euston-square 47½ *miles.* *Pop.* 3589
Dangerfield, R. J. (music) High-street
Donne, Edward B., High-street
Tibbett, James, High-street

LEIGHTON BUZZARD.
From Euston-square 40½ *miles.* *Pop.* 4465
Flint, Frank (printer) High-street
Partridge, Jesse, Leek-street
Young, James (printer) High-street

LUTON.
From King's-cross 28½ *miles.* *Pop.* 10,648
Hill, William, George-street
Wiseman, John, George-street

POTTON, &c.
From King's-cross 43 *miles.* *Pop.* 1922
Tebbutt, David, Market-square
Topham, James (printer) Market-square

SHEFFORD, &c.
From King's cross to Ashley 37 *mls.* *Pop.* 1052
Lewington, Francis, Bridge-street
Linford, James, Bridge-street

WOBURN.
From Euston-square 51 *miles.* *Pop.* 2042
Clarke, George B. (printer) Park-street
Crofts, William, High-street
Dodd & Peeling (publishers, printers, & binders) Bedford-street
Harland, Market-place

BERKSHIRE.

ABINGDON.
From Paddington 56 *miles.* *Pop.* 5954
Bezant, Aaron W. (music) Market-place
Cositer, Charles, Ock-street
Evans, Caleb (printer) Market-place
Faulkner, W., Bath-street
Parsons, J. R., Bridge-street
Payne, Charles, High-street
Staniland, John (stationer) Lombard-street

BINFIELD.
Pop. 1280
Bartleet, Joseph (stationer) Bracknel

HUNGERFORD.
From Paddington 61¼ *miles.* *Pop.* 2235
Franklin, William (printer) High-street
Hincks, Mary, High-street

MAIDENHEAD.
From Paddington 22½ *miles.* *Pop.* 3607
Burnham, William, High-street
Haines, George, High-street
Hodges, Henry H. (library) High-street

NEWBURY.
From Paddington 52¾ *miles.* *Pop.* 6574
Adnams, Frederick S., North Brook-street
Ashley, Thomas Payne, Bridge-house
Blackett, James, Northbrook-street
Cole, Thomas, 143 Bartholomew-street
Dodson, Richard, 72 Northbrook-street
Fry, John, Cheap-street
Garlick, William (stationer) Northbrook-st
Hall, William (publisher) Speenhamland
Higgs, Thomas, & Co., Northbrook-street

READING.
From Paddington 35¾ *miles.* *Pop.* 21,456
Barcham, Thomas, 89 Broad-street
Benwell, Charles, 24 Minster-street
Blackwell, Edward, London-street

1

Clayton, Sarah (stationer) Chain-street
Clayton, William Charles, 76 Oxford-street
Crupp, J., & Son, Castle-street
Farrar, Thomas, 39 Broad-street
Groom, John, 40 Castle-street
Lovejoy, George, 116 & 117 London-street
Macauley, James, 113 Broad-street
Rusher & Johnson, 14 King-street
Shackelford, John, 13 Middle-row
Welch, Richard, 12 Market-place
Westbrook, A. & E., Twyford

WALLINGFORD.
From Paddington 47½ *miles.* *Pop.* 8064
Bradford, John, Fish-street
Jenkins, Thomas (library) Fish-street
Payne, John G., Market-place
Wood, W. T. (music) High-street

WANTAGE.
From Paddington 60 *miles.* *Pop.* 3056
Belcher, James, Mill-street
Lewis, Joseph & George, Market-place
Saunders, Charles, Market-place
Yateman, Edward, Church-street

WINDSOR.
From Paddington 21 *miles; from Waterloo*
25½. *Pop.* 9596
Brown, John B. (library) Castle-street
Taylor, William F. (music) High-street
Willmore, William, Thames-street

BUCKINGHAMSHIRE.

AMERSHAM.
Pop. 2093
Broadwater, William (printer) High-street

AYLESBURY.
From Euston-square, 43½ *miles.* *Pop.* 26,794
Marlin, Henry, Market-square
Marshall, J. H., Temple-street
Muddiman, Joseph, Market-square
Muddiman, J. D., Junr., Judge's-lodge
Pickburn, J., Temple-street
Payne, S., Bourbon-street
Walker, J., Bourbon-street

BUCKINGHAM.
From Euston-square 61 *miles.* *Pop.* 8069
Chandler, Richard, Market-square
Stalworthy, W., Butchers'-market

CHESHAM.
Pop. 2496
Reading, J. A. (stationer) High-street
Sexton, Edward (printer) High-street

GREAT MARLOW.
Pop. 6523.
Anthony, C., West-street
Cannon, George (printer) High-street
Pearce, G. S., High-street
Segrave, E., High-street

NEWPORT PAGNELL.
Pop. 3312
Carr, A., High-street
Croydon, E. H., High-street
Tite, C., High-street

OLNEY.
Pop. 2265
Collingridge, T. (printer) High-street

STONY STRATFORD.
Pop. 1757
Nixon, William, High-street
Walford, Alfred, High-street

WINSLOW.
From Euston-square 54 *miles.* *Pop.* 1889
Twining, David, Market-square
Wigley, Henry, Market-square

WYCOMBE (WEST).
Pop. 2000
Butler & Co., Church-square
Forster, Charles (library) Market-place

Paper Makers.
Edmonds, Thomas, Rye-mill
Galliver, A., Loudwater
Lane, Alfred, Bowden-mill
Saunders, T. F., Beech-mill
Spicer, J. F. G., Glory-mill
Wheeler, Henry, Marsh-mill

CAMBRIDGESHIRE.

CAMBRIDGE.
From Shoreditch 57½ *miles.* *Pop.* 27,815
Marked thus * are also Publishers.
Allies, Matthew, Willow-walk
*Deighton, Bell, & Co., 12 Trinity-street
Frank, Charles, 46 Sidney-street
*Grant, William P., 8 Trinity-street
*Hall, John, 51 Trumpington-street
Hankin, James, Rose-crescent
Hutt, John (library) Peas-hill
*Johnson, Elijah, 1 Trinity-street
Johnson, James, Sidney-street
King, Mary, 10 Petty-curry
Lake, H. E., Bridge-street
*Metcalf & Palmer, Green-street
*Macmillan & Co., 1 Trinity-street
*Meadows, Edward, King's-parade
Morris, Edward, Downing-terrace
Page, J., Market-street
Sandifer, M., Freeschool-lane
Smith, W. H., Rose-crescent
Thornton, L. S., Rose-crescent
Wallis, Henry, Sidney-street
*Wheeler, J. T., Rose-crescent
Whittaker, Thomas, Sidney-street

Law Stationers.
Allen, Thomas, 7 Fitzwilliam-street
James, G. H., Orchard-street
Markham, Henry, New-square

Music and Instrument Sellers.
Barker, William, Benet-street
Eastes, John, Trumpington-street
Ling, S., King's-parade
Simmons, George, Regent-street
Sippel, F., St. Mary's-passage
Wood, Thomas, Market-street

Printers, &c.
Dickie, John (publisher) Sidney-street
Forster, M., 14 Church-street
Hall, John, Trumpington street
Metcalf & Palmer, Green-street
Naylor, C. W. (publisher) Market-hill
Parker, John, Trumpington-street
Purser, Henry, Silver-street
Smith, Henry (publisher) Market-hill
Talbot, Henry, Sussex-street
Wilson, S., Bridge-street
Printsellers.
Dunmock, James, Sidney-street
Frank, Charles, Sidney-street
Hoppet, Frank, St. John-street
Mutton, Henry, All Saints'-passage
Mutton, William, Trinity-street
Roe, Robert, King's-parade
Wilson, Samuel, Bridge-street

CHATTERIS.
From Shoreditch 83 miles.   Pop. 3738
Southwell, Joseph (printer) High-street

ELY, &c.
From Shoreditch 72½ miles.   Pop. 6176
Bradfield, A., Fore-hill
Clement, John, Market-place
Creak, W. B., Gaol-street
Hills, T. A. (music) Minster-street

LINTON.
Pop. 2061
Sergeant, Joseph, Linton

MARCH.
From Shoreditch 93½ miles.   Pop. 4171
Gales, J. (printer) Whittle-end
Glazier, William, High-street
Tyler, W. F., High-street
Ward, D. J., Market-place

NEWMARKET, &c.
From Shoreditch 72½ miles.   Pop. 3356
Rogers & Clark, High-street
Simpson, Allen (library) High-street

ROYSTON, &c.
From King's-cross   Pop. 2061
Flood, James, Melbourne
Pickering, Thomas, John-street
Warren, S. & J., High-street

SOHAM, &c.
Pop. 2756
Playford, William (library) High-street

WHITTLESEA.
From Shoreditch 96½ miles.   Pop. 7687
Crofts, T. J., Whitmore-street
Green, J., Almshouse-street

WISBEACH.
From Shoreditch 95½ miles.   Pop. 10,954
Marked thus * are also Printers.
Anderson, Robert, Blackfriars-road
Balding, James, Little Church-street
Collyer, Charles, Church-terrace
*Gardiner, John, Union-street
*Goddard, Samuel, High-street
Hudson, W. B., Maishland-road

*Johnson, E., Bridge-street
*Leach, John, High-street
Rutter, T. G., Lower Hill-street
Walker, Richard, Bridge-street

CHESHIRE.
ALTRINGHAM.
From Manchester 8 miles.   Pop. 4488.
Balshaws, Charles, Higher-town
Balshaws, Thomas, Church-street

BIRKENHEAD.
From Euston-square to Liverpool 201 miles.
Pop. 24,285.
Cross, James (library) Ivy-street
Dare, George, Seacombe
Griffiths, Joseph, Hamilton-street
Knowles & Co., Argyll-street
Law & Pinkney, Hamilton-street
Lomax. M. (stationer) Rock-ferns
Osborne, William, Chester-street

CHESTER.
From Euston-square 178½ miles.   Pop. 27,766.
Catherall, Thomas, Eastgate-street
Clarke, Thomas (binder) Watergate
Ducker & Minshull (binders & library) Watergate
Evans, Frederick (and printer) Towgate-street
Parry & Son (binders & printers) Eastgate-st
Pritchard and Roberts, Bridge-street
Roberts, William (binder) City-walls
Smith, Henry & Son (printers) Bridge-st-row
Suarbrick, John (second-hand) Bridge-st-row
Thomas & Son (printers) Bridge-st-row
Thompson, Thomas (printer) Bridge-st-row
Libraries, &c.
Albion News Room, Bridge-street
Chester Public Library, St. Peter's Church-yd
Commercial News Room, St. Peter's Church-yd
Mechanics' Institution, Newgate-street
Chester Chronicle, Friday, Bridge-st-row
Chester Courant, Wednesday, Northgate-st

CONGLETON.
From Euston Square, via Stafford   m.
Pop. 10,520.
Brightmore, Thomas (printer) Mill-street
Clarke, William (printer) High-street
Crouther, Charles, Lawton-street
Joyce, Edward (printer) High-street
Athenæum News Rooms & Library, High-st
   William Clarke, *Librarian*

CREWE.
From Euston-square 157¼ miles.   Pop. 4491.
Bennion, Edwin, High-street
Cotton, Mary, High-street
Neven, M., Coppenhall-terrace
Roberts, Hugh, Coppenhall-terrace
Walton, John, High-street

DISLEY.
From Euston-square.   Pop. 2255.
Collier, Robert, (library) New-mills

DUKINFIELD.
From Euston-square to Stockport 182½ miles.
Pop. 22,394.
Broderick, Samuel, Oxford-road

Burgess, Henry, Davis-street
Cook, William (and binder) Town-lane

FRODSHAM.
From Chester 10 *miles.   Pop.* 1010.
Badger, William

HYDE.
From Stockport 5 *miles, from Manchester* 7.
Pop. 11,569.
Booth, George, North Cheshire Herald Office, Market-street
Collier, Samuel, Hyde
Knowles, Willis, Hyde
Slater, Henry, Market-street
Public Library, Hyde-lane

KNUTSFORD.
From London 176 *miles.   Pop.* 3127.
Houarth, Thomas (binder) Princess-street
Siddeley, John, King-street
Working Man's Library, Market-place

MACCLESFIELD.
From Euston-square 170 *miles.   Pop.* 39,048.
Burgess, Matthew, Market-place
Brown & Swinnerton (printers) Mill-street
Chorley, John, Mill-street
Dunstan, W. Mill-street
Finney, Isaac, Chester-gate
Higginbotham, Henry (printer) Mill-street
Miage, Benjamin, Mill-street
Rowley, James, Mill-street
Stubbs, John (printer) Mill-street
Smith, William, Park-green
Surmurton, James, (printer) Chester-gate
Shuttleworth, Thomas, Chester-gate
Wilson, Thomas, Mill-lane
Wright John, (printer) Mill-lane
   Literary News Room, Duke-street
   Mechanics' Institution, Stanley-street
   Macclesfield Chronicle, Saturday
      Matthew Burgess, Market-place
   Macclesfield Courier, Saturday
      James Swinnerton, Chester-gate

MIDDLEWICH.
From London 167 *miles.   Pop.* 1235.
Jackson, L. (printer) High-town

NANTWICH.
From Euston-square 161 *miles.   Pop.* 5426.
Burgess, Thomas (printer) High-street
Griffiths, Edward (printer) High-street
Parratt, Thomas (printer) Welsh-row
Mechanics' Institution, High-street

NORTHWICH.
From Euston-square to Hartford-station 168¾
miles, from thence 2 *miles.   Pop.* 1377.
Burgess, Henry (library) High-street
Carnes, F., High-street
Hall Charles, High-street

RUNCORN.
From Chester 15 *miles, or to Preston-brook
from Euston-square* 175¾ *m.   Pop.* 8049.
Griffiths, Samuel, Church-street
Walker, William (library) Bridge-street
Walker, Charles (printer) King-street

STOCKPORT.
From Euston-square 182½ *miles.   Pop.* 53,835.
Burgess, John, Hill-gate
Claye, Thos. & Son (binder, music, & library) Little Underbank
Gill, Edmund (music) Hill-gate
Haigh, Brothers (binders & printers) Little Underbank
Holme, Edward, Queen-street
Kent, Joseph (binder) Queen-street
King, Edward, H. (printer) Bridge-street
Lambert, William (printer) Little Underbank
Lomax, Jas. & Sons (printers) Great Underbank
Martin, Thomas (music) Hillgate
   Mechanics' Library, Princes-street
   Tradesman & Operative's Library, Astley's-yd
   Stockport Advertiser, Friday
      James Lomax, Great Underbank
   Stockport Mercury, Friday
      W. & S. Haigh, Little Underbank

STALBRIDGE.
From Euston-square 190¼ *miles.   Pop.* 21,092.
Barnfard, John, High-street
Buck, William (printer) High-street
Brierley, John & Chas. (binders & printers) Rasbottom-street
Cunningham Ann (printer) Rasbottom-street
Davies, John (printer) Grosvenor-street
Harrop, Edward, Melbourne-street
Spencer William, High-street
   Mechanics' Institution, Bennett-street

CORNWALL.
BODMIN.
Pop. 6337
Drew, Henry, Fore-street
Liddell, S., Fore-street

CALLINGTON.
Pop. 2146
Philp, Edward

CAMBORNE.
Pop. 6547
Edwards, Elizabeth
Newton, Llewellyn
Thomas, Susan
Wear, Thomas

FALMOUTH, &c.
Pop., with Penryn, 13,656
Dixon, T. P., Market-street
Duckham, A. J., Arwenack-street
Lake, J. H. (library) Market-street
Lake, R. G., Market-street
Lancaster, J., Arwenack-street
Tratham, J., Market-strand
Tregoning, E. S. (library) High-street

HAYLE.
Harris, John O.
Williams, James, & Co.

HELSTON.
Pop. 7321
Carlyon, E., Coinage Hall-street
Cannack, R. J., Coinage Hall-street
Edwards, J., Wendron-street

Penalunn, W., Meneage-street
Woolcock, R., Meneage-street

LAUNCESTON.
Pop. 6005

Bray, H., High-street
Cater, J., Church-street
Dymond, W. (library) Southgate-street
Maddox, T. M., Southgate-street
Phillip, W., Broad-street

LISKEARD.
Pop. 6224

Bennicke, M., Fore-street
Keast, T. N., Tavern-hill
Matthews, J., Church-street
Peters, Thomas, Russell-street
Philp, John, Fore-street

LOSTWITHIEL, &c.
Pop. 1053

Stephens, J. E., St. Blazey
White, Richard

PADSTOW.
Pop. 2224

Allport, Samuel
Docton, Thomas
Still, James (stationer)

PENRYN.
Pop., with Falmouth, 13,656

Gill, John, Broad-street
Pearce, Thomas, Market-street

PENZANCE.
Pop. 9214

Beare, Thomas, Market-place
Lavin, Edward, Chapel-street
Paddy, Edward, Chapel-street
Rosse & Son, Market-place
Saundry, H. M., Chapel-street
Thomas, Charles, Market Jew-street
Virbert, F. T. (library) Market-place

REDRUTH, &c.
Pop. 7095

Bennett, A., Redruth
Daniel, Samuel, Redruth
Jewell, Frederick, Chasewater
Michell, John W., Redruth
Phillips, W., Redruth
Symons, F., Redruth
Tregaskis, J., St. Day

SAINT AGNES, &c.

Gripe, James

SAINT AUSTELL.
Pop. 3565

Andrew, James, Fore-street
Drew, J. H., Fore-street
Hodge, William, Fore-street
Physick, F. (stationer) Fore-street

SAINT COLUMB.
Pop. 5183

Drew, G. S. (printer)
George, C.

SAINT GERMANS.
Pop. 2969

Down (Brothers), Torpoint
Rimdale, William, Saltash

SAINT IVES, &c.
From Shoreditch 72 miles.   Pop. 3522

Kerwick, John May, Fore-street
Rodda, R. D., Tregenna-place

SAINT JUST.
Pop. 1557

Warren, John (printer)

STRATTON.
Pop. 1696

Bray, P. W. (printer)
Perry, W.
Porter, Thomas

TREGONEY, &c.

Roberts, James

TRURO.
Pop. 10,733

Brokenshire, John (music) Duke-street
Clyma, W. J., Lemon-street
Endean, J. R., Lemon-street
Heard & Sons (music) Boscawen-street
Hearne, George, Pydar-street
Lake, Samuel, New Bridge-street
Netherton, James R., 7 Lemon-street
Pascoe, Eldred R., St. Nicholas-street
Wicks, George (binder) Pydar-street

WADEBRIDGE.

Knapp, William Marshall

CUMBERLAND.

ALSTON.
From London 281 miles.   Pop. 2005

Guy, William
Pattinson, John (printer)

BRAMPTON.
*From Milton Station, on the Newcastle and
Carlisle Railway, 1 mile.   Pop.* 3074

Coulthard, Joseph, Front-street
Hodgson, John S., Back-street
Lancaster, Henry, Front-street
Nicholson, Joseph, High Cross-street

CARLISLE.
From Euston-square 300½ *miles.   Pop.* 26,310
Bookbinders.

Fidler, William (printer) English-street
Harris, Thomas W., Castle-street
Johnstone, John, 41 King-street
Slee, John, Annetwell-street

Booksellers, &c.

Arthur, James, Rickergate
Fishburn, William (library) Botchergate
Foster, James (printer) Scotch-street
Halton, Jeremiah (news) Scotch-street
Jackson, M. (new & old) 2 Botchergate
Johnstone, John (printer) King-street
Scott & Benson (printer) English-street
Steel, James (printer) 3½ English-street

Stewart, Charles, 139 Botchergate
Thurman, Chas. (printer & library) English-st
Whitridge, J. F. (binder) 34 Scotch-street
Willan, Robt. (printer & stationer) 36 Castle-st
   Commercial News Room, English-street
   Mechanics' Institution, Lowther-street ;
     W. J. Fisher, *Librarian*
   Carlisle Journal, Friday, Jas. Steel, English-st
   Carlisle Patriot, Friday, Theatre-lane.

COCKERMOUTH.
From London 305 miles.   Pop. 7275
Bailey, Thomas, junr., Main-street
Fidler, Daniel, Main-street
   News Room, Bank-buildings, Main-street

EGREMONT.
From London 291 miles.   Pop. 2049
Harrison, George (paper maker)

KESWICK.
From London 293 miles.   Pop 2618
Bailey & Son
Dixon, George
Ivison, James

LONGTOWN.
From London 309 miles ; from Carlisle 8½.
Pop. 2142
Henderson, Matthew (printer)

MARYPORT.
From London 309 miles.   Pop. 5698
Adair, Robert (printer & news) Senhouse-st
Harrison, John, High-street
Maugham, Christopher, John-street
Ostle, Joseph (lithographer) High-street

PENRITH.
From London 283 miles.   Pop. 6668
Atkinson, William, Market-place
Brown, H. (library & music printer) Market-pl
Sweeten, Benjamin Thomas (music & printer)
   Great Dockray
Walters, Robert (binder) Great Dockray
   Mechanics' Institution, Churchyard

WHITEHAVEN.
From London 296 miles, via Ulverstone.
Pop. 18,916
Boustead, Thomas, 18 Lowther-street
Callander, Dixon (binder & news) 3 Market-pl
Crosthwaite & Co. (binders & news), 3 Market-pl
Gibson, Robert, & Sons (binders & printers)
   26 King-street
Gaythorpe, John, 80 King-street
Glendenning, Charles, Roper-street
Ogden, Charles, Roper-street
Robinson, John (binder & printer) Strand-st
Wilson, Thomas (printer) 22 King-street
   Cumberland Pacquet, Tuesday, Robt. Gibson,
     26 King-street
   Whitehaven Herald, Saturday, Geo. Irwin,
     13 Louther-street
   Subscription News Room, Louther-street

WIGTON.
From London 305 miles.   Pop. 4224
Hoodless, Henry (printer, binder, & library)
   Market

M'Mechan, Joseph, King-street
Robertson, William (library) High-street
   News Room, Market-pl. ; H. Hoodless, *Sec.*
   Mechanics' News Room, High-street

WORKINGTON.
From London 312 miles.   Pop. 5837
Dickinson, James, Browtop
Dixon, William (library) Wilson-street
Kirkconel, James (library) Wilson-street
Mordy, John, Wilson-street
McGar, James, Wilson-street
   News Room, Portland-square

DERBYSHIRE.

ALFRETON.
From Euston-square 138¼ miles.   Pop. 8326
Coates, George,
Rowbottom, Samuel

ASHBOURNE.
From Euston sq. 147½ miles.   Pop. 2418
Hobson and Son, Market-place
Hoon, Mary, Butchers'-row
Howell, Ann, Post-office
Parkes, J., Digg-street

BAKEWELL.
From Euston-sq. 154 miles.   Pop. 2217
Goodwin, John, 9 Market-place
Gratton, James, Mattock-street

BELPER.
From Euston-sq. 139¼ miles.   Pop. 10,082
Kiddy, John (stationer) Bridge-street
Lowe, Edward, Market-place
Moss, John, Queen-street
Rosenarne, John, Bridge-street

BUTTERLY.
Rowland, George, Ripley
Whightman, James, ditto

BUXTON.
From Euston-square 154 miles.   Pop. 1235
Clayton, John, Spring-gardens
Moreland, James, Crescent
Sutton and Dennis, Spring-gardens

CHAPEL EN LE FRITH.
Pop. 3214.
Carrington, Wm. (printer and stationer)
Hughes, James (ditto)
Taylor, Josiah (ditto)

CHESTERFIELD.
From Euston-sq. 156¼ miles.   Pop. 7101
Barnes, Edward, Pucker's-row
Cooper, Sam., Low-pavement
Gallimore, Cornelius, Irongate
Pike, Thomas, Low-pavement
Roberts, John, High-street

DERBY.
From Euston-sq. 132 miles.   Pop. 40,609
Allen, J., St. Peter-street
Bemrose, Wm. (printer) Irongate
Chadfield, Joseph (printer) Friargate

Ford, John G. (printer) King-street
Frost and Lockyer (printers) King-street
Fuller, Edward, Victoria-street
Hobson, William (printer) Irongate
Horsley, W. (printer) Saddlergate
Keene, R., Irongate
Mozley, J. & C. (printers & publishers) Friargate
Newbold, J., Mercury-office
Peal, P. (and printer) Corn-market
Pike, W. & W. (printers) Corn-market
Poulton, R., Willow-row
Richardson, Thos. & Sons (pr. & pub.) Ashbourn-rd
Stour, James (and printer) Victoria-street
Stenson, John, Corn-market
Wilkins, G. & Son (printers) Queen-street
Watson, Henry, Friargate

Dealers in Periodicals.

Bestwick, James, Jury-street
Brooks, L., St. Alkmund's-churchyard
Hill, John, Morledge
Jones, W. H., Sitwell-street
Smith, John, Midland-road

News Agents.

Blundston, Samuel, St. Peter-street
Bradbury, Cornelius, Brook-street
Brookes, L., St. Alkmund's-churchyard
Clulow, Edward, Railway-terrace
Poynton, P., Middle Brook-street
Roberts, Thomas, James's-lane
Rowbottom, W., St. Mary-gate
Smith, John, Midland-road
Wilkinson, T., Park-house

GLOSSOP, &c.
Pop. 5467

Dawson, Henry, Hall-street
Islam, John, Howard's-town
Nutter, John, Green-vale
Scholefield, Chas. (binder) Howard's-town

ILKESTON.
Pop. 6122

Wombwell, John

MATLOCK, &c.
From Euston-square 148½ *miles.*   *Pop.* 1327

Adam, John W. Jun. (library)
Cotes, Elizabeth, Cromford

MELBOURNE.
Pop. 2680

Barker, Charles-street
Coxon, James

NEW MILLS.

Collier, R. (printer)

WIRKSWORTH.
Pop. 2632.

Cotes, Elizabeth, Market-place
Deakin, William, St. John-street
Whittaker, James, Market-place

DEVONSHIRE.

ASHBURTON.
Pop. 3432

Burton, John, West-house

Mann, Samuel (news) North-street
Subscription Library, North-street;
   Peter Foot, *Librarian*

Stationers and Printers.

Chappel, James M., West-street
Creagh, Henry C., Western-road
Dobell, Robert, North-street
Stentiford, George (library), East-street

AXMINSTER.
Pop. 2769

Pryer, William S., West-street
Pulman, W., Lyme-street
Wills, Emanuel, Lyme-street

BARNSTAPLE.
Pop. 11,371

Avery, William, High-street
Baker, John, 131, Boatport-street
Carter, George, 95 High-street
Cornish, Thomas, 33 High-street
Evans, John, 54 High-street
Jenvy, G. J.
Hearson, Thomas, 89 High-street
Hearson and Knibb (printers) High-street
Hadrew, Thomas, High-street
Hayman and Petter, High-street
Jones, John (printer) Quay
Searle, S., High-street
Waterfield, J., High-street

BIDEFORD.
Population 5775

Bishop, John, Mill-street
Blight, William, High-street
Cole, William, Allhallow-street
Griffith, Thomas, High-street
Hayman, John G., Grenville-street
Hogg, John J. (printer and binder) Bridge-st
Jacobs, S. (stationer) High-street
Wilson, John (printer) Allhallow-street

BRIXHAM, &c.
Pop. 5627

Ford, James, Fore-street
Goodwin, Enoch (printer) Beach-street
King, A., Fore-street

CHUDLEIGH, &c.
Pop. 2401

Searle, George (binder)
Searle, James (printer and stationer)

CHUMLEIGH, &c.
Pop. 1711

Nott, John (stationer)

COLYTON.
Pop. 2504

Hutchins, Henry (stationer)
Kittle, John (printer)

CREDITON.
From Paddington 197 *miles.*   *Pop.* 3934

Elston, William, High-street
Luxmoor, John V. (printer) High-street
Wreford, S., High-street

COLLUMPTON.

From Paddington 181¼ *miles.   Pop.* 2765

Frost, Isaac (library) Fore-street
Rowe, William (printer) Fore-street
Voisey, M., stationer, Fore-street

DARTMOUTH.

Pop. 4508

Blondett, Mary (library) New-road
Butteris, Valentine (music) New-road
Crauford, Robert, Quay
Jones, M. A. and M., Fosse-street
Maddick, N. & M., Quay

DAWLISH.

From Paddington 206 *miles.   Pop.* 2671

Bond, Elizabeth, 15 Strand
Crowther, A. G., 6 Strand
Westcott, L. (printer) 8 Strand

EXETER.

From Paddington 193¾ *miles.   Pop.* 40,688

Balle, William, 56 High-street
Clifford, William, 25 High-street
Curzon, George, 17 High-street
Drayton, Sarah and Sons, 201 High-street
Evans, J., High-street
Fitze, James, 39 High-street
Glanville, A., Bedford-street
Holden, Adam, 60 High-street
Jessep, James, 31 High-street
Roberts, William, 197 High-street
Shanley, M. A., Mint
Spreat, Jane, 263 High-street
Stone, Robert, 10 New Bridge-street
Vaughan, Dennis, 62 South-street
Wallis, H. J., 20 High-street
Welsford, Harriett, Upper Paul-street
Wheaton, Mary Ann, 185 Fore-street

EXMOUTH.

Pop. 1623

Baker William, Salterton
Bounsall, W. N. (music) Groyder-place
Parsons, John, Salterton
Spencer, Charles, Shepherd's-walk

HOLSWORTHY.

Pop. 1833

Croker, Charles
Jolliffe, John

HONITON.

Pop. 3427

Knight, John, High-street
Spurncey, Mary, High-street
Tucker, Richard (stationer) High-street

ILFRACOMBE.

From Paddington 179 *miles.   Pop.* 2919

Banfield, John, High-street
Lammas, Edwin H., High-street
Wills, Jemima (stationer) High-street

KINGSBRIDGE.

From Paddington 231¾ *miles.   Pop.* 1679

Friend, George, Fore-street

King, George, Fore-street
Pearce, Samuel, Salcombe

MODBURY.

Pop. 1679

Daw, George (printer)

MOLTON.

Pop.

Searle, Geo., East-street
Tepper, Amos, Broad-street
Tucker, William, Broad-street

NEWTON ABBOTS.

From Paddington 214 *miles.   Pop.* 3147.

Daimond, Richard, Courtenay-street
Elms, Jno., East-street
Jacobs, Henry, Bridge-street
Jacobs, Thomas, East-street
Vinning, Fanny, Bridge-street

NORTH TAWTON.

Pop. 1906.

Blight, Samuel

OAKHAMPTON.

Pop. 2165.

Simmonds, Thomas
Townshend, John

OTTERY ST. MARY.

Pop. 2534.

Mayne, Charles D., Silver-street

PLYMOUTH.

From Paddington 246¾ *miles.   Pop.* 52,221.

Albin, Edward, Squire-terrace
Bates, William, Old Town-street
Blackie and Son, York-street
Bass, Henry G. (agent) York-street
Brenden, Fred., 5 Cornwall-street
Briggs, Covn. R., 40 Exeter-street
Bully, Charles, Union-street and High-street
Byne, George, A., Saltash-street
Cole and Land, 18 George-street
Davy, John, 45, High-street
Fullaton and Co., agents, 7 Coburg-street
Henry Jones, agent, 7 Coburg-street
Heydon, Henry H., Tavistock-street
Hyne, Simon, 22 Russell-street
Keys, Isaiah, W. N., Bilbury-street
Lee and Palmer, Bedford-street
Lee, Geo. Samuel and Co. (and mill board
    manufacturers, Tamar-hill)
Lidstone, Roger, 16 George-street
Nettleton, Edward, 30 Whimpole-street
Nicholson, Felix, 16 Bedford-street
Rowe, J. B., Whimpole-street
Rogers, ——, Andrew-street
Sims, ——, Whimpole-street
Stevens, R. W., Parade
Tallis, Jno. and Co., Maley-street
Edwd. Mullins, agent, Maley-street
Tatton, Anthony, High-street
Ward, Mary, North-street
West, ——, Bilbury-street
Jewett and Micklewood, George-street

Bookbinders.
Cann, Edward J., 6 Morley-place
Dingle, William, 4 Briton-side
Gilbert, W. S., 29 King-street
Hayes, Rt., 13 York-street
Hyne, Simon, 22 Russell-street
Martin, Jno., 2 Morley-street
Newcombe, Geo., 9 Old Town-street
Sellick, James, Whimpole-street
Smith, John and Henry, 40 and 41 Treville-st
Tanner and White, Buckwell-lane
Walker, Wm., Finewell-street
Ward, Mary, Old Town-street

DEVONPORT.
Pop. 88,339
Colman, Wm. and Son, 51, Fore-street
Harris, Henry V., 15 Fore-street
Hearle, Geo. W., 118 Fore-street
Heydon, Jno., 104 Fore-street
Keys, Elias, 6 James-street
Lewis, John, 16 Cumberland-street
Lidstone, Roger, 107 Fore-street
Manicom, Edward, Tavistock-street
O'Neill, Andrew, 7 Mary-row
Pearse, John, Marlborough-street
Pengelly, Thos., H., 91 Fore-street
Rattenbury, E. J. 52 Queen-street
Frend, Samuel, 68 St. Aubyn-street
Watson, Alex., 17 Navy-row
Wood, Charles, 5 Stafford's-hill
Wood, William, 55 Fore-street

STONEHOUSE.
Bluckwell, Fred. and Thos. (fancy repository)
  59 Union-street
Cole, Edward, 12 Edgcumbe-street
Doidge, Jno. S., Union-street
Huss, Mary, 24 Chapel-street
Pollard, Wm. N., Edgcumbe-street

SIDMOUTH.
Pop. 2516.
Barnet, Rewlen, Market-place
Harvey, John, Fore-street
Hoyte, Susannah, Fore-street

TAVISTOCK.
Pop. 8086.
Adams, Alex. (library) Market-street
Chase, Thos. and Samuel, Buck-street
Commins, Jno. Locke, West-street
Feaston and Bounsall, West-street

TEIGNMOUTH.
From Paddington 209 *miles.* *Pop.* 5013.
Allen, Jno. Edward, Fore-street
Collings, Geo., Bank-street
Croydon, Edward (publisher) Regent-place
Croydon, Edward and Geo. Henry (printers)
Westcott, Leonard D., Station-row

TOPSHAM.
Pop. 2717.
Ford, Jno. (library) High-street

TIVERTON.
From Paddington 184 *miles.* *Pop.* 11,144.
Dunn, Susan, Fore-street

Marshall, Matthew, Fore-street
Mead, Thos. F., Bampton-street
Parkhouse, Thomas, Fore-street
Sharland, Jno. and Co. (library) Gold-street

TORQUAY.
From Paddington 219 *miles.* *Pop.* 7903.
Cockrem, Edward (library) 10 Strand
Croyden, Edw. (binder) Victoria-parade
Elliott, William, Vaughan-parade
Hall, Wm. H., Lower Union-street
Matthews, Edward James, Braddon's-row
Mudge, Elizabeth (stationer) Market-street
Narracott, Jno. L., Tor-place
Richards, Grace (stationer) Lower Union-st
Robinson, Jno. (library) Paignton
Wreord, R. T., Torwood-row

TORRINGTON, &c.
Pop. 3308.
Fowler, Mary, High-street
Sellick, William, South-street

TOTNESS, &c.
From Paddington 222¾ *miles.* *Pop.* 4419.
Bearne, Jno. behind the Wall
Denner, Jno., Fore-street
Hannaford, Samuel (library) Fore-street
Taylor, Jno. (library) Fore-street

DORSETSHIRE.
BEAMINSTER.
Pop. 2085.
Coombs, Edwin, Hogshill-street
Oliver, Isaac, Market-place
Spink, Samuel, Fore-place

BLANDFORD.
Pop. 3913.
Henville, Chas., Salisbury-street
Hobbs, James, West-street
Shipp, William, Market-place

BRIDPORT.
Pop. 7566.
Brown, John, West-street
Frost, Wm. C. (printer) East-street
Prince, John (printer) East-street
Stroud, Thos. (binder) East-street
Tucker, Francis (printer) South-street

DORCHESTER.
From Waterloo 140¼ *miles.* *Pop.* 6394.
Barclay, Wm. (library) Cornhill
Foster, James, West-street
Mepham, Samuel (binder) South-street
Patch, Thos. (library) High West-street
Simonds, Geo. (printer) South-street
Treeves, Rebecca, High East-street

GILLINGHAM.
Pop. 3775.
Neave, Edward

LYME REGIS.
Pop. 3516.
Dunster, Daniel, Broad-street
Landray, Susan, Church-street

Lock, Henry, Church-street
Moore, Edward, Horse Fair

POOLE.
From Waterloo 122 miles. Pop. 6718.
Fox, George (stationer) Bourne-mouth
Justican, Jas. R., High-street
Lankaster, Jno., High-street
Sydenham, E. M. (fancy stationer) Bourne-m
Turner, John, Bourne-mouth
Tribblett and Mate, Herald Office

SHAFTESBURY.
Pop. 9404.
Bastable, Chas., High-street
Highman, William, High-street
Hurd, R., High-street
Roberts, Geo. and David, High-street
Rutter, Clarence (library) High-street

SHERBORNE.
Pop. 3878.
Cooper, Samuel (binder) Cold-harbour
Kingdon, E. M., Cheap-side
Lavender and Co. (library) Cheapside
Penny, W. S. (library) Halfmoon-street

STALBRIDGE.
Pop. 1326.
Whelpton, Jno. (printer)

STURMINSTER.
Pop. 1916.
Trite, William (stationer and printer)

WAREHAM.
From Waterloo 125 miles. Pop. 7218.
Best, Geo. junr., North-street
Dugdale, E., South-street
Groves, Chas., West-street
Shipp, A., North-street

WEYMOUTH.
Pop. 9548.
Archer, David (printer) Esplanade
Benson and Co., St. Mary-street
Groves, Elizabeth, St. Mary-street
Jeffery, William V. (printer) St. Mary-st
Sherrian, James (printer) St. Mary-street
Tucker, Abraham (music) Charlotte-street

WIMBORNE.
From Waterloo 114½ miles. Pop. 2295.
Boore, Chas. (printer) The Square
Clarke, W. H. (printer) High-street
Housden, J., Westborough
Low, W. (printer) High-street
Purkiss, Alf. (binder) Church-street

DURHAM.
BARNARD CASTLE.
From London 244 miles. Pop. 828.
Atkinson, Jane, Market-place
Atkinson, Jno. R. & Wm., Market-place
Barker, Robert, Horse-market
Clifton, Thomas, Market-place

BISHOP AUCKLAND.
From London 255 miles. Pop. 4400.
Braithwaite, Matthew, Market-place
Fair, Peter (library) 4 Market-place
Hollis, Joseph, Market-place
Lowry, Joseph, Tenter-street

CHESTER LE STREET.
From London 262 miles. Pop. 20,907.
Coates & Farmer (printers) High-row
Dent, George (music) High-row
Jamieson, William (wholesale) Skinner-gate
Manley, John (printer) High-row
Oliver, William (printer) Skinner-gate
Penny, Harrison (printer) Prebend-row
Sams, Joseph, Prebend-row
Stockdale, George, Prebend-row
Watson & Co. (lithographers) Horse-market

CITY OF DURHAM.
From London 259 miles. Pop. 13,188.
Ainsley, William (printer) 74 Saddler-street
Andrews, George (music) 64 Saddler-street
Coward, George, 58 Clay-path
Dickons, John R., 6 Market-place
Franklin, William E., Railway-station
Murray, Mrs. W., 75 Clay-path
Ord, John (stationer & paper dealer) 27 Silver-st
Procter, Geo. (music & printer) 8 Market-place
Walker, George (printer & publisher)
  Mechanics' Institute and Library, Giles-gate
  Library and News Rooms, Queen-street,
  John Shields, *Sec.*; J. Hager, *Librarian.*

GATESHEAD.
Pop. 25,568.
Chambers, James (periodical) 52 High-street
Douglas, William (printer) 14 High-street
Hedley, Joseph (printer) 23 High-street
Jackson, Robert (printer) 31 Bridge-street
Jackson, Thomas (periodical) Oakwell-street
Kelly, Henry (printer) 227 High-street
Rankin, Robert (printer) 38 Bottle-bank
Watson, Geo. (music & library) 35 Bottle-bank
  Gateshead Observer,
    William Douglas, 14 High-street
  Mechanics' Institution, West-street,
    Richard Cooke, *Librarian*
  Public Library, High-fell,
    George Pearson, *Librarian*

HARTLEPOOL.
From London 250 miles. Pop. 9503.
Merryweather & Pearson, High-street
Ord, Ben. Thomas, High-street
Procter, John, High-street
Rymer, John (stationer) Jackson's-dock
  Mechanics' Institute and News Room,
    John Sanderson, *Librarian*

HOUGHTON LE SPRING.
From London 269 miles. Pop. 3224.
Morton, Robert (printer) Sunderland-street
Richardson, William, Sunderland-street
  Mechanics' Institute and News Room,
    Robert Wilkinson, *Librarian*

SAINT JOHN'S, WEARDALE.
Miners' Reading Room and Library,
John Walton, *Librarian*

SEAHAM HARBOUR.
From London 266 miles. Pop. 4042.
Atkinson, David, Rutherford's-buildings
Richardson, John, South-crescent
Mechanics' Institute, North Terrace,
George Stokeld, *Secretary*

SHOTLEY BRIDGE.
From Gateshead 13 miles.
Annandale, John, & Sons (paper-makers) Shotley-grove
Bushby, John, Black-hill
Leslie, Elizabeth (library) Shotley-bridge
Maughan, Mary, Berry-edge
Mechanics' Institute,
John Annandale & John Appleby, *Secs.*

SOUTH SHIELDS.
From London 281 miles. Pop. 28,974.
Coxon, Henry, 25 East King-street
Dobby, Robt. (printer & binder) 48 King-st
Hewison, Hy. (printer & binder) 34 Market-pl
Kelly, R. M., 2 Market-place
Lackland, Jas. (printer) 37 East Holborn
Kidd, Sarah, 32 Thrift-street
Sharp, Geo. B. & Son, 2 Dean-street
Tate, Geo. A. (printer) 16 Market-place
Exchange News Rooms, Town-hall,
John Paxton, *Secretary*

STAINDROP.
From London 246 miles. Pop. 1429.
Harrison, Maria
Heppel, William (printer and binder)
Mechanics' Institute,
William Heppel, *Librarian*

STOCKTON ON TEES.
From London 242 miles. Pop. 9808.
Appleton, John, 20 Bishop-street
Jennet & Co., 58 High-street
Redman, James, 66 High-street
Robinson, W. (library) 42 High-street
Subscription Library, 27 High-street,
John A. Dain, *Librarian*
Mechanics' Institute, Corporation-hall,
W. Holt, & W. Hornsby, *Secretaries*
News Room, Town-hall,
Thomas Appleby, *Secretary*

SUNDERLAND.
From London 302 miles. Pop. 67,974.
Atkinson, M. (printer) Church-street
Atkinson, Robt. (binder) 22 Coronation-street
Barnes, W. B. (binder) 135 High-street
Burnett, George (binder) 210 High-street
Capon, Robert, 189 Market
Comin, Thos. (binder) Little Villiers-street
Dixon, Hy. J. (printseller) 216 High-street
De Lacy, Charles (binder) 12 Sans-street
Garbut, George (library) 190 High-street
Graydon, Robert (printer) 149 High-street
Hills, William H., 186 High-street

Hodge, John B., 74 High-street
Huison, Robert, 106 Coronation-street
Huntley, Joseph, 233 High-street
Marwood, Thomas June, 141 High-street
Morrison, David, 245 High-street
Reed, Thomas & Co., 185 High-street
Smith, Edmund & Son, 188 High-street
Tarbut, William, 41 Church-street
Thompson, Thomas, 11 High-street
Vint and Carr, 175 High-street
Williams, James, 129 High-street
Williams, John R., 11 High-street
Yallowley, Jane, 57 High-street
Athenæum Library, 27 Fawcett-street,
James Stevenson, *Librarian*
Law Library, Lambton-street,
Thomas Burn, *Secretary*
Subscription Library, 190 High-street,
George Garbutt, *Librarian*
Subscription & News Room, Barclay-street,
M. Atkinson, *Librarian*
Mechanics' Institute,
Thomas Dixon, Jun. *Secretary*

WOLSINGHAM.
From London 256 miles. Pop. 4585.
Chapman, John, High-street
Knapton, James, High-street

ESSEX.
BARKING.
From Shoreditch 7 miles. Pop. 493.
Nash, James (stationer) High-street
Welch, Eliza (stationer) North-street

BILLERICAY.
From Shoreditch 24 miles. Pop. 1533.
Eccardt, F. W. (stationer)
Keircher, W. H. R. (stationer)
Nix, J. K. (Stamp Office)

BRAINTREE.
From Shoreditch 44¾ miles. Pop. 4340.
Coote, Wm. (stationer) High-street
Joscelyne, Jas. & Son (printers & stationers) High-street
Shearcroft, Jno. F. (printer) Bank-street
White, Jas. (binder) London-road

BRENTWOOD.
From Shoreditch 19 miles. Pop. 2205.
Corden, W. (stationer and printer)
Twinn, L. Miss (stationer)

CHELMSFORD.
From Shoreditch 29 miles. Pop. 7795.
Arthy, T. B. (music, binder, and library) High-street
Bond, Geo. Thos. (music) Springfield-lane
Boobyer, Adam, New Bridge-street
Burrell, T. H. and W. D. (binders & library) High-street
Dutton, T. D. (printer, pub. and news) Conduit-st
Edwards, Chas. (law stationer) High-street
Fry, Josh. (printer, binder, and news) High-street
Shearcroft, J. (printer & stationer) High-st

Woolnough, T. (binder) Union-yard
Literary Institution ; J. E. Bailes, *Sec.*, New
    London-road
Chelmsford Chronicle ; Meggy & Chalk, High-st

CHIPPING ONGAR.
From Shoreditch 20 miles. Pop. 843.
Scruby, Wm. (stationer)
Slocombe, Chas. (printer)

COGGLESHALL.
From Shoreditch 44 miles. Pop. 4010.
Coventry, Alf. (stationer, &c.) Market-end
Coventry, Jas. (printer) Market-end
Durrant, S. (printer) Market-hill
    Literary Institution and Reading-rooms,
    S. Jackson, *Sec.*; E. Fenn, *Librarian.*

COLCHESTER.
From Shoredtch 51¼ miles. Pop. 19,443.
Avey, J. H. (binder) Balkerne-hill
Bacon, Thos. (printer and binder) St. John-st
Benham, Edward (binder, stationer, and library
    and news) High-street
Brackett, J. (also printer, stationer, binder, and
    news) High-street
Corder, Jno. (news) North-street
Dennis, C. Mrs. (printer, binder, and stationer)
    High-street
Essex Gazette, W. A. Warwick (pub.) 19 High-st
Essex Standard, John Taylor, jun. (pub.)
    27 High-street
Fenton, C. F. (printer, &c.) 51 High-street
Fincham, W. (repository Christian knowledge)
    91 High-street
Harvey, J. B. (printer, stationer, and news)
    166, High-street, publisher of
Ipswich Express and Essex and Suffolk Mercury
Mattacks, H. Miss (stationer) 14 Hyre-street
Rudkin, Jno. (printer, binder, and stationer)
    7 Crouch-street
Totham, W. (also printer, binder, & stationer)
    24, High-street
    Conservative Reading-rooms, Three Cups
    Hotel, George Chaplin.
    Literary Institution, Thos. Bacon, St. John-st

DUNMOW.
From Shoreditch 35 miles. Pop. 3235.
Brown, E. Miss (stationer)
Carter, D. (stationer)
    Church of England and Union Society's Li-
    brary, J. J. Britton
    Literary Institution, Thos. Williss, *Librarian*

EPPING.
From Shoreditch 15 miles. Pop. 1821.
Clements, H. A. (stationer)
Griffiths, F. (printer and stationer)
    Literary Institution, Jno. Thurlow, *Librarian*

GRAYS.
From Shoreditch 20½ miles. Pop. 1713.
Henderson, M. A. (stationer) High-street

HALSTEAD.
From Shoreditch 46 miles. Pop. 6982.
Carter, Alfred (printer & stationer) High-street

Clarke, R. (depository of Christian knowledge)
    High-street
Gilbert, Hy. (printer) High-street
Riddell, R. (wholesale stationer) North-street
    Mechanics' Institution, Thos. Swindells,
    High-street

HARLOW.
From Shoreditch 26½ miles. Pop. 2198.
Whittaker, Charles, High-street

HARWICH.
From Shoreditch 71½ miles. Pop. 3383.
Rawlings, Jno. (stationer) Market-street
Saxby, Jos. (stationer) Church-street
Smith, Jas. (printer and publisher) Church-st

HAVERHILL.
From Shoreditch 54 miles. Pop. 2278.
Bigmore, Samuel (printer)
Dearsley, W. (printer and stationer)
Stams, H. J. (stationer)
    Library and Lecture Society, W. W. Boreham

HEDINGHAM.
*From Shoreditch to Braintree 44½ miles, and
7 miles from there to Hedingham. Pop. 2346.*
Carter, Jeffery (stationer) Post Office

ILFORD.
From Shoreditch 7 miles. Pop. 3746.
Bayley, Jno. (depository of Christian knowledge)
Chapman, Joseph (stationer and news)

KELVEDON.
From Shoreditch 41¾ miles. Pop. 1633.
Eley, Josh. (printer and binder)
Sadler, Isaac (stationer)
    Literary Institution, J. G. Mechi, *Chairman*
    J. D. Eley and J. D. Bennell, *Librarian*

MALDON.
From Shoreditch 44 miles. Pop. 4558.
Bridge, Geo. D. (printer and news) High-street
Youngman, P. H. (printer) High-street
    Mechanics Institution, High-st, J. Everard,
    Librarian
    Library, Rev. E. R. Horwood, *Librarian.*

MANNINGTREE.
From Shoreditch 60 miles. Pop. 2692.
Watts, Thos. High-street
    Mechanics' Institution, South-street, John
    Sizer, *Secretary*

PLAISTOW.
From Whitechapel 4½ miles. Pop. 2668.
King, Mrs. S. (stationer) Balaam-street

RAYLEIGH.
From Shoreditch 34 miles. Pop. 1463.
Rissey, William

ROCHFORD.
From Shoreditch 40 miles. Pop. 1704.
Arthy, Thos. B.
Raymond, Jno. (binder)
Scott, Mrs. M. M. (stationer)

ROMFORD.

From Shoreditch 13 miles. Pop. 5868.

Bridge, Samuel (printer) Market-place
Jull, Thos. (stationer) High-street
Robinson, Thos. (stationer) Market-place
Literary Institution, A. F. Merrett, *Sec.*

SAFFRON WALDEN.

From Shoreditch 40 miles. Pop. 5911.

Hart, Henry (printer) Market-street
Youngman & Son (printers and stationers)
    Market-place
Literary Institution, W. F. Ackland, *Sec.*

STRATFORD.

From Shoreditch 3¼ miles. Pop. 10,586.

Burton, Miss M. (stationer) Broadway
Edgar, Jno. (library) Broadway
Morris, M. Mrs. (library) Broadway
Morris, Sept. (stationer) High-street
Showell, James, sen. (stationer) Broadway
Tennant, Wm. (printer & stationer) Broadway

WALTHAM ABBEY.

From Shoreditch 14 miles. Pop. 4303.

Clements, Henry (stationer) High Bridge-st
Littler, Edmd. (printer) Sun-street
Marshall, J. A. (stationer) High Bridge-street
Smith, J. S. (library) High Bridge-street

WALTHAMSTOW.

From Shoreditch 6 miles. Pop. 4959.

Baalham, Ann Mrs. (stationer) Church-end
Pringle, Geo. (stationer, &c.) Marsh-street
Ralph, Thos. (stationer) Wood-street

WANSTEAD.

From Shoreditch 7 miles. Pop. 2207.

Scales, Miss Julia (library)

WITHAM.

From Shoreditch 37 miles. Pop. 3303.

Cheek, R. F. (printer and binder)
Knight, K. Mrs. (printer)
Literary Institution and News-room, James
    Warden, *Librarian*

WOODFORD.

From Shoreditch 8 miles. Pop. 2774

Badrick, William, Woodford-green
Echford, M. A. Mrs. (news) Snake's-lane
Newman, Edward (stationer) Woodford-green

GLOUCESTERSHIRE.

BRISTOL.

From Paddington 118½ miles. Pop. 137,328

Ackland, James, Dolphin-street
Andrews, William, Corn-street
Arrowsmith,
Barton, James, Dardham-downs.
Bevan, George, Hotwells-road
Bingham, Mary, Broad-street
Burbidge, John, Clifton
Chandler, Jos., Castle-street
Chiltoh, Jno., Clare-street
Clarke, Chas., Castle Mill-street
Clements, William Henry, High-street
Coombs, William, Horse-fair

Cheese, J. R., Broadmead
Curry, Jno. J., Queen-street
Cook, W. H., Broadmead
Evans and Abbott, Clare-street
Foulder, Jno., King's-square-avenue
George, William, Bath-street
Haggett and Trew, Park-street
Hobbs, John, Nelson-place
Honiwell, William, Temple-street
Jones, J. M., 6 Clare-street
Kerslake, Thos., Park-street
King, H. H., Small-street
Lancaster, Thos., Portland-place
Lander, Samuel, Stokes-croft
Lanbury, Oliver, Park-street
Lavans, John, Bridge-street
Morgan, William, Clare-street
Newcombe, J. W., John-street
Oldland, Henry, Corn-street
Palmer, Jno., College-green
Parsons, William, Upper-arcade
Parsons, William, Kingsdown
Pickering, Alfred, Broad-street
Prescott, W. T., Milk-street
Probert, William, Kingsdown
Reader, Samuel, Park-street
Reed, Henry, West-street
Rose, Philip, Broadmead
Shepherd, B., Mall-place
Tanner, Jacob G., Redcliffe-street
Tolemon, H., Christmas-street
Virtue, Francis, Pembroke-street
Waite, Jos. and Hen., Broadmead
Way, William, 69 College-street
Weston, Thos. Henry, Corn-street
Wharton, G. M.
Whearat, Wm., sen., St. Michael's-hill
Wood, George, Wine-street
Wright, James, Bridge-street

Stationers.

Adams, James, W., Peter-street
Aldridge, William, Redcliffe-street
Bissell, William, sen., James-parade
Brown, And., West-street
Chandler, Mary, Welsh-back
Chapman, Abraham, Broad-quay
Coombs, Jas., Park-street
Cross and Cox, Bridge-street
Freame, W. H., Castle-street
Gowen, Samuel, Clifton-place
Holden, Jacob, Old-market-street
Jones, William, Nelson-street
Matthews, Edw., Upper-arcade
Miller, Samuel, Park-street
Morrish, Henry, Narrow Wine-street
Page, Jno. A., Broad-street
Payne, Jas., Castle-street
Price and Co., Bridge-street
Richards, Nelson-street
Robinson, E. S., Redcliffe-street
Rose, Henry, West-street
Simeon, Felix, Old-market-street
Smith, William, Orchard-street
Tanner, Brothers, St. Stephen-street

Tongue, Jas. Alf., Wine-street
Wainsbrough, Jno., and Sons, Redcliffe-street
Workman, Ryland Floyd, 11 Narrow Wine-st

CHELTENHAM.

From Paddington 121 miles. Pop. 35,051.

Alder, Daniel, Promenade
Baily, William, 5 Queen's-circus
Bormor, Geo. F., 95 Winchcomb-street
Bunting, Jos., Westall-place
Cowling, Geo., 14 Suffolk-parade
Davies, Henry, 1 Montpellier-street
Dight, Lewis, 333, High-street
Edwards, Rd., 82 High-street
Gardner, Mary, 62 Winchcombe-street
Grove, Jas. (Catholic) 6 Chester-walk
Harper, Thos. (vendor of patent medicines)
     318 High-street
Henley, Eley, 23, Pittville-street
Hendrigues, M. Q., 286 High-street
Long, Jos., 7 Well-walk
Maynard, Geo. M., 84 High-street
Mew, Jas., 11¼ Colonnade
Palmer, Henry, 5 Keynsham-bk
Shenton, Thos. B., 90 Winchcombe-street
Shipton, Thos., 13 Promenade-villas
Webb, Chas., 7 Winchcombe-street
Westley and Co., 96 High-street
Wight and Bailey, Promenade
Williams, Geo. A., 393 High-street

CIRENCESTER.

From Paddington 95 miles. Pop. 6096.

Bailey and Jones (bookbinders) Market-street
Hart, Step., John, Gosditch-street
Ovens, Jos. (old bookseller) Dyer-street
Smith, Hen. (bookbinder) Market-place

COLEFORD.

Hough, Jno. Jas. (printer)
Watts, Sarah and Hannah (Berlin wool
     dealers)

DURSLEY.

Pop. 2617.

Rickards and Workman, Market-place
Stephens, Jno., Parsonage-street
Workman, Rufus (and printer) Market-place

GLOUCESTER.

From Paddington 114 miles. Pop. 17,572.

Davies, T. R., 5 Northgate-square
Henley, Wm. (bookbinder and machine ruler)
     47 Eastgate-street
Jew and Waring, 153 Westgate-street
Power, Edw., 6 Westgate-street
Stokes, William, College-court
Lea, Ann, 2 Westgate-street
Mansell, William, F., College-court
Thomas, Chas., 28 Westgate-street
Whitehead, Alf., 90 Southgate-street

MINCHINHAMPTON.

Pop. 4469.

Partridge, Wm. (stationer) Nailsworth
Sims, Anthony (stationer) Nailsworth

STOW.

Lane, Rd. Waite

STROUD.

From Paddington 101½ miles. Pop. 36,535.

Bailis, William, High-street
Brisley, Jno. P., High-street
Bucknall and Son, King-street
Harmer, Fredk., George-street
Poole, Catherine, Cairnscross
Watts, Jos., Cairnscross
Brierley, J. P.
Webb
Pritchard, H. G.

TETBURY.

From Paddington 91 miles. Pop. 2615..

Goodwin, Jno. G.

TEWKESBURY.

Pop. 5878.

Bennett, Jas., 139 High-street
Garrison, Jno. (library) 139 High-street
Jenner, Isaac (library) Cross
Lawler, Jno., 146 High-street

THORNBURY.

Pop. 1470.

Brown, Jno. (binder)
Eley, Martha
Hughes, Griffith

WOOTTON-UNDER-EDGE.

Pop. 4224.

Hunt, S. A., Long-street
Page, Sophia, Long-street
Povey, Lewis, Long-street
Pressley, Rd., Market-street

HAMPSHIRE.

ALRESFORD.

Moody, Jas. B.

ALTON.

Pop. 2828.

Barnfield, Geo., High-street
Beale, Francis (stationer) High-street
Walden, John, High-street

ANDOVER.

From Waterloo 58 miles. Pop. 10,582.

Brown, Fred. J. J., High-street
Dyson, Johd, High-street
Marcer, George, High-street

BASINGSTOKE.

From Waterloo 47¾ miles. Pop. 4263.

Chandler, Samuel, Winchester-street
Cottle, Robert, Winchester-street

BISHOPS WALTHAM.

From Waterloo to Bottley 78¾ mls. Pop. 2265.

Ellyett, E., High-street
Roberts, W., Bank-street

CHRISTCHURCH.

From Waterloo 99 miles. Pop. 7475.

Tucker, W. (printer) High-street
White, Josh., High-street

FAREHAM.
From Waterloo 84¼ miles.   Pop. 5842.
Annett, Edward, West-street.
Gough, Fredk., Tichfield

FORDINGBRIDGE.
Pop. 3096
Jubb, Jas. (music) High-street
Fulford, W. L. (stationer) Salisbury-street

HAVANT.
From London-bridge by Brighton-line 88 mls.
Pop. 2416.
Baker, W. S., High-street
Cobby, S., Queen-street
Freeland, Henry, Bedhampton
Jones, John, High-street
Lock, Charles, Earl-street
White, George, West-street
Stride, John (library) The Square

LYMINGTON.
Pop. 5282.
Galpine, W. L., High-street
King, Richard, High-street
Watterson, Charles, High-street

ODIHAM.
Pop. 2811.
Gotilee, Henry, High-street

PETERSFIELD.
Pop. 5550.
Duplock, G., High-street
Minchin, W. A., jun., High-street

PORTSMOUTH.
From Waterloo 94¼ miles; from London-bridge
95 miles.   Pop. 72,096, including Portsea.
Batchelor, Thomas (binder) High-street
Bonney, C., Broad-street
Charpentier, W. H. (printer) 60 High-street
Comelford, S., Penny-street
Gardner H. (binder & printer) St. Mary-street
Godfrey, W., 100 High-street
Lewis, Henry, 114 High-street
Legg, George, High-street
May, James, St. Thomas-street

PORTSEA.
From Waterloo or London-bridge.
Pop. 72,096, including Portsmouth.
Bonney, W. C., Hanover-street
Betts, Mary, 90 Queen-street
Chark, G. H. (binder) Union-street
Griffin, Samuel, Queen-street
Gardner, Henry, sen., Queen-street
Hinton, Thomas, Hanover-street
Horsey, Samuel (printer) Queen-street
Jones, James, Union-street
Moxon, George (printer) Queen-street
Nightingale, Henry, Southsea
Trives, J. (binder & printer) St. George's-sq.
Woodward, Wm. (printer) Common Hard
Williams, E. (printer) Queen-street
Weeks, W., Queen-street

RINGWOOD.
From Waterloo 105 miles.   Pop. 3928.
Wheaton, W. A., High-street
Woodford, Spencer, High-street

ROMSEY.
From Waterloo 80½ miles.   Pop. 2080.
Chignell, William, Market-place
Medley, John (binder) Bell-street
Lorden, J., (printer) Market-place

SOUTHAMPTON.
From Waterloo 78¾ miles.   Pop. 35,305.
Bookbinders.
Bradsheet, Thomas, College-street.
Brown, A., 141 High-street
Cawte, Charles, Castle-lane
Marshall, G. L., High-street
Paul, E., High-street
Peirce, W., Bevois-street
Roberts, Edmund, High-street
Booksellers, &c.
Bleekley, G. W., Oxford-street
Bonner, Alfred, East-street
Bown, Ann (library) High-street
Cox, J. C., St. Mary-street
Colborne, J., 25 Above Bar
Davies, George, Canal-walk
Forbes and Marshall, High-street
Foster, J. and G., High-street
Marshall, John L., High-street
Paul, Edward, High-street
Phillips, J., High-street
Rayner, C., High-street
Rayner, J. F., High-street
Roberts, M. S. (library) St. Mary-street
Sharland, W., High-street
Webb, W., High-street
Watts, James, Totton

WINCHESTER.
From Waterloo-bridge 66½ miles.   Pop. 13,704
Allen, George, Jury-street
Gilmour, D. E. (printer) High-street
Jacob and Johnson (printer) High-street
Nutt, David, College-street
Tanner, William, (printer) College-street
Warren, Matthew (printer) High-street
Barclay, H., High-street

ISLE OF WIGHT.

COWES.
Pop. 4786.
Hillyer, William, High-street
Pinhorn, James, High-street
Richardson, William (stationer) Bath-road
Symonds, John, Bath-road

NEWPORT.
Pop. 8047.
Denyer, R. J., 35 Pyle-street
Gubbins, J. and W., 27 High-street
Neat, John, 98 High-street
Snooks and Upward, 96 High-street
Upward, Edward, 52 High-street
Yelf, W. W., 12 and 13 Holyrood-street

RYDE.
Pop. 7147.

Beazley, William J., High-street
Butler, George (printer and binder) Lind-street
Briddon, James, Cross-street
Burt, Helen (stationer) Union-street
Gabell, William (printer) Union-street
Hebert, Charles D., Pier-street
Hellyer, P. S., Union-street
Turtle, S. and C., Union-street
Wagner, Ann, Union-street

VENTNOR.
Pop. 2569.

Butler, Thomas, High-street
Johnson, Thomas, Shanklin
Moore, F. (music) Marine Library
Printz, J. (stationer) High-street
Squire, W. F. (printer and library) High-street

HEREFORDSHIRE.
BROMYARD.
From Paddington or Euston-sq. Pop. 3093.

Eckley, Harriet
Gardner, E. and A., Library

HEREFORD.
From Paddington 145 miles; Euston-square
via Shrewsbury 212 miles. Pop. 12,108.

Davies, Thomas, High Town.
Gardner, John, Church-street
Head, Joseph, High Town
Jones, Joseph, Broad-street
Merrick, F. and A., High-street
Parker, John, High-street
Parry, W., Bye-street
Phillips, High Town
Bookbinders only.
Bather, John, Maylord's-lane
Roberts, W., Victoria-street
Musicsellers, &c.
Bradley, Edward, Commercial-road
Chilk, Ellen, Broad-street

KINGTON.
From Paddington to Hereford 145 miles;
thence by coach. Pop. 2871.

Humphreys, Charles, High-street
Went, Francis, High-street
Wilson, John (printer) Bridge-street

LEDBURY.
From Paddington to Worcester 120½ miles;
thence by coach. Pop. 3027.

Baylis, Philip, High-street
Gibbs, James J., Home End-street
Roberts, W. A., New-street

LEOMINSTER.
From Euston-square via Shrewsbury 199¾ mls.
Pop. 5214.

Chilcott, J. V. (library) Broad-street
Went, F. and Son, High-street
Woolley, T. and J., Broad-street

ROSS.
From Paddington 131 miles. Pop. 4071.

Counsell, W. F., High-street
Dobles, G. C. (library) High-street
Farrer, T. J., High-street
Vaughan, Thomas, Broad-street

HERTFORDSHIRE.
BALDOCK.
From King's-cross 37 miles. Pop. 1920.

Thody, S. J. (stationer and news) High-street
News and Reading Room, Uigh-street

BARNET.
From King's-cross 9¼ miles. Pop. 2379.

Baldock and Son (printers) Dyrham-place
Baldock, William (stationer) New-road
Cook, John, (stationer) Uadley
Cowing, S. A., Mrs.(printer & binder) High-st.
Ellis, W. (stationer) High-street
Matthews, M. A., High-street, Hadley

BERKHAMPSTEAD.
From Euston-square 28 miles. Pop. 3395

Thane, George D. (printer) High-street
Mechanics' Institute, High-street, S. Crewe

BISHOPS STORTFORD.
From King's-cross 18 miles. Pop. 5280.

Bradfield, Thomas (printer, binder, & library)
Ellison, Robert (fancy stationer) Potters-street
King, J. M. (stationer) Hockerill
Mullinger, J. M. (binder) North-street
Library and Reading-room, Corn Exchange

BUNTINGFORD, &c.
From King-cross 34¼ miles. Pop. 6590.

Nicholls, Charles (stationer) Post-office

CHESHUNT.
From Shoreditch 16¼ miles. Pop. 5579.

Buck, Thomas (library) Turner's-hill
Properjohn, Mrs. M. (stationer) Cheshunt-st.
Threader, George (stationer) Cheshunt-street
Literary Institution, Turner's-hill, J. B.
Chaplin, *Secretary*

HARPENDEN.
From King's-cross 25¼ miles. Pop. 1980.

Vallance, William (stationer)

HATFIELD.
From King's-cross 17¾ miles. Pop. 3862.

Cox, Stephen (stationer) Fore-street

HEMEL HEMPSTEAD.
From Euston-square 23½ miles. Pop. 7073.

Girl, C., Mrs. (stationer) High-street
Mason, Frederick (printer) High-street
Depository of Christian Knowledge, William
Frowd, High-street
Literary Institution, J. Hailes, *Secretary*

HERTFORD, &c.
From Shoreditch 26 miles. Pop. 6605.

Austin, S. (printer and binder, &c.) Fore-street
Cobb and Co., Fore-street
Huchs, W. H. (law stationer) Castle-street

Munday, W. G. (stationer) Maidenhead-street
Pollard, W. (printer and publisher) Old-cross
Prior, William (stationer) The Wash
Rose, John, Fore-street
Simson, G. & S. E. (printers, binders, &c.)
  Market-place
  Literary Institution, G. A. Towers, *Secretary*
  County Press and Hertford Mercury, S.
  Austin, Fore-street
  Hertford Guardian, W. Pollard, Old-cross

HITCHIN.
From King's-cross 32 miles.   Pop. 7077.
Palmer, John, Cock-street
Paternoster, Charles and Thomas (printers,
  binders, &c.) Sun-street
Tonson, Samuel B. (printer, binder, &c.) Market-
  place and Post-office

HODDESDON.
From Shoreditch 17 miles.   Pop. 1854.
Cheffins, S. & M., Misses (fancy) High-street
Dickenson, Geo. (stationer & printer) High-st.
  Literary Institution, Charles Christie, *Sec.*

KING'S LANGLEY, &c.
From Euston-square 21 miles.   Pop. 1599.
Butcher, W. *Manager*, Messrs. Dickenson's,
  paper-makers, Home Park Mills
Caslon, H. and Co. (type-founders)
Dickenson, J. & Co. (paper-makers) Apsley Mill
Pearman, Edward (stationer)
Peacock, *Manager*, Mach Mills

RICKMANSWORTH.
From Euston Square 20¾ miles.   Pop. 4851.
Dickenson and Longman, Batchworth-mills,
  J. Tolley, *Manager*
Dickenson and Longman, Croxley-mill, Thos.
  Allcock, *Manager*
Harvey, Geo. (news) High-street
Ingram, H. (paper) Loudwater-mills
Newman, Misses S. E. and S. (fancy) High-st
  Literary Institution, D. Beaumont, *Secretary*,
  High-street

ROYSTON.
From King's-cross 44¾ miles.   Pop. 2061.
Warren, Jno. (publisher, binder, &c.) High-st
Wilkerson, Jas. (stationer and binder) Knees-
  worth-street
  Subscription Library and Reading-room,
  Thos. Pickering, *Librarian*, John-st
  Subscription Library and Reading-room,
  Jno. Warren, *Librarian*, High-street

ST. ALBANS.
*From King's-cross to Hatfield 17¾ miles, and
  6 beyond.   Pop. 7000.*
Bayly, A. T. (news) Verulam-street
Boobyer, Adam, Verulam-street
Gibbs, Rd., and Son (printers) Market-pl
Langley, Wm. (printer) High-street
Potts, R.
Rayment, Edwd. (stationer) Holywell-st
Stracy, Miss S. (stationer) High-street

TRING.
From Euston-square 31¾ miles.   Pop. 3218.
Bird, E. C. (printer) High-street
Gates, Thos., High-street
Kindell, J. Depository of Christian Knowledge,
  High-street
Mechanics' Institution, C. Grace, *Sec.*

WARE.
From Shoreditch 24¼ miles.   Pop. 4882.
Ffrost, Joseph P. B. (printer and binder)
  High-street
Peacock, W. (stationer) High-street
Price, Mrs. E. (stationer) High-street
  Library and Reading-room, Geo. Price, *Sec.*

WATFORD.
From Euston-square 17¼ miles.   Pop. 3800.
Bigg, Thos. (news) High-street
Gibbs, R. (stationer) High-street
Litchfield, Miss A. (fancy) High-street
Morley, Jas. (library) High-street
Peacock, Jno. and Son (printers and publishers
  of the Watford Weekly Advertiser) High-st
Slowgrove, Rd., High-street
Young, Wm., Depôt of Religious Tract Society,
  High-street

WELWYN.
From King's-cross 22 miles.   Pop. 1557.
Lawrance, Philip (stationer)

HUNTINGDONSHIRE.
HUNTINGDON.
*From King's-cross 58¾ miles; or Shoreditch
  viâ Cambridge.   Pop. 6219.*
Edis, Rt. (library) High-street
Hatfield, Jas., High-street
Wood, A. P., High-street

KIMBOLTON.
Pop. 1633.
Brewster, Wm. (stationer) Back-street
Craddock, Geo., Front-street
Gudgeon, G. B. (stationer) Church-lane
Hall, Chas., Front-street
Ibbs, Chas., Front-street

RAMSEY.
Pop. 2641.
Mutton, Wm., Gt. White
Palmer, Isaac, High-street

ST. IVES.
From Shoreditch 72 miles.   Pop. 3522.
Chapman, M., Crown-street
Gardner, S., Crown-street
Skeles, Geo., Sheep-market

ST. NEOTS.
From King's-cross 51½ miles.   Pop. 2951.
Emery and Son, Market-place
Thomson, D. R. (printer) Market-place
Topham, Jas. (printer) High-street

SOMERSHAM.
From Shoreditch 77½ miles.   Pop. 1653.
Bayes, Chas., Somersham
Wiles, Jas., Somersham

2

KENT.

ASH.

From London 64 miles; from Canterbury 10.
Pop. 2095
Adkins, J. T. (stationer)

ASHFORD.

From London-bridge 67 *miles. Pop.* 5007
Elliott & Son (binders, printers, & library)
　High-street
Igglesden, Henry (binder & printer) High-st
Moore, George (news) High-street

BEXLEY HEATH & WELLING.

From London 12 *miles. Pop.* 2098
Lovelace, John
Mesnard, John (stationer & news agent)
Temple, Thomas (printer & binder)

BLACKHEATH.

From London-bridge 6 *miles.*
Arnott, George (stationer) Tranquil-vale
Burnside, William, Tranquil-vale
Earl, E. S. (music) Tranquil-vale
Howell, Miss E. J. (stationer) Grote's-place
Wray, A. H. (fancy) Spencer-place
　Institution & Reading Room, John Huggett,
　　Librarian
　Subscription Library, W. Burnside, *Librarian*

BROADSTAIRS.

From London 98 *miles. Pop.* 2975
Barnes, David (marine library) Albion-st
Cantwell, Edward, 28 Albion-street

BROMLEY.

From London 10 *miles. Pop.* 4127
Taylor, George (printer) High-street
　Literary Institution, B. Wood, *Librarian*
　District Society for Promoting Christian
　　Knowledge, Thomas Campling, *Secretary*,
　　High-street

BUCKLAND.

From London 69 *miles. Pop.* 1895
Ashdown, Charles (paper maker)

CANTERBURY.

From London-bridge 81 *miles. Pop.* 18,398
Ashdown & Co. (wholesale stationers) High-st
Ashton, John (binder) Burgate-street
Austen, W. & R., Burgate-street
Bundock, John (stationer) St. Peter's-street
Caldwell, Samuel (stationer) Northgate-street
Chivers, Henry (printer) Palace-street
Colegate, Robert (printer) Parade
Davey, W. (news) Guildhall-street
Deverson, J. (binder) Castle-street
Ginder, A., St. George's-hall
Goulden, Charles, High-street
Hayward, Charles (binder) Burgate-lane
Jennings, William (printer) St. George's-street
Ladd, G. W. (news) Burgate-street
Maiten, Charles (printer) High-street

Mudford, Mrs. A. (printer & publisher of the
　Kentish Observer & Canterbury Journal)
　47 St. George-street
Pullen, Charles (printer) Guildhall-street
Ward, Henry (printer & publisher) 31 High-st
Ward, Henry W. (printer) Mercery-lane
Wood, W. (law stationer) St. Margaret-street
　Literary Institution, Guildhall-street; J. W.
　　Pilcher, *Secretary*
　Church of England Young Men's Literary
　　Institution, St. George's-hall; Rev. H.
　　Curtis, *Secretary*; James Reed, *Librarian*
　Clerical Library, Precincts
　Kentish Library & Reading Room, 6 Parade

CRANBROOK.

From London 48 *miles. Pop.* 4020
Dennett, J. T. (stationer) High-street
Waters, — (printer) Church-gates

CRAYS (THE).

From London 12 *miles. Pop.* 2893
Balls, Stephen (stationer) Post-office, Foot's Cray
Joynson & Son (paper makers) St. Mary Cray
Nash, Thomas & William (paper makers)
　St. Paul's Cray
Woodfall, Henry (paper maker) Foot's Cray
　Literary Institution, J. S. Featherstone, *Sec.*

DARTFORD.

From London-bridge 17 *miles. Pop.* 6054
Dunkin & Son (printer & publisher) High-st
Golding, Thomas (stationer) Spital-street
Reeves, J. A. (printer & binder) High-street
Saunders, T. H. (paper maker) Phœnix-mills
　Literary Institution, High-st.; J. A. Reeves,
　　Secretary

DEAL.

From London-bridge 102 *miles. Pop.* 7067
Cavell, Thomas V. (news) 201 Lower-street
Deveson, John (printer & stationer) Lower-st
Hayward, Edward (printer) 7 Lower-street
Hayward, Thomas (printer) 23 Lower-street

DEPTFORD.

From London-bridge 4 *miles.*
Bowles, C. J. (news) Broadway
Goldfinch, Mrs. P. (fancy) High-street
Paine, Daniel George, High-street
Porritt, Isaac (printer) High-street
Warcup, William, Broadway
　Mechanics' Institution, High-street; Henry
　　Goodwin, *Secretary*

DOVER.

From London-bridge 88 *miles. Pop.* 22,244
Amos, John (binder) 53 Biggin-street
Batchelor, William (Dover Telegraph, & printer
　& publisher) 1 Snargate-street
Bowles, W. J. (news) 164 Snargate-street
Binfield, George (music) 44 Snargate-street
Brett, William (printer) Fishmongers'-lane
Briggs, John (printer & proprietor of the
　Dover Chronicle) King-street
Cozens, Thomas (news) Castle-street
Fox, John (binder) 119 Snargate-street
Gardner, Thomas (printer) 146 Snargate-st

Garnett, Rebecca (depository for religious tracts) 40 Biggin-street
Harris, Henry (printer) 2 New-bridge
Hart, Henry (printer) 175 Snargate-street
Igglesdon, S. P. (news) 35 St. James's-street
Johnson, John (printer) King-street
Judge, John, 24 Snargate-street
Mate, Miss E. (stationer) King-street
Paine, William (news) 23 Biggin-street
Rigden, Thomas (printer & stationer) 66 Snargate-street
Sutton & Potter (music) 3 New-bridge
Warren, Geo. (marine library) Marine-parade
Williams, Charles, 7 Town-hall-street
Williams, Thomas (stationer) 37½ Snargate-st

EASTRY.

From London 102½ miles.　Pop. 1697
Foord, George, Post-office

ELTHAM.

From London 8 miles.　Pop. 2437
Edlon, Mrs. J. (stationer) High-street
Lacy, John (binder & news) Court-yard
Pike, Mrs. R. (stationer) Post-office

ERITH.

From London-bridge 14 miles.　Pop. 2231
Allen, James (stationer)

FAVERSHAM, &c.

From London 47 miles.　Pop. 7450
Boulden, Henry (stationer) West-street
Harding, John (printer, binder, & library) Market-place
Monk, Frederick (library and reading-room) Court-street
Literary Institution, Court-street; William Maile, *Secretary*

FOLKESTONE.

From London-bridge 82 miles.　Pop. 6726
Creed, Edmund (printer) High-street
Davis, John Oliver, High-street
English, John, High-street
Hunt, John (fancy) High-street
Stock, Henry (library) High-street
Tiffin, William (library) Kingsbridge-street

GOUDHURST.

From London 56 miles.　Pop. 2595
Stevens, William

GRAVESEND.

From London-bridge 24 miles.　Pop. 21,782
Acklam, John, Kentish Independent Office, 34 Wakefield-street
Baker, James (stationer) Milton-road
Baynes, G. J. (printer) Windmill-street
Caddell, R., & Son (printers) King-street
Davis, Thomas (news) 14 King-street
Edwards, Mrs. C. (stationer) 16 West-street
Fraser, Robert (news) 25 High-street
Hall, Thos. (printer & binder) 4 Windmill-st
Hopkins, Thomas (stationer) 8 New-road
Langstone, C. P., 11 Harmer-street

Large, James (printer) 46 Harmer-street
Raspirod, Mrs. M. (stationer) 80 High-street
Wroe, Benjamin (printer)

GREENWICH.

From London-bridge 5 miles.　Pop. 34,801
Allen, Miss C. (stationer) Stockwell-street
Beaver, J. W., 16 Nelson-street
Berryman, E. G. (printer) Blackheath-road
Boorne, William (printer) Cold Bath-street
Burt, Eliz. (stationer and library) South-street
Butter, Charles (news) Church-street
Clifford, William (and news) 2 London-street
Cooper, Alfred (stationer) 40 Trafalgar-road
Crocker, L. Th. (fancy) 22 Nelson-street
Crockford, W. H. (printer) 7 Blackheath-road
Flashman, William (printer) Blackheath-road
Gibbons, Henry, Market-street
Glaisher, Henry, 2 London-street
Helyer, W. H. (printer) 2 London-street
Horn, James (stationer) Trafalgar-road
Horton, W. N. (and printer) Royal-hill
Kennedy, Robert (and news) Blackheath-hill
Kreckeler, Philip (news) 7 London-street
La Feuillade, James (music) Blackheath-road
Lucas, H. (publisher of Kent and Surrey Mercury) Maize-hill
Morgan, J. (news) Lewisham-road
Moyes, P. S. (stationer) Deptford-bridge
Notley, Mrs. Rebecca (fancy) Blackheath-road
Powell, Henry (news) Pelham-road
Richardson, H. S., Church-street
Seaward, Jas. (printer & publisher) London-st
Somerford, Thomas (music) 24 Nelson-street
Weale, Mrs. M. (stationer) Trafalgar-road
Wilson, Joseph (stationer) Blackheath-road
Wright, Mrs. J., 1 Crooms-hill
West Kent Guardian, W. N. Horton, *Publisher*, 1 Royal-hill
Lecture Hall and Library, Royal-hill
Mechanics' Institute, Trafalgar-road

HADLOW.

From London-bridge 45 miles.　Pop. 2395
Briggs, F. M. (binder and fancy) Post-office

HARDRES, UPPER.

From London 80 miles.　Pop. 266
Barwood, Hammond (stationer)

HAWKHURST.

From London-bridge 62 miles.　Pop. 2704
Doubell, James (news)
Hartley, Mrs. E. (fancy)

HERNE BAY.

From London-bridge to Sturry 74 mls.　Pop. 1361
Tupper, John (library and fancy) Parade
Literary Institution, William-street

HORTON KIRBY.

From London-bridge 21 miles.　Pop. 747
Hall, Henry (paper-maker) South Darenth

HYTHE.

From London-bridge 77 miles.　Pop. 2857
Burgess, John (and stationer) High-street
Halke, George John (fancy) High-street

King George (binder) High-street
Paine, W. S. (fancy) High-street
Shrewsbury, Thomas (printer) High-street
Tiffin, William, High-street
 Library and Reading Society, Bank-street,
  Edward Ashdown, *Librarian*

LEE.
From London-bridge 6 miles.   Pop. 3552
Collins, C. G. (binder and printer) High-road
Freer, Thomas (stationer) High-road
Horne, Thomas (and printer) High-road

LEEDS.
From London 39 miles.   Pop. 663
Whitnall (stationer)

LEWISHAM.
From London-bridge 5 miles.   Pop. 15,064
Blackett, Mrs. Ann (news) Lewes-grove
Butler, Miss C. (fancy) Avenue-place
Downes, Mrs. S. (library) Exchequer-place
Day, Thomas (news) High-road
Holmes, Mrs. E. (fancy) the Village
Williams, Jas. jun. (library) Granville-terrace

LOOSE.
From London 36½ miles.   Pop. 1542
Allnutt and Sons (paper-makers)
Gurney and Son (millboard)

LYDD.
From London 83 miles.   Pop. 1605
Gilbert, James (stationer)

MAIDSTONE.
From London-bridge 34 miles.   Pop. 20,801
Allnutt and Sons (paper-makers) Tovil-mill
Austen, Amb. (printer and music) Week-street
Back, Thos. (stationer) 18 Week-street
Brown, Josh. (printer)
Cocks, William, 76 Bank-street
Cooke and Co. (printers & publishers) Bank-st
Cooke,Chas.Jas. (pub.Maidstone Jour.) Bank-st
Cutbush, F. W. & H. R. (printers and pub. of
  South Eastern Gazette) Week-street
French, S. (music) King-street
Green, J. B. (paper-maker) Hayle-mill
Green, T. B. (law-stationer) St. Faith-street
Hobbs, W. (stationer, &c.) Stone-street [mill
Hollingworth, T. & J. (paper-makers) Turkey-
Hook and Simpson (straw-paper makers) Tovil
  Upper-mills
Joslen, J. P. (wholesale stationer) Earl-street
Lurcock, John (news) Earl-street
Monckton, Wm. (printer and wholesale sta-
  tioner) King-street
Moore, C. F., Week-street
Morfill, William (music) Week-street
Ostler, Charles (binder) Union-street
Peters, George (stationer) Stone-street
Smith & Son (printers & binders) 10 Week-st
Thomason, William (printer) Mill-street
West, William (printer) High-street
Wickenham and Son, Week-street
 Literary and Mechanics' Institute, High-street,
  Thomas Clayton and Geo. Edmett

MALLING, EAST AND WEST.
From London 26 miles.   Pop. 2021
Busbridge,G.F. (paper-makers) East Malling-st
Carpenter, Thomas (and fancy)
Nicholl, Arthur, Post-office

MARDEN.
From London-bridge 50½ miles.   Pop. 2296
Cornwell, Thomas

MARGATE.
From London-bridge 101 miles.   Pop. 10,099
Brazier, H. Charles, 20 High-street
Denne, Mrs. M. (printer) 4 Queen-street
Dixon, C. Dixon, 22 High-street
Keble, Thos. Hy. (printer) 137½ High-street
Perry, William, 4, Broad-street
Sau, Wm. (binder) 5 St. John-street
Turner, P. T. (stationer) 3 Addington-street
 Literary Institution, 53 Hawley-square,
  Richard Edwards, *Librarian*

PENSHURST.
From London 36¼ miles.   Pop. 1628
Turner, Richard (paper-maker) Chafford-mill

RAMSGATE.
From London 97 miles.   Pop. 11,838
Armstrong, George (binder) 134 High-street
Atkins, T. S. (stationer) 7½ Queen-street
Brewer, William Henry, Goldsmid street
Griggs, George (stationer) 30 Addington-st
Harnett, Joseph (stationer) 40 Queen-street
Hawkes, George (stationer) 8 Portland-place
Hunter, Richard (news) 76 High-street
Hunter, Mrs. S. (stationer) 46 Queen-street
Hunt, James, 4 Addington-place
Hunt, Wm. Alex. (library) 64 Queen-street
Knott, Frederick, 21 Harbour-street
Mudford, Mrs. A., 57 High-street
Paton, Andrew (printer) 5 Queen-street
Pilcher, John, 109 High-street
Pilcher, Thomas (music) 115 High-street
Sturgess, Thomas, 13 York-street
Thistleton, William, 17, Harbour-street

ROCHESTER, &c. &c.
From London-bridge 29 miles.   Pop. 43,362.
Bartlet, Jno. (binder) 101 High-street
Berry, Miss M. (stationer) 216 High-street
Berry, Mrs. S. (library and news) High-street
Burch, Henry (printer & stationer) 72 High-st
Caddell, S. & Son (Rochester Gazette) High-st
Edmed, Henry (stationer) 82 High-street
Fraser, Miss C. (news) 45 High-street
French, Thos. (music) 176 High-street
Phippen, Jas. F. (printer) St. Margaret-bk
Reynolds, G., High-street
Shadbolt, William, 196 High-street
Troup, Jas. (music) 165 High-street

CHATHAM.
Armstrong, Jno. (binder) 8 Military-road
Austen, Thos., 8 Hammond-place
Beck and Brooks (reading room) 58 High-st
Burch, Caroline (fancy) 80 High-street
Fordham, A. T. (printer) 127 High-street

Love, Mrs. S. (fancy) 11 Chatham-side
Milton, Thos. (news) 156 High-street
Taylor, Rd. (printer) 15 Watts-place
Wilstead, Geo. (printer) 351 High-street
Windeyer, G. H., 300 High-street

STROOD.

Harden, William (fancy) 28 High-street
Sweet, J. and W. H. (and printer) 28 High-st

BROMPTON.

Beck and Brook, 51 High-street
Pearce, Stephen, 21 High-street
Tracey, Alb., 3 High-street
Woolley, Thos. (stationer) 27 High-street

ROMNEY.

From London 84 *miles.   Pop.* 1053.

Parsons, Isaac (printer and binder)
Vidgen, Jas. (stationer) Post-office

SANDGATE.

From London 80½ *miles.   Pop.* 1399.

Purday, S. and M. A. (library) Post-office

SANDWICH.

From London by rail 98 *miles.   Pop.* 2966.

Baker, Henry, Market-street
Hayward, Thos. (printer) New-street
Thom, Fredk., High-street

SEVENOAKS.

From London-bridge 24 *miles.   Pop.* 4178.

Harrison, Geo. W. (printer)
Philpot, Rd. (fancy)
Seymour, William
Sutton, Thos. (fancy)
    Literary Institution, Jno. Fitness and W. S.
        Burton, *Secs.*

SHEERNESS, &c.

From London-bridge.   Pop. 8578.

Anstey, Jas. (stationer) High-street, Mile-town
Batcheldor, H. P. (printer) Post-office, Blue-
    town
Felkin, Edwd. (news) Post-office, Mile-town.
    Mechanics' Institute, Edward-street, Banks-
        town, Alfred Walker, *Librarian*

SHOREHAM.

From London 29 *miles.   Pop.* 1192.

Willmott, George (paper-maker)

SITTINGBOURNE.

From London 39 *miles.   Pop.* 5304.

Dorrell, J. A. (stationer)
Read, Jno. (printer and fancy)
Tidy, Henry (and news) Stamp-office
    Mechanics' Institution and Reading-room,
        Edwd. Knowles, *Librarian*, Milton

SNODLAND.

From London to Rochester 6 *miles beyond.
    Pop.* 625.

Wildes, Henry A. (paper-maker)

STAPLEHURST.

From London 53 *miles.   Pop.* 11,660.

Hickmott, Jno. V.

SWANSCOMBE, &c.

From London 21 *miles.   Pop.* 1763.

Payne, Jno. (newsvender)

SYDENHAM.

From London-bridge 7 *miles.   Pop.* 4501.

Andrews, Wm. (stationer) Post-office
Blake, Chas. (printer) High-street
Bennett, Jno. (news) Lower Sydenham
Hailes, Jas., Forest-hill
Jeffries, Mrs. E. (and library) High-street
Quiddington, Mrs. H. (stationer) Lower
    Sydenham
Scott, Rd. (fancy) High-street
    Literary Association, Upper Sydenham,
        Chas. Blake, *Librarian*

TENTERDEN.

From London to Staplehurst 53 *miles, and*
    12¾ *miles beyond.   Pop.* 3782.

Ballard, Samuel (printer)
Bolton, Thos. (stationer)
Bourner, William (stationer)

TUNBRIDGE.

From London-bridge 41 *miles.   Pop.* 16,548.

Bridger, Wm. and Son (and library) High-st
Crabb, J. A. (stationer) High-street
Dickenson, Miss A. (fancy) High-street
Hall, Mrs. A., High-street
Hutchings, Wm. (music) 9 Terrace
Ware, Wm. (printer and binder) Post-office
    Literary Institution, F. Cobham, *Sec.*

TUNBRIDGE WELLS.

From London-bridge 46 *miles.   Pop.* 10,587.

Clifford, J. B. (printer) Parade
Colbran, Hy. S. (printer) Calverley-road
Colbran, Jno. (library) High-street
Hasting, Mrs. S. (stationer) Church-road
Jones, Mrs. C. (fancy) High-street
Larmouth, Thos. Hy. (news) High-street
Lucas, Miss E. (fancy) Calverley-promenade
Nash, Wm. (library) Parade
Nye, Hy. (librarian and news) Grosvenor-road
Pearce, Jno. (fancy) Mount-pleasant
Stidolph, Thos. and Sons (printers) Parade
Syme, Alex., Parade
    Literary Society, Parade
    Mechanics' Institution, Belgrave-road

WESTERHAM.

From London to Sevenoaks 6½ *west from there.
    Pop.* 1247.

Clare, Thomas
    Literary Institution, Wm. Pywell, *Librarian*

WHITSTABLE.

From London 87 *miles.   Pop.* 2746.

Fullagar, Jas. (stationer) Harbour-street
Tuddeman, Thos. (binder and news) High-st

WEST WICKHAM.

3½ *miles from Bromley.   Pop.* 732.

Jones, Mrs. Rebecca (librarian) of the Paro-
    chial Library

WINGHAM.

From London 62 miles. Pop. 1083.

Sells, Robert (stationer)

WOOLWICH.

From London 8 miles. Pop. 32,177.

Black, Jas. (printer) Powis-street
Boddy, J. M. (binder) Artillery-place
Boddy, J. Juan, Wellington-street
Chasteaneuf, Mrs. E. (binder) Samuel-street
Cherry, M. (printer and news) Beresford-street
Edwards, J. 125 High-street
Greenleaf, Jno., 122 Powis-street
Henby, Mrs. M. (news) New-road
Jackson, W. P. (printer and pub.) Wellington-street
McKenzie, Geo. (music) Thomas-street
Miskin, J. S. (binder) Market-street
Mountier, J. (printer and pub.) King-street
Muckle, Rd., George-street
Orr, Matthew (pub. and news) 49 Wellington-street
Piper, Jos., Prospect-row
Rixon, Rd. (printer) Beresford-street
Pargeant, Chas. 33 High-street
Savage, Francis, Thomas-street
Steele, Jno. (stationer) Church-street
Wates, Miss J. (stationer) 145 Powis-street
Watt, Mrs. S., 46 Wellington-street
    Mechanics' Institution, High-street, Mr. Hudson, *Sec.*

LANCASHIRE.

ACCRINGTON, &c.

From Euston-square, 255½ *miles.   Pop.* 7481.

Bowker, E. (printer, binder, and music), Piccadilly
Broadley, John, Enfield
Catlow, James, Church
Duckworth, James, Oak-street
Fish, Richard, Abbey-street
Holt, Robert. Blackburn-street
Hutchinson, Elizabeth (printer) Blackburn-st.
Riley, John, Abbot-street
Salter, Catherine, Church-street
Shuttleworth, James B. (library and news) Warner-street
    Mechanics' Institution, Bank-street

ASHTON-UNDER-LYNE.

From Euston-square, 188¾ *miles. Pop.* 27,791.

Bennett, Christopher J., Park-street
Cunningham, Thomas and Son (printers) Stamford-street
Fowler, Daniel, Portland-street
Hilton, William (printer) Old-street
Hobson, Edward (printer) Stamford-street
Holding, James, Delamere-street
Kerrison, John Thomas, Old-street
Lingard, Joseph (printer) Warrington-place
Micklethwaite, Wm. B. (publisher and printer) Old-cross
Orme, George (printer) Stamford-street

Porter, Henry, Stamford-arcade
Quarmby, William, Stamford-street
Swallow, L., Delamere-street
Williamson, John (library) Stamford-street
    Mechanics' Institute, Church-street

BACUP.

From Rochdale 7 *miles.*

Anderton, John (library and printer) Market-place
Ashworth, Richard (printer) Church-street
Brown, Thomas (printer) Market-place
    Mechanics' Institution, Irwell-terrace

BLACKBURN.

From Euston-square viâ *Derby.   Pop.* 46,536.

Cooper, Robert (binder) 7, Mount-street
Douglas, James (binder, &c.) Northgate
Haworth, John N., Church-street
Holt, Richard (binder) Clayton-street
Mitchell, John (news) Fleming-square
Pemberton, Thomas, Darwen-street
Riley, Edgar, Astley-gate
Tiplady, Charles (binder) Church-street
Walkden, James (binder) William-street
Wharton, Edward (news) Church-street
Wood, William (binder) Darwen-street
Woods, Thomas (printer) 7 Lord-street
    Mechanics' Institution News-room, Church-street

BLACKPOOL.

From Euston-square viâ *Preston,* 228 *miles.*

Banks, Thomas, St. John's-market
Butcher, John, South-shore
Dean, Arthur, St. John's-market
Porter, Thomas, North-beach
Simpson, John, St. John's-market
Waddington, Michael, Victoria-street

BOLTON-LE-MOORS.

From Euston-square, 200¼ *miles. Pop.* 61,171.

Ainsworth, James, Market-street
Bradbury, Henry, jun., Deans-gate
Cooke, Joseph (printer) Farnworth
Chadwicke, John, Deansgate
Dawson, George, Kay-street
Gardner, Samuel (printer) Bradshaw-gate
Gray, A. (library) Newport-street
Hargreaves, James (printer) Bradshaw-gate
Harrison, Robert, Derby-street
Heaton, John (binder) Deans-gate
Joyce, John, Deans-gate
Kenyon, Robert (printer) Market-street
Lawson, Joseph, Market-street
Lowe, Josiah (binder and printer) Fold-street
Mather, James, Derby-street
Moss, John, Market-street
Ogle, John (binder) Market-street
Roberts, Thomas, (binder) Bradshaw-gate
Reid, Thomas, Deans-gate
Tillotson, John (binder and printer) Meal-house-lane
Whewell, Robert, Barn-street
Winstanley, William, Barn-street

Winterburn, John, Deans-gate
  Bolton Chronicle, Saturday
  Mechanics' Institute, Bridge-street

BURNLEY.

To Manchester 188½ miles, thence by the East
Lancashire Line. Pop. 20,828.

Clegg, John (binder) St. James's-street
Edwards, George, Goodham-hill
Frankland, William (binder) Howe-street
Greenall, Thomas and James, St. James's-st.
Nuttall, James (binder) Cheapside
Richard, Thomas, 14 Blucher-street
Spencer, John, Market-street
Sutcliffe, James (printer) Yorkshire-street
Sutcliffe, Thomas (binder) St. James's-street
Waddington, William, New Market-street
  Literary Institution, 39 Market-street
  Mechanics' Institution, St. James's-street

BURY.

From Euston-square. Pop. 31,262.

Barker, Dennis, Union-street
Crompton, Thomas, Fleet-street
Davenport, Henry, Croston-lane
Dearden, Henry, 9 Fleet street
Glover, Benjamin, Agar-street
Heap, John, Union-square
Hill, Edward, New-market
Jones, John (news) Princes-street
Kaye, Robert John, Rock-street
Thomas, David, Stanley-street
Trimble, John, Silver-street
Vickerman, John, Union-square
Woods, S., Bury-lane
     Musicsellers.
Openshaw, Ormrod, Stanley-street
Randle, Hannah, Union-square
  Mechanics' Institution, News-room, Broad-st.

CHORLEY.

From Euston-square 210¼ miles, near Bolton-
le-Moors. Pop. 8907.

Houghton, George (musicseller) Market-street
Lawson, Horatio Nelson (library) Market-street
Waddington, Michael (library) Fazakerley-st.

CHOWBENT.
From Euston-square.

Ryland, George W. (news agent) Tylderley

CLITHEROE.
From Euston-square. Pop. 11,480.

Whalley, Henry (printer) Castle-street
Whewell, William (printer) Castle-street

COLNE.
Pop. 6644.

Baldwin, Thomas, Church-street
Bannister, Thomas, Barrowford
Firth, William (binder) Colne-lane
Hartley and Earnshaw (printers) Church-st.

DARWEN.
From Euston-square. Pop. 7020.

Duckworth, John, Spring-gardens
Greenwood, Margaret, Bolton-street
Greeson, Edward (news) Market-street

ECCLES.
From Euston-square. Pop. 8509.

Norris, William, Patricroft
Shuttleworth, Richard (printer) Market-place

FLEETWOOD.
From Euston-square, 230½ miles. Pop. 3121.

Aston, William Twining, Dock-street
Porter, William, Dock-street
Stanley, Isabella, 7 Albert-street
  Fleetwood Chronicle, Friday

GARSTANG.
Pop. 2756.

Clarke, Thomas Walker (printer) Market-pl.
Threltall, Lawrence, Market-place

HASLINGDEN.
From Euston-square, 207¼ miles. Pop. 6154.

Cockcroft, Henry, Regent-street
Kemp, Henry (binder) George-street
Read, John, Church-street

HEYWOOD.

Cook, Mary, Market-place
Heywood, John, Market-street
Kent, George Henry, York-street

LANCASTER.
From Euston-square 231¾ miles. Pop. 16,168.

Barwick, James and Jane, 75 Market-street
Clark, George Christopher, 129 Market-street
Edmondson, Thomas, 38 Market-street
Milner, Anthony, 37 Church-street
Nevatt, Isaac, 16 New-street
Nixon, James, 108 Church-street
Quittenton, Josh., New-street
Richmond, George, New-street
Whittam, Thomas W., Cheapside

LEIGH.
From Euston-square to Manchester 188½ miles;
from there 12 miles. Pop. 5206.

Cook, James (news) Newton-square
Halliwell, Thomas, (news & music) Market-st.
Williams, Frederick, Market-street

LIVERPOOL.
From Euston-square 201 miles. Pop. 375,955.
Bookbinders, &c.

Brakell, Richard (printer) 11 South Castle-st.
Carroll, Henry, 76 Lord-street
Daniell, John, 65 Vauxhall-road
Dilworth, Alice, 65 Shaws-brow
Fazakerley, Thomas, 4 School-lane
Fearnall, William, & Co. (printers) Bassett-st.
Fraser, James (printer) 6 Church-street
Gregory, James, 17, Stafford-street
Hall, Lund, and Co., 23 Lord-street
Hayman, John, 21 Basnett-street
Hetherington, William, 30 St. James's-street
Hodgson, John, 13 Parker-street
Law, James, 15 Cases-street
Lewis, Joseph S. (printer) 8 Basnett-street
Lovatt, Robert Ashton, 10 Temple-street
McKewen, Robert, 1 Dale-street
Mitchelson, George, 83 St. James's-street

Molloy, James, 20, Fenwick-street
Parker, Henry, Morley-street, Kirkdale
Quilliam, Joseph, & Co., Church-street
Santley, William, 19 North John-street
Selig, Obadiah, 10 Copperas-street
Smith, Thomas, Brunswick-buildings
Stanley, Thomas, 34 Clarence-buildings
Thredder, William H., Laws-buildings
Tyerman, William S., 4 Walter-street
Underhill, John, London-road
Walker, James, 17 Lord-street
Wardlow, Henry, Russell-street
Webb and Co., Castle-street
Whewell, John, 6 Ranelagh-place

Booksellers and Stationers.

Arnold George S. (news) 20 South John-st.
Ashton, E., 7 George-street
Blain, Joseph, 35 Bold-street
Blevin, James (printer) 17 Leece-street
Bradshaw, Thomas, 32 Soho-street
Braithwaite, H., 1 Mill-street
Brown, William, Burlington-street
Christie, E. and S. (library) Bootle
Chaffin, Eugene (printseller) 22 Parker-street
Cooper, Christopher, Queen-street
Cornish, James, 37 Lord-street
Dailey, Michael, 38 Edmund-street
Davies, Thomas, 16 Christian-street
Deighton and Co., 46 Church-street
Evans, Isaac (library) 216 Falkner-street
Ewan, John C., Bootle
Fairbrother, Thomas, Old Hall-street
Forster, John (library) Whitechapel
Forsyth, John C., 24 Scotland-place
Gleave, John, 80 Dale-street
Gregory, James, 17 Stafford-street
Griffiths, L., 60 London-road
Groom, George, and Son, 42 Lord-street
Grundy, R. H. (printseller) Church-street
Harrold, John, 80 Great Horner-street
Hawksworth, Thomas, Simpson-street
Hays, Francis, Post Office-place
Hetherington, William, St. James's-street
Herbert, W. G. (printseller) Exchange-street
Hindley, Thomas, Waser-street
Hopkins, John, West-street
Howell, Edward (printer) Church-street
Isaac, John R. (printseller) Castle-street
Jackson, Peter, Post-office-place
Jenkins, John, Paddington
Johnson, Samuel, Berry-street
Jones, David, Tithebarn-street
Jones, Thomas, Clayton-street
Kaye, Thomas (printer) Castle-street
Kearney, Patrick, Dale-street
Kellet, Thomas, & Son (printers) Old Hall-st.
Kent, Samuel, 85 Paradise-street
Kirby, Robert, 93 Bold-street
Knight, Mary (library) 61 Islington
Knipe, William (library) 24 St. James's-street
Lane, George, 86 Paradise-street
Lea, William, Dale-street
Levi, Godfrey (news) London-road
Loader, John, 5 Brunswick-road

Longton, M. (library) 42 Park-lane
Lonsdale, Brothers (printers) 123 Park-road
M'Donnell, M. A. (printer) St. James's-place
Mather, George, 55 St. James's-street
Meyric, A. (library) Hanover-street
Mitchell and Co., 73 St. Ann-street
Molyneux and Co., Scotland-road
Morris, William, Paradise-street
Myers, John, 166 Dale-street
Newling, Arthur (printer) 27 Bold-street
Newton, Thomas, 29 Church-street
Noonan, 18 Hawke-street
O'Brien, John, Much Woolton
Palmer, William, 7 Leece-street
Parry, Henry (library) 85 Renshaw-street
Payne, James, 97 Bold-street
Phillips, George, and Son, Castle-street
Quilliam, Josh. and Co., Church-lane
Robinson, George and Joseph, 32 Castle-street
Rock, Patrick, 13 Lime-street
Rockliff and Son (printers) Castle-street
Scragg, Richard (printer) 73 Renshaw-street
Shepherd, Joseph (library) Scotland-road
Smith, Benjamin (printer) South Castle-street
Simpson, Thomas, Vauxhall-road
Smyth, G. H. & J., & Co. (printers) 12 Berry-st.
Sutton and Co., Paradise-street
Sutton, J. G., & Son, Old Hall-street
Taylor, Thomas (printer) Church-street
Thomas, Joseph (printer) Scotland-road
Thompson, Richard, St. James's-street
Townsend, Henry, Lord-street
Turner, John (printer) 2 James's-street
Underhill, John, 68 London-road
Walmsley, Joshua, Lord-street
Whewell, John (printer) 6 Ranelagh-place
Whitford, Robert Henry, 235 Scotland-road
Williams, George (library) Bootle
Willmer & Co. (news & printers) 32 Church-st.
Willmer, Charles (news) South John-street
Wood, P., Bold-street
Woollard, James (printer) 54 Castle-street
Wagg, George, Cleveland-square
Young, Henry (library) South Castle-street

Musicsellers.

Beswick, Thomas J., 9 Berry-street
Clarke, James, 11 Jones-street
Hime & Son, 57 Church-street
Magill, John, 16 London-road
Shade, George, 4 Bury-street
Smith, James, 66 Lord-street
Taylor, G., & Son, Roscoe-street

News Agents.

Aylward, Michael, 82 Lord-street
Bailey, Josh., 75 Whitechapel
Benson, Peter, 307 Scotland-road
Brett, Josh., 33 Old Hall-street
Carter, Joseph, 9 Williamson-street
Chester, John, Hardwick-street
Dobson, H. M., 73 Park-road
Evans, J. M., Pembroke-place
Gerrard, James, 28 Manchester-street
Hughes, Samuel, 50 Hill-street
Jones, Thomas, Richmond-row

Kirk, George, Scotland-road
Lancaster, John, Kirkdale-road

News Agents.

Lowe, Thomas, 160 Park-lane
Morgan, John, 288 Scotland-road
Pearson, William, 93 Lord-street
Powell, J., 3 Greenland-street
Preston, Thomas, 17 Paddington
Pugh, John, Tithebarn-street
Roughley, M. J., Bootle-road
Shepherd, Joseph, 99 Scotland-road
Stewart, James, Whitechapel
Titford, Charles, Curry-street
Walker, George, 23 Copperas-hill
Willmer and Co., 32 Church-street
Willmer, Charles, 19 South John-street

Newspapers.

Albion, Castle-street, Monday
Chronicle, Church-street, Saturday
Courier, Castle-street, Wednesday
Journal, Castle-street, Saturday
Mail, Castle-street, Saturday
Mercury, 44 Lord-street, Tuesday and Friday
Standard, George's-street, Tuesday
Telegraph, Redcross-street, Daily
Times, Castle-street, Tuesday and Thursday

Printers.

Baines and Herbert (stationers) 12 Castle-street
Bean, A. (stationer) 36 Castle-street
Bower, Samuel, 10 Williamson-street
Davidson, John F., 9 Paradise-street
Doran, Edw. J. (stationer) 44 Duke-street
Dunsford, Fredk. (stationer) South Castle-street
Egerton and Co. 44 Lord-street
Ellis, William and Co., Castle-street
Forshaw, William (stationer) 7 Dale-street
Hurton, Stephen A., 7 Queen-square
Jones, Edward (stationer) 64 Castle-street
Knight, William, and Co., Derby-square
Lace and Addison (stationers) St. George's-stN.
Mawdsley, James (stationer) 4 Castle-street
Mead and Co., 18 Redcross-street
McCorquodale, George (stationer) 38 Castle-st
Nelson, John, 40, Pitt-street
Potts, James (stationer) 37 Great Crosshall-st
Poore, George James (stationer) 42 Castle-street
Richardson, John, 13 Lower Castle-street
Shaw, Richard and Co., Clayton-square
Shaw, William and Co., Lancaster-buildings
Smith, Watts, and Co., Lancaster-buildings
Sutton, J. G. and Co. (stationer) Old Hall-st
Tyreman, Wm. S. (stationer) 4 Water-street
Whitty, M. J., 18 Castle-street
Williams, John R., Whitechapel

Stationers.

Bailey, Joshua, 75 Whitechapel
Brett, Joseph, 157 Great Howard-street
Harris and Co. (wholesale) Moorfields
James, Richard, South Castle-street
Keet, George, 90 Renshaw-street
Lace and Addison, 4 St. George's-crescent

Levi, Godfrey, 26 London-road
McCorquodale, George (wholesale) Castle-street and Pitt-street
Molyneux and Co., 120 Scotland-road
Pannell and Sons (wholsale) Cable-street
Parry, Robert, 192 Mill-street
Phillips, George and Son (wholesale) South Castle-street
Pitt, William (wholesale) 2 Strand-street
Poore, George J. (wholesale) 42 Castle-street
Roughsedge, Thomas (wholesale) 12 Cable-st
Rogers, Thomas L. (wholesale) 18 John-street
Wade, George, J. (wholesale) 13 Canning-place
Webb, Wareing (wholesale) 9 Castle-street
Auxiliary Bible Society, 8 Slater-street
Church of England Institution, 33 Bold-street
Church of England Tract and Book Society, 27 Bold-street
Church of England Young Men's Society,
Albion News Rooms, 8 Great Charlotte-street
Athenæum News Room and Library, 40 Church-street
Exchange News Rooms, Exchange-buildings
Law Society's Library, South John-street
Liverpool Library, 1 Bold-street
Lyceum News Room, 1 Bold-street
St. George's News Room, Gt. Charlotte-street
Union News Room, Duke-street
Dictrict Committee for Promoting Christian Knowledge, 93 Bold-street

MANCHESTER.

From Euston-sq. 188½ miles, or King's-cross via Sheffield. Pop. 316,213

Bookbinders.

Affleck, Thomas, Kent-street, Pall-mall
Ainsworth, James, 93 Piccadilly
Boardman, Samuel, 26 St. Ann-street
Bradshaw & Blacklock, 47 Brown-street
Cathrall and Beresford, Newhall's-buildings, Market-street
Coy, James Crew, 18 Lloyd-street, Cooper-st
Dean, Joseph, Barlow's-court, Market-street
Dickinson, John, 5 Cannon-street
Ellerby & Cheetham, 3 Oldham-street
Ellerby, Richard, 30 New Cannon-street
Fletcher & Tubbs, 49 Cross-street, King-st
Gardner, John, 97 Gt. Ancoats-street
Gibbons, Matthew, 10 Cooper-street
Harris, Peter, 23 Princess-street
Hatton, George, 39 Victoria-street
Heralo, Joseph, 7 Police-street, King-street
Irwin, William, 53 Oldham-street
Leonard, James, 5 Abraham's-ct, Market-st
Love & Barton, 70 Market-street
Lowndes, James, 118 Deansgate
Marsden, Thomas, 23 Half-st, Cathedral-yard
Megson, Albert, 103 Market-street
Parr, Thomas, 8 Cross-street, Hanover-street
Poulson, Thomas, & Son, 2 Bow-street
Riley, Thomas, 8 Clarence-street, Princess-st
Slater, Isaac, 37 Fountain-street
Smith, Barnes, & Blackley, 23 Brazenose-st
Sowler, Thomas, 4 St. Ann's-square
Stones, Susannah, Bailey's-court, Market-pl

Thackray, Matthew, 51 Shudehill
Thompson, James and Joseph, 39 Market-st
Walker, William, and Co., 52 Cross-st, and
    180 Oxford-street, Chorlton-on-Medlock
Wallwork, Henry, 20 Kennedy-street
Ward, Peter, 35 Spring-gardens
Warner, William, 20 Fennel-street
Whitehead, John, 17 Port-street, Piccadilly
Whitmore, Henry, 121 Market-street
Wilde, Frederick, 9 Half-st, Cathedral-yard
Winstanley, John, 35 Cooper-street
Wroe, Alice, 101 Great Ancoats-street
Wroe, James, 57 Oxford-street, St. Peter's

Booksellers & Stationers.

Ainsworth, James, 93 Piccadilly
Anderson, Thomas, & Son, 58 King-street
Ardrey, William, 117 Market-street
Armstrong, William, 25 Bond-street
Barlow, Richard, 22 Portland-street
Bentham, George, 16 Market-place
Boardman, Samuel, 26 St. Ann-street
Bradshaw & Blacklock, 47 Brown-street
Bramell, John, 38 Lime-street, Oldham-road
Burge, Richard, 15 Princess-street
Cooper, James Renshaw, 1 Bridge-street
Cooper, Stephen, 104 Red-bank
Dearman, Richard, 25 Great Ducie-street,
    Strangeways
Dunnill & Palmer, 3 Bond-street
Ellerby & Cheetham, 3 Oldham-street
Emmins, John, 68 Faulkner-street
Fletcher & Tubbs, 49 Cross-street, King-street
Galt, James, & Co., Ducie-street, Exchange
Gleave, Joshua, 7 Liverpool-road, Deansgate
Goodall, George Henry, 26 Princess-street
Gould, John, Exchange-arcade, Cross-street
Greenwell, Thomas, 6 South-parade, St. Mary's
Hale & Roworth (English & Foreign) 45 King-st
Hale, Bowden, 78 Cross-street, King-street
Hatton, George, 29 Victoria-st, Smithy-door
Haycraft, Joseph, 52 Market-st, & 33 Pall-mall
Hebden, John, 83 Stretford New-road
Heywood, Abel, 58 Oldham-street
Heywood, John, 170 Deansgate
Hilton, John, Broad-street, Pendleton
Higginbotham, Charles, 133 Oxford-street,
    Chorlton-on-Medlock
Hutchenson, William, 43 Oxford-st, St. Peter's
Irwin, William, 53 Oldham-street
Johnson, Joseph, 10 Market-street
Johnson, Martha, 2 Liverpool-road, Deansgate
Johnson, Richard, 74 Market-street
Kenworthy, Leon, 9 Cateaton-street
Lewis, Chas. Hucklebridge, 11 Market-street
Lockwood, Joseph, 19 Shudehill
Long, John, 6 Back King-street
Love & Barton, 70 Market-street
Lowndes, James, 118 Deansgate
Lynch, Richard, 20 Back King-street
M'Cann, Margaret, 81 Oldham-street
M'Quin, Edward, 275 Deansgate
M'Whinnie, James, 31A Rochdale-road
Megson, Albert, 103 Market-street
Mellor, Thomas, 34 St. Ann-street

Miller, James, 15 Oxford-street, St. Peter's
Moore, Nathan Newfold, 5 Deansgete
Moreland, James, Cambridge-street, C. on M.
Morrison, Christopher, 127 London-road
Palmer, Jno., 157 Higher Chatham-st, C. on M.
Parker, Alfred, 85 Brook-street, Garratt-road
Parkes, Jas. Thos., 89 Market-street
Pickford, Edward, 87 Oldham-road
Pratt, Joseph, 57 & 58 Bridge-street
Richards, Thos., Oxford--street, St. Peter's
Richardson, Reginald John, 10 Victoria
    Bridge-street, Salford
Riley, Thomas, 13 Hanging-ditch
Roberts, Fred., 36 Oxford-street, C. on M.
Rowbotham, John, 67 Oxford-street, St. Peter's
Simms & Dinham, 16 St. Ann-square
Smith, George, 11 Greengate, Salford
Smith, Thos., 211 Great Ancoats-street
Somerset, Geo., 53 Great Ducie-street
Sowler, Thomas, 4 St. Ann's-square
Tallis, John, & Co., 35 New Bridge-street,
    Strangeways—Edward Reid, *Agent*
Taylor, John, 3 Withy-grove
Thackray, Matthew, 51 Shudehill
Thomson, Jas. & Jos., 39 Market-street
Tyson, Edward, 55 Great Bridgewater-street
Walker, Wm., 187 Oxford-street, C. on M.
Weatherley, Jas., 10 Marshall's-c't, Fennel-st
Wheeler, Benj., Exchange-arcade, Cross-street
Whitmore, Henry, 121 Market-street
Wiley, Geo., 243 Chapel-street, Salford
Williamson, Jacob, 11 Smithy-door
Willis, William, Cathedral-yard
Wroe, Alice, 101 Great Ancoats--street
Wroe, James, 51 Oxford-street, St. Peter's

Libraries.

Ashworth, Samuel, 116 River-street, Hulme
Bamter, Robert, 135 Oldham-road
Bullough, Robt, 9 Gray-street
Charity, Henry, 96 Travis-street
Charlsworth, Robert, 16 Brazenose-street
Chetham's College (T. Jones), Hunts-bank
Cockcroft, Sarah, 91 Great Ancoats-street
Falconer, Martha, 11 Great Ducie-street
Foreign Library (F. Jackson) St. Ann's-sq
Frith, Sarah, 1 Rusholme-grove
Goring, Mary, 61 Chester-road, Hulme
Harrison, Sarah, 3 St. Ann's-place
Harrop, Robert, 8 Fairfield-street
Harwood, Mary, 9 Lloyd-street, Hulme
Hebden, John, 83 Stretford New-road
Higginbotham, Charles, 133 Oxford-street
Hobson, William, 47 Great Jackson-street
Houghton, Richard, 7 Medlock-street
James, Thomas, 136 Oldham-road
Kenworthy, Leon, 9 Cateaton-street
Law Library, 4 Norfolk-street
Leggett, William, 60 Medlock-street, Hulme
Lyceum News Room & Library, 107 Great
    Ancoats-street
M'Whinnie, James, Rochdale-road
Manchester Mechanics, Cooper-street
Manchester Subscription, Newall's-buildings
Manchester Old Subscription, Exchange-bldngs

Medical Society's, Nicholas-street
Morris, Christopher, 127 London-road
Morville, Ellen, 6 Upper Brook-street
Oerall, Elizabeth, 47 Bridge-street
Page, James, 47 Cross-street
Platting Mechanics, Argyle-street
Portico News & Library, 57 Mosley-street
Procter, Richard W., 105 Mill-gate
Richardson, Elizabeth, Exchange-arcade
Salford Royal Museum & Library, Mosley-st
Salford Mechanics, 76 Chapel-street
Salford Library & Reading Rooms, 12 King-st
Spurr, Thomas, 43 Chester-road
Stockdale, Ann, 10 Ernell-street, Salford
Syers, Ann, 24 Broad-street, Pendleton
Tomlinson, John, 31 Chancery-lane
Williams, Sarah, 40 Booth-street
Winterbottom, Samuel 148 Stretford New-road

Map Publishers.

Bradshaw & Blacklock, 47 Brown-street
Slater, Isaac, Fountain-street

Music Sellers, &c.

Andrews, Henry, 184 Chapel-street, Salford
Andrews, Richard, Hunts-bank
Haughton, Daniel, 42 John Dalton-street
Higham, Joseph, Victoria-terrace
Hime & Addison, 19 St. Ann's-square
Lock, Edward C., St. John-street, Deans-gate
Martin, Thomas, 4 Withy-grove
Molineux, Thomas, 37 John Dalton-street
Moore, Alice, 11 Clarendon-street
Moss, John, 14 Quay-street, Deans-gate
Pickering, Alice, 30 Princes-street
Powell, James, 43 Peter-street
Sharp, Thomas, 166 Chapel-street, Salford
Smith, Joseph Charles, 21 Lower King-street
Townsend, John, 3 King-street
Werton, Robert, 19 Granby-row
Woodney, Hugh, 5 Portland-street
Wroe, Alice, Great Ancoats-street
Wroe, Frederick, 7 John Dalton-street

News Agents and Periodical Dealers.

Andrews & Co., 12 Brown-street
Appleton, David, & Son, 70 London-road
Bailey, James, 42 Regent-street, Salford
Barker, Josiah, 21 Lower Mosley-street
Barlow, Richard, 22 Portland-street
Bamper, R., Oldham-street
Bartley, Susan, 153 Oxford-street
Beardsall, Mary, 25 Bridge-street
Bentham, George, 16 Market-place
Bohaund, Joseph, 36 Broughton-road
Booth, John, 9 Fairfield-street
Bowker, William, 452 Oldham-road
Bremner, William, 15 Piccadilly
Bullough, Robert, 9 Gray-street, Chorlton-on-
    Medlock
Chorlton, Charles, 77 Oldham-road
Cooper, Stephen, 104 Red-bank
Daily, Mark, 198 Chapel-street
Drury, Elijah, 86 Green-gate, Salford
Ellerby & Cheetham, 3 Oldham-street
Flitcroft, Thos. Ducie-bridge, Long Mill-gate

Goring, Mary, 61 Chester-road, Hulme
Hall, John, 51 Brook-street
Hall, Thomas, 125 Piccadilly
Harrop, Robert, 8 Fairfield-street
Hebden, John, 83 Stretford New-road
Heywood, Abel, 58 Oldham-street
Heywood, John, 57 Great Jackson-street
Heywood, John, 170 Deans-gate
Holker, Ralph, 277 Great Ancoats-street
Hutchinson, William, 43 Oxford-street
Jones, William Charles, 122 Medlock-street
Kenworthy, Leon, 9 Cateaton-street
Leggett, Francis W., 25 Red-bank
Leggett, William, 60 Medlocck-street
Lewis, Charles, H., 11 Market-street
Lynch, John, 105 Market-street
Lynch, Richard, 2 Back King-street
McKenzie, James, 87 Medlock-street
McPhinnie, James, 31 Rochdale-road
McQuin, Edward, 275 Deans-gate
Morrison, Christopher, 127 London-road
Owen, John, 10 Rochdale-road
Peck, William Frederick, 29 Downing-street
Pickford, Edward, 87 Oldham-road
Richardson, Reginald John, 10 Victoria-bridge
Reynolds, Kate, 5 Ducie-street, Exchange
Riley, Thomas, 13 Hanging-ditch
Smith, George, 10 Regent-road
Smith, Thomas, 211 Great Ancoats-street
Stokes, Jessie P., 9 Cross-street
Tomlinson, John, 31 Chancery-lane
Wainhouse, Thomas, 45 Portland-street
Warren, Joseph, 22 Medlock-street
Wheeler, Benjamin, Exchange-arcade
Wiley, George, 243 Chapel-street, Salford
Wroe, James, 57 Oxford-street, St. Peter's

Newspapers.

Courier, St. Ann's-square, Saturday,
    Thomas Sowler, Proprietor
Examiner, Market-street, Wednesday & Sat.
    Ireland & Co., Proprietors
Guardian, Warren-street, Wednesday & Sat.
    Taylor & Co., Proprietors
Spectator, Market-street, Saturday,
    Harrison & Co.

Printsellers and Publishers.

Marked thus * are Publishers also.

*Agar, Charles, 104 King-street
*Agnew, Thomas, 14 Exchange-street
*Bolougard & Son, 32 Market-street
Deeley, William, 152 Chapel-street, Salford
*Grundy, John C., 4 Exchange-street
Lloyd, Brothers, 46 Princes-street
Lomax, John, Exchange-arcade
Morney, James, 65 Bridge-street
Rowley, Charles, 38 Oldham-road
Whaite, Henry, 85 Bridge-street
Zanetti, Ann, St. Ann-street

Printers—Letter-press.

Ainsworth, James, 93 Piccadilly
Anderson, Thomas and Son, 58 King-street
Bardsley, John & George, 23 Oldham-street
Bayley, John, Mary-street, Strangeway

Bottomley, George, 37 Spring-gardens
Bradshaw & Blacklock, 47 Brown-street
Bradshaw, John, 4 Church-street
Brewster & Leeuning, 41 York-street
Broad, Jesse, & Co., 43 Barlow's-ct., Market-st
Brown, David, 7 Broom-street, Shudehill
Brown, Thomas James, Parsonage
Buck, James, 17 Market-place
Burgess & Peck, Victoria-arches, Victoria-street
Bury, Wm. H., Victoria-bridge-street, Salford
Cathrall & Berresford, Newall's-buildings, Market-street
Cave & Sever, 18 St. Ann-street
Cheetham, Jas. & Son, Wright's-ct., Market-st
Cheetham, James, 23 Cannon-street
Chorlton, Charles, 77 Oldham-street
Clarke, Joseph, 128 Cross-street, Market-street
Corner, Charles Tinsley, New Cannon-street
Corrigan, Michael, 81 Shudehill
Dalton, Hugh, Market-place
Demeza, William, 16 Old Mill-gate
Dunnill & Palmer, 3 Bond-street
Ellerby & Cheetham, 3 Oldham-street
Falkner, George, 49 Brown-street
Fleming, Edmund Lionel, 1 Victoria-street,
    Market-place
Fletcher & Tubbs, 49 Cross-street, King-street
Forsyth, John, 14 Fennel-street
Fothergill, John, 31 Booth-street, Mosley-st
Fothergill, William, Exchange-arcade
Galt, James, & Co., Ducie-street, Exchange
Grant, Philip, 6 Corporation-street
Hampson, Benjamin, 14 Fountain-street
Harrison, John, Abraham's-court, Market-st
Haycraft, Joseph, 33 Pall-mall & 52 Market-st
Herald, Joseph, 7 Police-street, King-street
Heywood, Abel, 58 Oldham-street
Hilton, James, & Co., 42A Fountain-street
Hind & Brabner, 12 Dale-street
Hodgson, James, 21 Cannon-street
Hopkinson, Kezia, 81 Bennett-st., Oldham-rd
Hopper, Thomas, Back King-street
Horsfield, Thomas, Riding's-court, St. Mary's
Horton, Henry, Angel-yard, Market-place
Hulme, Charles Enoch, 22 Chapel-street, S.
Hulme, Henry, 97 Clarendon-street, Hulme
Irlam, William, 54 King-street
Irwin, William, 53 Oldham-street
Jackson, Wm. Francis, 40 New Bailey-st., S.
Johnson, Rawson, & Co., Corporation-street
Johnson, Richard, 74 Market-street
Johnson, Thomas, 62 Livesey-street
Kiernan, James, 25 George-Leigh-street
Latham, Thomas, 99 Great Ancoats-street
Le Blond & Co., 12 Norfolk-street
Leech, James, 42 Turner-street, High-street
Leigh, John, 95 Market-street
Leonard, James, Abraham's-court, Market-st
Lewis, Charles Hucklebridge, 11 Market-street
Livsey, John, Whittle-street, Oldham-road
Love & Barton, 70 Market-street
Maclean, John, Hanging-ditch
McWhinnie, James, 31A Rochdale-road
Maplestone & Co., 14 Lloyd-street, Cooper-st
Megson, Albert, 103 Market-street

Megson, Edward Benjamin, 14 Market-place
Metcalfe & Lavender, 14 Riding's-court, St.
    Mary's-gate
Parker, John, 2 Cannon-street
Patrick, Joseph, 20 Cannon-street
Petty, Ernst, & Co., 69 King-street
Plant, William, 38 Long Mill-gate
Powlson, Thomas, & Son, 2 Bow-street
Pratt, Joseph, 56 Bridge-street
Roberts, John, 146 Chapel-street, Salford
Rogerson, William, Hardman-street, Deansgate
Sale, John Joseph, 1 Spring-gardens
Shaw, William, 104 Market-street
Sherratt, James, Broad-street, Pendleton
Shields, Frederick, 20 Brazenose-street
Simms & Dinham, 14 St. Ann's-square
Simms, Charles & Co., 50 Pall-mall
Simpson, William, 7 Police-street
Slater, Isaac, 37 Fountain-street, and 36 Port-
    land-street
Smith, Barnes, & Blackley, 23 Brazenose-street
Smith, James, 38 Brazenose-street
Sowler, Thomas. 4 St. Ann's-square
Sowood, Thomas, 5 Blue Boar-court
Stanley & Read, 90 King-street
Swain, Charles, 58 Cannon-street
Swindells, Henry Allsop, 22 Deans-gate
Swindells, John, Pall-mall
Taylor, David, & Co., 9 Cannon-street
Taylor, Garnett, & Co., 4 Warren-street
Taylor, John, 18 Ashton-street, London-road
Thompson, James, 30 New Cannon-street
Thomson, James & Joseph, 39 Market-street
Varey, William D., 5 Red Lion-street
Walker, William, & Co., Cross-street
Wilcock & Norbury, 26 Faulkner-street
Wilkinson, Thomas, 8 Lloyd's-street
Willis, William, Cathedral-yard
Wright & Whittaker, Byron's-ct., St. Mary's-gt

Stationers, &c.

Agnew, Thomas, (fancy) 14 Exchange-street
Ainsworth, James, 93 Piccadilly
Anderson, Thomas & Son, Cable-street
Anthony, George W., 125 Oxford-street
Ashworth, Samuel, River-street, Hulme
Bailey, James, 42 Regent-street, Salford
Barker, Josiah, 21 Lower Moseley-street
Barlow, Richard, 22 Portland-street
Bartley, Susan, 153 Oxford-street
Beardsall, Mary, 25 Bridge-street
Bloomer, William, Upper Medlock-street
Bohanna, Joseph, Broughton-road
Booth, John, 9 Fairfield-street
Bowker, William, Oldham-road
Brandreth, William, 4 Pall-mall
Brenner, William, 15 Piccadilly
Broad, Jesse, & Co., Market-street
Bullough, Robert, 9 Gray-street
Bushell, Ellen, Bury New-road
Cartwright, William, 11 White-cross-court
Charity, Henry, 96 Travis-street
Charlton & Co., Market-street
Chorlton, Charles, 77 Oldham-street
Clarke, Samuel, 89 Moss-lane

Collins, James, 76 King-street
Cooper, Stephen, 104 Red-bank
Coy, James C., & Sons, 18 Lloyd-street
Crean, Daniel, 120 Moss-lane
Daggatt, James, Union-street
Daly, Mark, 198 Chapel-street, Salford
Dibbs, Charles, 15 New York-street
Dickenson, John, 5 Cannon-street
Drury, Elijah, 85 Greengate-street
Farrington, Roger, 252 Oldham-road
Flitcroft, Thomas, Ducie-bridge
Gasgoine, James, Great Jackson-street
Grant, Philip, Corporation-street
Grundy, John C. (fancy) 4 Exchange-street
Hall, John, 51 Brook-street, David-street
Hall, Thomas, Piccadilly
Harrop, Robert, 8 Fairfield-street
Hatton, George, 29 Victoria-street
Herald, Joseph, King-street
Hilton, Jomes, & Co., Fountain-street
Hindle, Samuel, Chester-road
Hitchin, Thomas, Newton-heath
Hobson, William, Great Jackson-street
Holden, James (wholesale) 6 Palace-street
Holmes, William, 105 Chapel-street
Islam, John, Major-street
Jackson, William F., New Bailey-street
Jones, William C., 122 Medlock-street
Kerr, Archibald, & Co., 2 Essex-street
Latham, Thomas, 99 Great Ancoats-street
Le Blond & Co., 12 Norfolk-street
Leigh, John, 95 Market-street
Leonard, James, 5 Abraham's-court
McKenzie, James, Medlock-street
Morville, Ellen, Upper Brook-street
Mowbray, George, 9 St. Mary's-street
Owen, John, Rochdale-road
Page, Richard, 74 Cross-street
Parnell, William, Peter-street, Deans-gate
Peck, William F., 29 Downing-street
Powlson & Son, 2 Bow-street
Riddle, James, 145 Butler-street
Shaw, William, 104 Market-street
Simms, Charles, & Co. (wholesale) Pall-mall
Smith & Co., 23 Brazenose-street
Spurr, Thomas, 43 Chester-road, Hulme
Swindells, John, 1 Pall-mall
Turner, John, Oldham-street
Wain, William (fancy) 58 Cross-street
Warren, Joseph, 22 Medlock-street
Wilkinson, Edwin, 86 Bury-street, Salford
Williams, John P., 23 Rusholme-road
Winterbottom, Samuel, Stretford New-road
Wood, James, River-street, Hulme
Wright, Son, & Co. (wholesale) Cross-street, Market-street

MIDDLETON.
From Manchester 6 miles.
Horsman, William, Long-street
Wigley, John, Long-street
    Mechanics' Institution, Blackley
    Mechanics' Institution, Long-street

NEWCHURCH, &c.
From Rochdale 9 miles. Pop. 16,915
Hindle, John, Waterfoot

King, Edwin (binder) Rawtenstall
Lonsdale, James (news) Newchurch
    Mechanics' Institution, Rawtenstall
    Rossendale Working Man's Institution, Waterside, Newchurch

OLDHAM.
From King's-cross, viâ Knottingley. Pop. 72,357
Buckley, Edmund, Shaw
Clegg, William, Yorkshire-street
Dawson, James (library, binder, printer, and news) Market-street
Dawson, John, Waterhead-mill
Dodge, John (binder, printer, and library) Market-place
Evans, Daniel (printer) 22 Yorkshire-street
Green, Robert (printer) Yorkshire-street
Harrison, John, Yorkshire-street
Jackson, H. (binder) George-street
Lees, Joseph, 35 West-street
Nicholson, John (printer) Lees
Quarmby, Joseph, Mumps
Travis, John, Shaw
Wild, Samuel, Yorkshire-street
    Mechanics' Institution, Hollingwood

ORMSKIRK.
From Liverpool, re-book by the East Lancashire Railway. Pop. 5548
Jeffryes, John (binder) Church-street
Leake & Co. (binders) Church-street
Smith, William, Houghton-street

PADIHAM.
From Burnley 3 miles. Pop. 4509
Croushaw, Richard, Church-street
Nuttall, George, Church-street
Pate, James, Church-street

POULTON.
From London 234 miles, near Fleetwood. Pop. 1120
Smith, M. (printer) Market-place

PRESCOTT.
From London 197 miles. Pop. 7393
Culshaw, John, Market-place
Travers, Thomas, Church-street
    News Room, Royal Hotel

PRESTON.
From Euston-sq. 210¼ miles. Pop. 67,542
Addison, Philip & Charles, Church-street
Ambler, Edward (printer) North-road
Bailey, William, 107 Fishergate
Banks, Thomas, 23 Market-place
Barton, Henry, 96 Fishergate
Buller, E. C., Cannon-street
Burrows, G. H., 168 Friargate
Chew, Edward, Church-street
Clarke, W., Fishergate
Cuff, Brothers, Fishergate
Dobson & Son (printers) Market-place
Dobson, jun., Fishergate
Dixon, Friargate
Harkness, John (printer) 121 Church-street

Hartley, A., 66 Park-road
Heyward, Philip Henry, Friargate
Heyward & Hargreaves, Friargate
Lambert, Railway-station
Livesey, Messrs. (wholesale printers & stationers) Cheapside
Oakey, Henry, 25 Fishergate
Ogle, Thos. (binder) Fishergate.
Sherrington, Wm. (binder) Avenham-lane
Thomson, A. 25 Fishergate
Walker, John (printer) 1 Church-street
Wilcock, Edward (printer) 27 Fishergate
Worthington, J., & Co., Church-street
   Institution for Diffusion of Useful Knowledge, Avenham-lane
   Law Library, Chapel-walls
   Literary Institution, Winckley-square

RADCLIFFE, &c.

Pop. 5022.

Heaton, John, Blackburn-street
Wheelhouse, Samuel (library) Blackburn-st

RAMSBOTTOM.

From Manchester 14 miles.

Holden, James, Bridge-street
Kelly, Sarah (stationer) Market-place
Whittaker, Robert, Market-place

Paper Makers.
Ingham, S. B. & James, Shuttleworth

ROCHDALE.

From King's-cr. viâ Knottingley. Pop. 29,195.
Bookbinders.

Ashworth, J. (printer) Orchard-street
Day, Abraham, 58 High-street
Wildee, John, 16 Hunter's-lane

Booksellers, &c.
Ashworth, Misses (binders, music, &c.) South-parade
Apsden, Richard, 119 Yorkshire-street
Brearley, Joseph, Yorkshire-street
Butterworth, William (binder & printer) St. Mary's-gate
Gill, John M., St. Mary's-gate
Croskill, Henry (binder & printer) 86 Yorkshire-street
Cheetham, Edward, Yorkshire-street
Hartley & Howarth (fancy) 20 Yorkshire-st
Huddlestone, John (binder & stationer) Whitworth-road
Mills, John & James (binders & printers) 96 Yorkshire-street
Mills, William, 24 Drake-street
Milne, M. (binder & printer) Exchange-street
Magson, Henry, Exchange-street
Turner, James, Exchange-street
Westall, James (old) Market-place
Wrigley, Edmund (binder, printer, and music) Yorkshire-street
   People's Institute, Baillie-street

SAINT HELEN'S.
From Liverpool 10 miles.
Blanshard, George, New-market

Butler, Thomas, New-market
Foreman, William, Church-street
Kean, Patrick (stationer) East-street
Sharpe, Isaac (library) Church-street
Travers, Mary (stationer) Tontine-street

SOUTHPORT.
From Ormskirk 9 miles.
Fleming, Ann, Neville-street
Hudson, John, Neville-street
Johnson, Robert (publisher) Lord's-street
Wilson, E. (printer) Neville-street

TODMORDEN.
From King's-cross, viâ Nottingley. Pop. 4532
Chambers, Brothers (printers) Cheapside
Walton, James N. (printer, news, and music) Pavement

ULVERSTONE.
From Lancaster 22 miles.   Pop. 6433
Atkinson, David, King-street
Jackson, John (printer) Market-place
Kitchen, William, Market-street
Soulby, Stephen (printer & publisher) King-st
   Ulverstone Advertiser, Thursday ; J. Soulby, King-street
   Athenæum & News Room, Theatre-street

WARRINGTON.
From Euston-square 181½ miles.   Pop. 23,363
Booth, William, Sankey-street
Connor, George, Sankey-street
Farnell, William, 62 Bridge-street
Furnival, George, Bridge-street
Haddock & Son (printers) Market-place
Hatton, Richard (printer) Butter Market-st
Hurst, Thomas (printer) Sankey-street
Rome, Thomas, Sankey-street
Sutton, Thomas, Market-place
Tuston, William, Market-place
   Exchange News Room, Market-gate
   Mechanics', Academy-place
   Museum & Library, Friarsgate

WIGAN.
From Euston-square 195¼ miles.   Pop. 31,941
Birch, J., Market-street
Hutching, W. H., Wiend
Jackson, Thomas, Wiend
Pollard, John, Market-place
Ramsdale, John (music & news) Market-place
Reckett, Henry B. (library) Standishgate
Stickland, William (library) Wallgate
Thomas, David (publisher) Market-place
   Wigan Times, Friday, Market-place ; David Thomas, publisher & proprietor

LEICESTERSHIRE.
ASHBY DE LA ZOUCH.
From Euston-square 124¼ miles.   Pop. 3762
Goadby, James, Market-street
Hextall, W. & J., Market-street
Wayte, Thomas (library) Market-street

CASTLE DONNINGTON.
Pop. 2297.

Cowlishaw, John
Popple, M.
Richardson. Thomas, & Son (publisher)

HINCKLEY.
Pop. 6111.

Baxter, John (binder) King-street
Chawner, William (news) Market-street
Lee, G. F. (news) Market-street
Shaw, William, Market-place
Short, Thomas (news & library) Borough

LEICESTER.
From Euston-square 102¾ *miles. Pop.* 60,584.

Adams, J. B. (stationer) Humberley-road
Allen, Edward (printer) King-street
Billson, John (news) Belgrave-gate
Bent, John (news) Town Hall-lane
Brown, T. C. (print. pub. news & music) Mkt-pl
Brown, John (stationer) Pocklington-walk
Barton, John (printer) Haymarket
Burton, W. H. (printer) Northampton-street
Chamberlaine, B. S. & Son (printer) East-gate
Chamberlain, George (binder) St. George-st
Chew, Edward, High-street
Cook, Thomas (news) Granby-street
Crossley, S. S. & Co., (printer) Gallowstree-gate
Fieldwick, Henry (news) Granby-street
Fowler, John, St. Martin's
Fowler, J. S. (binder & printer) Church-gate
Hammersley (binder) Freeschool-lane
Jackson, R., Market-street
Jones, M. (stationer) Granby-street
Long, M. A. (printer) High-street
Payne & Co. (printers) Market-place
Plant, R. F. (binder & stationer) King-street
Rowe, J. R. (printer) Granby-street
Ward, John (music) Belvoir-street
Wheeler, J. (news) London-road
Winks, J. F. (news & pub.) High-street
Wright, John (binder) Hill-street

LOUGHBOROUGH.
From Euston-square 115¼ *miles. Pop.* 10,900.

Dauks, Thomas, Market-place
Griffin, R., Swan-street
Lee, Samuel, High-street

LUTTERWORTH.
From Euston-square to Welford, 92¼ *miles.*
Pop. 2446.

Bottrill, E. & Son (library) High-street
Woodward, Misses, Church-street

MARKET BOSWORTH.
Pop. 1058.

Burton, T. E. (library)

MARKET HARBOROUGH.
From Euston-square 100½ *miles. Pop.* 2325.

Abbott, E. A. (binder) High-street
Eland, W. (binder & printer) Church-street
Gurden, M. N., Church-square
Wood, B. H. (stationer & music seller) High-st

MELTON MOWBRAY.
From Euston-square 118 *miles. Pop.* 4391.

Day John (printer) Cornhill
Towne, John, Cornhill

ALFORD.
From King's-cross 130 *miles. Pop.* 2262.

Leake, John, Church-street
Mountain, John (binder & printer) Market
Townsend, C., Market

BARROW-UPON-HUMBER.
Pop. 2283.

Robinson, John B. (stationer)

BARTON-UPON-HUMBER.
Pop. 2048.

Ball, Charles (printer) Market-place
Tomlinson, Henry J., Market-place

BOSTON.
From King's-cross 107 *miles. Pop.* 17,518.

Bowtoff, C., & Son, High-street
Brown, E. (news room)
Buck, James (library) Bar-gate
Clarke, Joseph, Market-place
Morton, John, Market-place
Noble, John, & Co., Market-place
Porter, James, Bar-gate
Royce, W. (library) Market-place

BOURNE.
Pop. 2789.

Bell, Thomas (printer) West-street
Daniel, William, Market-place

BRIGG.
Pop. ——.

Atkinson, F. H. Bridge-street
Cressey, William, Wraby-street
Leaberry, Robert (binder) Rigby-street
Palmer, Henry, Market-place

LINCOLNSHIRE.

CAISTOR, &C.
Pop. 2166.

Parker, George (binder) Grimsby-road
Wigglesworth, Thomas, Market-place
Witham, John (printer) South-street

CROWLAND.
From King's-cross to Peakirk, 80½ *miles.*
Pop. 2446.

Burrus, John, East-street
Harker, Edward, South-street
Sutton, E. (stationer)

GAINSBOROUGH.
Pop. 8293.

Amcoats & Co. (binders) Loud-street
Bowden, J. W., Market-place
Caldicott, W. H., Market-place
Smith, Alfred, Beast-market

GRANTHAM.
From King's-cross 105¼ *miles.   Pop.* 10,873.
Bushby, Thomas, Vine-street
Jackson, W., Swine-street
Lyne, Thomas, West-gate
Mousir, John, Water-gate
Ridge, Samuel, High-street
Rogers, Joseph, Water-gate
Todd, West-gate
Thompson, J. Swine-gate

GREAT GRIMSBY.
Pop. 8860.
Leigh, W. M., Baxter-gate
Margerum, W., Left-street North
Skelton, W. Market-place
Skelton, W. J., Left-street North
Tessyman, W., St. Mary's-gate

HOLBEACH.
Pop. 2245.
Ibbs, Charles W.
McDonald, John Charles

HORNCASTLE.
From King's-cross to Kirkstead 122¾ *miles.*
Pop. 4921.
Boulton, John, High-street
Cussons, David, High-street
Simpson, John, Bull-ring

KIRTON.
From King's-cross 103¼ *miles.   Pop.* 1948.
Spring, R.

LINCOLN.
From King's-cross 138½ *miles.   Pop.* 17,536.
Akville, Charles, High-street
Bellatti, W. Henry (printer) 170 High-street
Cousans, E. R., High-street
Brogden, T. S. (printer) 24 Silver-street
Brooke, W. & B. (printers) 290 High-street
Brown, David, Steep-hill
Drury, John W. (printer) 312 High-street
Drury, James (printer) 224 High-street
Hall, John (printer) Butcher-street
Keyworth, Edward (binder) Butcher-street
Leary, R. E. (binder) Strait
Lockyer, J. G., High-street
Peck, William (binder) Bailgate
Shaw, William, 192 High-street
Stainton, John (printer) Cornhill

LOUTH.
From King's-cross 140½ *miles.   Pop.* 10,467.
Edwards, William, Corn-market
Jackson, John & Thomas, Market-place
Marshall, A. G., Mercer-row
Preston, Thomas, Market-place
Shepherd, William, Market-place
Squire, Edwin, Market-place

MARKET DEEPING.
From King's-cross 83½ *miles.   Pop.* 1294.
Croft, M. E., Market-place
Wherry, John (stationer) Market-place

MARKET RASEN.
Pop. 2110.
Cabon, John G. (binder & library) Queen-st.
Pearson, John, Queen-street
White, J., Queen-street

SLEAFORD.
From King's-cross 96¾ *miles.   Pop.* 3729.
Creasey, James (library & music) Market-place
Smedley, Josh. (library) Market-place

SPALDING.
Foom King's-cross 93 *miles.   Pop.* 7627.
Albin, Thomas, Bridge-street
Ashwell, Joseph, Bridge-street
Gilbert & Son (library) Market-place
Watkinson, Henry (publisher) Market-place

SPILSBY.
Pop. 2586.
Hoff, Elizabeth, Stamp-office
Morton, John
Rhoades, John (printer)

STAMFORD.
From Euston-square viâ Rugby 124 *miles.*
Pop. 8933.
Bagley, Robert, Ironmonger-street
Johnson, Henry (publisher) St. Mary's
Langley, William, High-street
Sharpe, Samuel, High-street

SUTTON.
From King's-cross 141½ *miles.   Pop.* 1436.
Swaine, John, High-street

WAINFLEET.
From King's-cross.   Pop. 1365.
Clayton, W. R. (printer)
Tickler, R. & S. (printers)

MIDDLESEX.

ACTON.
From London 5 *miles west on the Oxford Road,*
or by rail from Fenchurch-st. Pop. 2582.
Bunney, Wm. P. (stationer) High-street
Hays, Mrs. S. (stationer) High-street

BRENTFORD.
From London 7 *miles, or by rail from Water-*
loo, or Fenchurch-street. Pop. 8870.
Gregge, John (news)
Knight, Mrs. M. (stationer)
Maberley, George (stationer)

NEW BRENTFORD.
Biggars, John (librarian) Town-hall
Norbury, Miss M. A. (printer) Post-office
Murphy, Chas. J. (printer & binder)
Woodbridge, Mrs. A. (stationer)

CHISWICK AND TURNHAM GREEN.
From Hyde-park-corner 5 *miles.   Pop.* 6303.
Carter, Mrs. A. (stationer)
Cooke, George (news)
Platrier, William (stationer & printer)

CLAPTON.
From Shoreditch 3 miles. Pop. 2500.
Gribble, John, Lower Clapton
Jones, John Alfred (stationer) Wood-street
Pearson, John (fancy) Hill-street
Upcraft, Mrs. L. (stationer) Upper Clapton

EALING.
From Paddington 5½ miles. Pop. 3771.
Ackworth, James Edward (news) Post-office
Watts, Mrs. L. (stationer)
Literary Institution,
   John Rymer, *Secretary*

EDMONTON.
From Shoreditch Church 6½ miles. Pop. 9708.
Corker, Miss E. (stationer) Fore-street
Fox, Mrs. S. (stationer) Fore-street
Heyward, Robert George, Fore-street
Rowley, Mrs. John (library & fancy) Fore-st
Salmon, Henry James (printer & fancy) Lower
   Edmonton
Schleucker, Mrs. M. (fancy) Fore-street
Shadbolt, Mrs. H. (stationer) Post-office-green

ENFIELD.
From Shoreditch 10 miles. Pop. 9453.
Ainger, Miss E. (fancy) Enfield-town
Barrow, Mrs. K., 3 Charles-place, Baker-street
Belchsr, Thomas (stationer) Highway
Fraser, Mrs. C. (stationer) Enfield-town
Meyers, John Henry (news) Enfield-town
Pratt, William (stationer) Baker-street
Smith, George Joseph (stationer) Highway
Young, Jane & Ann (stationers) Silver-street

FINCHLEY.
From the General Post-office 8 m. Pop. 4120.
Evans, Evan (stationer) Common
Gwillin, John (stationer) Chapel-street
Lawrence, Joseph (stationer) Market-place

FULHAM, ETC. ETC.
From Hyde-park-corner 4 miles. Pop. 11,886.
Lavis, John (stationer) High-street
Wilson, George (printer) Walham-green

HACKNEY.
Collins, Miss C. Y. (fancy) Gwynne-place
Darley, William (binder) Norway-place
Rider, James Thomas (library) Cambridge-pl
Smith, Wm. & Bros. (news) Kettesford-place
Slater, Miss M. A. (stationer) Suffolk-place
Taylor, John (fancy) London-terrace

HAMMERSMITH, ETC.
From Hyde-park-corner 3½ miles. Pop. 17,760.
Alais, William (printer & stationer) King-street
Allen, Mrs. M. (library) 2 Britannia-place
Barker, Fred., & Son (news) Dorcas-terrace
Carter, William (printer & stationer) Broadway
Davis, Edward & Co. (music & library) King-st
Eldridge, Mrs. E. (stationer) New-road
Froy, William (news) 11 Dorville's-row
Hambridge, Wm. (stationer) King-street
Jackson, Thomas (stationer) Grove-road

Lock, Miss M. (stationer, &c.) New-road
Marlow, Thos. L. (stationer) 5 Lower Vale-pl
Marshall, Mrs. S. (fancy) King-street
Moody, Thomas (news) King-street
Otridge, Thomas, 7 Angel-terrace
Page, Edward (printer) 9 Angel-terrace
Thompson, John (printer & stationer) Broadway
Tuck, William (printer & binder)

HAMPSTEAD.
Pop. 11,986.
Bluck, Miss L. J. (library) Heath-street
Carter, George (stationer) Rosslyn-street
Shaw, James Jessie (printer & binder) High-st
Smith, George Edward
Public Library, Heath-street,
   Henry Wash, *Librarian*

HAMPTON, ETC.
From Waterloo 15 miles. Pop. 4802.
Bradley, Richard Edward (stationer)
Blakeley, Frederick (stationer)
Lindsey, William (printer)
Piper, Mrs. M. (stationer)

NEW HAMPTON.
Austin, William (stationer)
Miller, Mrs. S. (fancy)

HAMPTON WICK.
Ayliffe, George (stationer)
Register, Benjamin (library)

HARROW, ETC.
From Euston-square 11½ miles. Pop. 4951.
Balls, John V.
Longworthy, William (binder)
Winkley, William, jun. (printer)
Literary Institution,
   John Chapman & John Quilton, *Secs.*

HIGHGATE.
From General Post-office 5¼ miles. Pop. 4502.
Broadbent, Miss C. (fancy) High-street
Glead, John (news)
Sherar, Robert, High-street
Whitmore, Richard, South-grove
Literary Institution, South-grove
   Richard Whitmore, *Librarian*

HOMERTON, NEAR HACKNEY.
Smith, Samuel, High-street
Wharton, Thomas (library)
Homerton College. Training Institution of
the Congregational Board of Education
   Rev. Wm. Jordan Unwin, M. A. (*Principal*) High-street
   Samuel Morley, *Treasurer*
   William Rutt, *Hon. Sec.*, Depository,
   Homerton College

HORNSEY.
From King's-cross 5 miles. Pop. 7135.
Hannis, Mrs. E. (stationer) Manor-place
Page, Misses M. A. & S. (fancy) Maynard-st

HOUNSLOW.
From Waterloo 12½ miles. Pop. 3981.
Cooper, William L. (fancy) High-street

Everley, Thomas (news) High-street
Gotelee, John (printer & binder)
Lovegrove, William L. (stationer) Staines-road

ISLEWORTH.

From Waterloo 9 miles.   Pop. 7007.
Taylor, Mrs. Johanna (fancy) the Square

KILBURN.

From Hyde-park-corner 2½ miles.
Blakeley, Thomas (fancy) 7 Manchester-terrace
Bull, Mrs. G. (stationer) Post-office
Hunt, John, 5 Priory-terrace

SHACKLEWELL, NEAR HACKNEY.

Eyre & Spottiswoode (printer to Her Majesty)
Young, John, (stationer) the Green

SHEPHERD'S BUSH.

From Marble-arch 3 miles.
Hellewell, Henry (stationer) 39 Morland-road
Pierson, Robert (fancy) 8 Richmond-terrace

SOUTHGATE, ETC.

From London 8 miles, near Edmonton.
Pop. 2460.
Anscombe, Robert (stationer)

SOUTH MIMS.

From London 14½ miles, near Chipping Barnet.
Pop. 2825.
Baldock, Willim, & Son (printers) New-road

STAINES.

From Waterloo 19¼ miles.   Pop. 2577.
Norris, Mrs. Jane (reading rooms) Clarence-st
Watkins, William (printer) High-street
Literary Institution,
    Curtis & Richings, *Secretaries*

GREAT STANMORE.

From London 10 miles.   Pop. 1180.
Green, Alfred

STOKE NEWINGTON.

From Shoreditch-church 3 miles.   Pop. 5549.
Bentall, Charles A., 8 Rochester-terrace
Ferriday, William (stationer) 2 Brunswick-pl
Jefferson, William, 34 Church-street
Miller, Charles, Church-street
Munday, Miss Eliza, 5 Abney-park-terrace
Rendell, Miss Sarah (fancy) High-street
Smith, Charles (stationer) High-street
Sutton, Joseph, (stationer) 5 Glo'ster-place

SUNBURY.

From Waterloo 16 miles.   Pop. 2076.
Collett, Charles (library)

TEDDINGTON.

From Waterloo 12 miles.   Pop. 1146.
Lemon, George N. (stationer)

TOTTENHAM.

From Shoreditch 7¾ miles.   Pop. 9120.
Bourne, Misses A. & M. (fancy) High-street
Colyer, William, (news) Post-office
Coventry, George (printer) High-road

Gad, Mrs. S. (fancy) 20 Grove-place
Hennings, William B. (news) High-road
James, Wm. (stationer) Northumberland-park
Middleton, Miss Jane (fancy) High-road
Prior, Joseph F. (binder) High-road
Robinson, Mrs. S. (news) High-road
Taylor, Misses A. & E. (fancy) High-road
Warr, Richard Hale
Wood, Mrs. Ann (fancy) High-cross
    Literary Institution, High-road,
        S. L. Howard, *Secretary.*

TWICKENHAM.

From Waterloo 10 miles. pop. 6254.
Curtis, William, Post-office
Schutz, John (fancy) Church-street
Seymour, Misses S. & J., Church-street
Woods, Miss Emma (stationer) Church-street
    Literary Institution, King-street,
        Francis Ethrington, *Librarian*

UXBRIDGE, ETC. ETC.

From Paddington 17 miles, pop. 6341 ;
and Hillingdon, pop. 6352.
Birch, John T. (musicseller) London-street
Cosier, Henry G. (printer) High-street
Dancer, James, Windsor-street
Hethrington, R. W. (binder) London-street
Murray, G. W. (stationer) High-street
Prior, Robert (fancy) Windsor-street
Silver, James (fancy) High-street
Trenchard, Ben. (news) High-street
    News Rooms, London-street

WHETSTONE.

From King's-cross 8¾ miles.
Reynolds Thomas E. (stationer)

WINCHMORE HILL.

From London 8 miles, near Enfield.
Thomas, Mrs. H. (stationer.

MONMOUTHSHIRE.

ABERGAVENNY.

From Euston-square 233 miles, or Paddington
Pop. 4797.
Davies, Edward S., & Co., Cross-street
Morgan, J. H., High-street
Rees & Son

CHEPSTOW.

From Paddington 141½ miles.   Pop. 4295.
Clarke & Son, Back-street
Davis, Thomas (library) Moor-street
Taylor, Robert (library) High-street

MONMOUTH.

Pop. 5700.
Farror, Thos., Agincourt-square
Heath, Elizabeth, Agincourt-square
Jenkins, William, Monnow-street
Wightman, —, Agincourt-square
Yates, Charles, St. Mary-street

NEWPORT.

From Paddington 158½ miles.   Pop. 19,323.
Christopher, William, High-street

Dowling, Edward (printer) Corn-street
Evans, M. (library & printer) Corn-street
Edwards, Mrs., Corn-street
Jones, D. W. (library) Commercial-street
Loder, William, High-street
Mullock, Henry, High-street
Oliver, Charles, Commercial-street
Oliver, Thos., & Co. (printers) Commercial-st
Pitt, Wm. (publisher) Commercial-street
Partridge, John (printer) Stow-hill
Reed, Samuel, High-street

PONTYPOOL.
Pop. 16,864.

Hughes, Henry, Commercial-street
Wood, W. & Edward, Commercial-street

TREDEGAR.
Pop., with Pontypool, 16,864.

Bean, Henry (binder) Church-street
Davies, Edward, Circle
Peaty, Charles, Castle-street
Walker, Thos., Morgan-street
Thomas, John, Church-street

USK.
Pop. 1479.

Clarke, James Henry

NORTHAMPTONSHIRE.

BRACKLEY.
From Euston-square 68¼ *miles.   Pop.* 2157.
Green, Alfd. (printer & binder) High-street
Mee, William, High-street

DAVENTRY.
Pop. 4430.

Bailey, Thomas, High-street
Barratt, Thos. (printer & library) Sheaf-street
Bennett, Edwd. (printer & library) High-st
Tomalin & Potts (printers) High-street

HIGHAM.
Pop. 1140.

Ashby, David, Wood-street
Grindell, Robt., Market-street

KETTERING.
Pop. 5125.

Dash, Wm. (printer) Market-place
Toller, Joseph (printer) Market-place
Waddington, Thos. (printer) High-street
Wright, E., Market-place

NORTHAMPTON.
Pop. 26,657.

Abel & Sons (music & publishers) Parade
Dorman, William, Drapery
Cooper, M. A., Drapery
Freeman, John, & Son, Market-square
Harris, J., Bridge-street
Henson, Geo., Bridge-street
McPherson, James, Gold-street
McStay, Alice, Market-square
Phillips, Thos., Sheep-street
Snape, —, Drapery

Taylor, John, Gold-street
Wetton, Geo. (pub. & music) Drapery

Printers.
Burgess, John T., Gold-street
Dicey, Thos. E., Parade
Law, W. W., Sheep-street
Stanton, F. J., Wood-street
Vickers, John, Bearnard-street
Wetton, G. N., Drapery

OUNDLE.
From Euston-square.   Pop. 3108.
Todd, Richard, New-street

PETERBOROUGH.
*From Euston-square, King's-cross, or Shore-
ditch, 76 miles.   Pop.* 8672

Bairn, T. C., Bridge-street
Clarke, J. S., Market-place
Collyer, Chas., Long-causeway
Gardner, Robt., Bridge-street
Green, Henry, Long-causeway
Pentney, William, Long-causeway
Perkins, T. C. (binder) Westgate
Sargeant, E. B., Bridge-street

Printers.
Harley, John, Market-place
Wallis, John (binder) Priestgate

THRAPSTONE.
From Euston-square.   Pop. 1183.
Collin, Sarah, High-street
Notcutt, I. T. (printer) Bridge-street

TOUCESTER.
Pop. 2478.
Hurfurt, J. B. (library) High-street
Inns, Samuel, High-street
Rodhouse, T. B., High-street

WELLINGBOROUGH.
From Euston-square.   Pop. 5061.
Bearn, William, & Sons, Silver-street
Bellamy, William, High-street
Chesterton, John (printer) Silver-street
Saunders, John (printer, &c.) Silver-street
Wilkin (printer) Sheep-street

NOTTINGHAMSHIRE.

BINGHAM.
Pop. 2054.
Doncaster, Charles, Market-place

MANSFIELD.
Pop. 10,012.

Aves, O., Leeming-street
Collinson, Charles, Westgate
Clarke, T. W., Westgate
Langley, G. Market-place
Plumbe, C., Sutton
Thacker, W., Church-street

NEWARK-ON-TRENT.
From Euston-square 147½ *miles, or from
King's-cross.   Pop.* 11,330.
Bridges, James, Church-street

Brooke, Edwd., Stodman-street
Perfect, James, Market-place
Ridge, Chas. & W., Market-place
Tomlinson, —, Stodman-street
Wells, John (printer) Bambygate

NOTTINGHAM.
From Euston-square 130 *miles; King's-cross*
128 *miles.   Pop.* 57,407.

Addicott, Thos. (binder) Queen-street
Allen, M. A. & E., Queen-street
Allen, A., Audley-street
Allsop, W. & J. (music) St. Peter's
Batters, Geo. (printer) Chapel-bar
Bayne, Charles (binder) Warser-gate
Bull, Robt. (binder) Newcastle-street
Bunny, Wm. (printer) Bridlesmith-gate
Dearden, Wm. (printer) Carlton-street
Dunn, J., & Co. (printers) Parade
Farmer, Henry (music) High-street
Foster, Stephen, Count-street
Field, William (binder) Granby-street
Hall, William, Carrington-street
Hudstone, Henry (printer) Maypole-yard
Harrison, John, Swinton-street
Jeffs, E. S. (music) St. Peter's-gate
Kirk, Thos. (printer) St. Peter's-gate
Leighton, John, Lincoln-street
Mahon, J. L., Milton-street
Mercer, Richard, Chapel-bar
Porter, Robt., Beeston
Preston, R. W. (printer) Pelham-street
Shaw & Sons (printers) Wheelergate
Shepherd, Thomas, Angel-row
Stevenson, T. & T. H. (printers) Middle-pavement
Staveley, A., Pelham-street
Sutton, Richd., & Co. (printers) Bridlesmith-gate
Taylor, Wm. (printer) Long-row
Wilkinson, R., Back-lane
Williams, W. R. (printer) Carlton-street
Wheelhouse, Henry (binder) Back-lane
White, Jas. (music) Pelham-street
Winrow, W. (music) Hollowstone
Wright, C. N., Long-row

RETFORD.
From King's-cross 138¼ *miles.   Pop.* 46,054.

Dewhurst, B., Square
Hodson, F. (music) Carolgate
Kippax, John (music) Market-place
Metcalf, Anthony (library & music) Market-pl
Pennington, Wm. (music) Bridgegate
Whiteside, Joseph (binder) Carolgate

SOUTHWELL.
From King's-cross to Newark 120 *miles.*
Pop. 3516.

Ridge, C. & W., Market-place
Singleton, E. D., Farnsfield
Whittingham, Jas. (printer) Queen-street

WORKSOP.
From King's-cross 146¼ *miles.   Pop.* 7215.

Linet, J., Coney-street

Sissons, Sarah (library) Potter-street
White, Robert, Coney-street
White, W. (music & library) Bridge-street

NORFOLK.

ATTLEBOROUGH.
From Shoreditch 110 *miles.   Pop.* 2324.

Adamson, William
Parsons, A. & E.

AYLSHAM.
Pop. 2814.

Clements, Charles, & Son

BURNHAM MARKET.
Pop. 1214.

Hammond, William (printer)
Oakes, Francis (stationer & library)

DISS.
From Shoreditch 94¼ *miles.   Pop.* 2867.

Abbott, Robert (printer) Mere-street
Gostling, Thomas, More-street
Cupiss, Francis (printer) More-street

DOWNHAM MARKET.
Pop. 2867.

Brett, John (printer) Market-place
Cole, John L. (printer) High-street
Hutson, Edward, High-street
Lemon, H., High-street
Thorogood, R. (printer)

EAST DEREHAM.
From Shoreditch 127 *miles.   Pop.* 3372.

Barker, P., Market-place
Boyce, W., Market-place
Wigg, Henry C., High-street

FAKENHAM.
From Shoreditch 139 *miles.   Pop.* 2240.

Miller, T. J., Market-place
Stewardson, G. N. (library) Market-place

HARLESTON.
Pop. 1509.

Cannan, Samuel
Pratt & Cann

HARLING.
From Shoreditch 103¼ *miles.*

Gallant, James
Monday, Mark

HOLT.
Pop. 1726.

Colman, Josh., High-street
Younge, Edward, Market-place

LYNN.
From Shoreditch 98 *miles.   Pop.* 19,355.

Aiken, John, W., High-street
Bray, John (music) High-street
Cadman, T. F., St. James's-street
Garland, Thomas, High-street
Mutrell, John, High-street

Plowright, W. S., High-street
Reddie, J. F. (music) Buckingham-terrace
Smith, J. R., St. James's-road
Taylor, William, St. James's-road
Thew & Son (publishers) High-street
Wade, Frederick, St. James's-street

Bookbinders.

Carr, William, Norfolk-street
Inkson, Henry, Regent-street

NORTH WALSHAM.

Pop. 2911.

Mower, John F., Market-place
Plumby, John, Market-place

NORWICH.

From Shoreditch viâ *Colchester* 113¼ *miles.*

Pop. 68,195.

Bacon & Co., London-street
Blackie & Son, St. Giles's-street
Brown, Z., Ber-street
Cupper, James, Rampant Horse-street
Dullinger, J. A., Davey-place
Darken, James, London-street
Fletcher & Alexander (printers) Haymarket
Gooch, Robert, White Lion-street
Jarrold & Sons, London-street
Jeary, Robert, Bridewell-lane
King, J., Back of Inns
Lain, Edward, Elm-hill
Lemmon, James, The Walk
Matchett & Co., Market-place
Miller, G. R., St. Andrew's-hill
Muskett, Charles (music) Haymarket
Priest & Green, St. Stephen-street
Quinton, John, Pottergate-street
Rose, Sarah, Castle-street
Shalders, John, Bethel-street

Bookbinders.

Bush, George, Bridge-street
Charlwood, A., Orford-hill
Coote, G. M., Old Hay-hill
Dean & Co., St. Stephen-street
Gunter, C. E., St. George's
Oliver, Mark, St. Andrew-street
Priest & Co., St. Stephen-street
Read, Charles, St. Benedict-street
Smith, William, Post-office-court
Stevens, H. W., Pottergate-street
Steward, S., Elm-hill
Upcroft, W., Fishgate-street

Musicsellers, &c..

Cops, James, Chapelfield-road
Fish, William, Bridewell-alley
Howlett, William, London-street
Mudge, Giles, Botolph-street
Russell, H., & Son, Thorpe
Warnes, Elizabeth, Pottergate-street

Printers.

Daynes, Samuel, Plough-corner
Dean & Co., St. Stephen-street
Gilbert, James, Oak-street
Houghton, Henry, All Saints-green

Norman, B., Bethel-street
Priest & Co., St. Stephen-street
Sharpe, J. J., Colegate-street
Stevens, H. W., Pottergate-street
Thorndicke, Henry, Princes-street
Upcroft, W., Fishgate-street
Walker, Robert, St. Miles's-churchyard
Webster, Thomas, Pottergate-street

SWAFFHAM.

From Shoreditch 113 *miles.* *Pop.* 3858.

Floyd, J. & H., Castle-acre
Gowing, J. S. (music) Market-place
Philo, John, Market-place

THETFORD.

From Shoreditch 95¼ *miles.* *Pop.* 4075.

Bowering, Samuel, King-street
Carley, Robert, Market-place
Fleet, James, Earl's-lane

WATTON.

Pop. 1353.

George, G. (stationer)
Gowing, J. S. (library)

WELLS.

Pop. 3633.

Fryer, Thomas & Henry, Staith-street
Howard, Thomas, Butlands-street
Neville, Henry, High-street

WYMONDHAM.

From Shoreditch 116 *miles.* *Pop.* 2970.

Forster, Robert (printer) Church-street
Francis, M. A., Market-place
Francis, William, Market-place
White, M. (printer) Market-street

YARMOUTH.

From Shoreditch 146 *miles.* *Pop.* 30,879.

Cooper, J., Market-row
Duncan, Alexander, Market-row
Foreman, John, Theatre-plain
Gooch & Sons (library) Market-place
Gilham, James, Howard-street
Meall, T., Howard-street
Sloman, Charles (library) King-street
Sotheran & Sons, King-street
Thorndicke, James

Bookbinders, &c.

Denew, J. M. (printer) Row-quay
Diboll, J. W., Howard-street
Gyton, W. H. (printer) Howard-street
Purdy, H. G. (printer) Gaol-street

Libraries.

Alexander, W., King-street
Bates, James, Market-place
Wright, W., King-street
Smith, John, George-street
Thompson, M., George-street

Printers.

Alexander, William, King-street
Barber, Charles, Quay
Gooch & Sons, Market-place
Sloman, Charles, King-street

NORTHUMBERLAND.

ALNWICK.

From London 307 *miles. Pop.* 6231.

Blair, Henry H., 23 Bondgate
Davison, William, 22 Bondgate
Pike, George, 37 Market-place
Smith, Mark, 39 Bondgate
    Reading and News Room, Market-place ;
     William Dickson, *Secretary*
    Mechanics' Institute, Percy-street ; George
     Lingwood, *Librarian*

BERWICK-ON-TWEED.

From London 334 *miles. Pop.* 15,094.

Carss, Jas., & Co., Western-lane
Henderson, Alex. (news) Western-lane
Henderson, John (binder) Hide-hill
Melrose, Thos. (music) High-street
Rennison, John (binder) Bridge-street
Rennison, Margaret (binder) High-street
Wilson, John, Hide-hill
    Berwick Advertiser, Saturday ; Andrew
     Robson, Western-lane
    Warder, Friday ; Geo. Macaskie, Mary-gate
    Subscription News Room, Geo. K. Nicholson,
     Secretary

HEXHAM.

From London 280 *miles. Pop.* 4601.

Cooke, William, Fore-street
Pruddah, Edward, Market-place
    Mechanics' Institution, Golden Lion-lane ;
     Charles B. Smith, *Librarian*

MORPETH.

From London 289 *miles. Poy.* 5020.

Blair, Peter, Newgate-street
Flint, George, Bridge-street
Mackay, James, Bridge-street
    Mechanics' Institution, Market-place ; Wm.
     Wilson, *Librarian*

NEWCASTLE-ON-TYNE.

From London 273 *miles. Pop.* 87,784.

Atkin, Wm. (printer) 62 Quay-side
Bailey, Joseph, 49 Clayton-street
Barkas, Thos. P. (printer) 26 Grainger-street
Barlow, Joseph (printer) 28 Grainger-street
Brennan, Hugh, 40 Grainger-street
Charlton, Edwd., 46 Pilgrim-street
Charnley, Emmerson, 45 Bigg-market
Christie, John (printer) Nelson-street
Cowan, Robt. (binder) 95 Clayton-street
Crothers, Robt. (periodicals) 121 Pilgrim-st
Crowther, Isaac, 3 Denton-street
Dawson, Wm. (binder) St. Nicholas'-churchyd
Dodds, Matthew (printer) Quay-side
Dodsworth, Fred. & Wm., Collingwood-street
Denkin, Robert, Elswick-lane
Everatt, Alfred (periodicals & library) 82 New-
    gate-street
Farren, John, Mosley-street
Fordyce, Wm. (printer) 58 Pilgrim-street
Foster & Hara, 26 Side
France, Peter, & Co., 8 Side

Franklin, Wm. E., Royal-arcade
Garrett, Wm., Northumberland-place
Gilbert, John (printer) Royal-arcade
Gunn & Munro (binders) 29 Sandhill
Horn, Thos. (news) 32 & 33 Grey-street
Huntley, John (binder) 17 Side
Kaye, Wm. (library) Blackett-street
Kelly & Waters (binders) Nelson-street
Lambert, M. & M. W. (binders & printers)
    Grey-street
Lee, John, St. John's-lane
Loraine, Catherine (library) 23 Mosley-street
Mackey, Robt. (periodicals) 4 Westgate
McMinnies (periodicals) Nelson-street
Marston, Joseph (library) Mosley-street
Newlands, Thomas, 61 Side
Ormston & Smith (printers) 69 Quay-side
Phillipson & Hare (printers) Mosley-street
Pringle, Walter S., Collingwood-street
Richards, George, Clayton-street
Robinson, Robt., 116 Pilgrim-street
Sang, William, 61 Grey-street
Shield, Wm. (musical library) Market-street
Snowdon, Wm. & Son (binders) 10 Bigg-market
Sturrock, John (binder) 46 Grainger-street
Sharp, Jane, 33 Westgate-street
Sturrock, George, Westgate-street
Sutton, William, Collingwood-street
Turnbull, John, Butcher-bank
Turner, Robert, 72 Grey-street
Virtue, G., & Co., Collingwood-street ; Wm.
    Naismith, *Agent*
Watson, William, Marlborough-crescent
Wilson, George P., Side
Young, John (library) Nun-street
    Exchange News Room, Grey-street ; Francis
     Jackson, *Secretary*
    Exchange Subscription Room, Sandhill ;
     Thomas E. Wilkinson, *Secretary*
    Literary Society, Westgate-street ; John
     Thornhill, *Librarian*
    Mechanics' Library ; Arthur Robinson,
     Librarian
    Saint Nicholas Reading Room ; Robert
     Moffatt & John White, *Secretaries*

Musicsellers.

Binns, Thomas, Nelson-street
Graham, Wm., New Bridge-street
Horn, Thomas, Grey-street
Morland & Co., Collingwood-street
Paradise, Wm., Percy-street

Newspapers.

Newcastle Chronicle ; M. W. Lambert,
    Grey-street
Newcastle Courant ; John Blackwell & Co.,
    Pilgrim-street
Newcastle Guardian ; Macliver & Bradley,
    Grainger-street
Newcastle Journal ; Jno. Hernaman, Grey-st

Printers.

Benson, Michael, Dean-street
Blackwell, John, & Co., Pilgrim-street
Bostle, Wm., & Son, Grey-street
Christie, —, Nelson-street

Clarke, John, St. Nicholas'-churchyard
Collin, John, High-bridge
Collins, Nathaniel, 94 Side
Crow, W. S., 96 Side
Day, Thomas, 25 Percy-street
Dent, Roger, 112 Pilgrim-street
Gibson, M. H., Bigg-market
Green, George, 99 Side
Leighton, B. W., 7 Grainger-street
Reid, Andrew, 117 Pilgrim-street
Selkirk & Rhagg, 48 Pilgrim-street
Simpson, Thomas, & Son, 2 Side
Spens, Thomas, 8 Grainger-streeet
Ward, Robert, 3 Dean-street

NORTH SHIELDS, &c.

*From London 279 miles. Pop. 30,524 with
Tynemouth.*

Ditchburn, Gawin (binder) Camden-lane
Harrison, Robt. (binder) Tyne-street
Franklin, Wm. E. E., Railway Station
Hall, John, Camden-town
Hays, John, 54 Trout-street, Tynemouth
Henderson, Robt. (library) 5 Church-way
Orange, William, 4 Bedford-street
Phillipson and Hare, 7 Tyne-street
Stewart, James (news) Clive-street
Sutherlaud, William (news) Bedford-street
Turner, Daniel (binder) 2 Bell-street
Walker, George (binder) 12 Tyne-street
Watron, William, 47 Clive-street
Literary Institution, Tynemouth, John Robson, *Librarian.*

WOOLER.

From London 319 miles. Pop. 1911.

Brown, Robert (printer) Wooler
Brand, William (binder) Wooler
Carr, Jno. and Chas. (binders) Wooler
Little, Creighton, Wooler

OXFORDSHIRE.

BANBURY.

*From Euston-square, viâ Bletchley, 78 miles;
and from Paddington 86 miles. Pop. 8715.*
Bookbinders.

Godfrey, Francis, Calthorpe-lane
Golsby, William, North Bar-street

Booksellers, &c.

Cheney, Esther, High-street
Potts, William, Parsons-street
Rusher, John G., Market-place
Stone, Henry (library) High-street
Walford, George, High-street

Printers.

Brook, Thomas (stationer) Church-lane
Payne, William, (stationer) High-street

BICESTER.

From Euston-square 66¼ miles. Pop. 2763.

Hewiett, George, Market-end
Smith, James (binder) Market-end

BURFORD.

From Euston-square. Pop. 1593.

Burghope, William (printer) High-street

CHIPPING NORTON.

From Euston-square 74 miles. Pop. 2932.

Liddiard, John, High-street
Smith, George M. (printer) High-street
Stanbridge, Catherine, Middle-row

DEDDINGTON.

From Euston-square miles. Pop. 1543.

Hiron, John Samuel (publisher)

HENLEY ON THAMES.

From Paddington miles. Pop. 3369.

Hickman & Kinch (printers) Market-place

OXFORD.

From Paddington 63 miles. Pop. 27,843.
Bookbinders.

Bennett, Charles, High-street
Curtis, David, High-street
Grainger, William, Friars-entry
Hartley, Robert, St. Giles's-road
Hayes, William, Oriel-street
Kile, Frederick, St. Clement's
Maltby & Bloxham, College-lane
Mansell, William, High-street
Salter, William, High-street
Sanders, James, Blue Boar-lane
Shrimpton, William, St. Aldates-street
Trash, Frederick, Queen-street

Booksellers, &c.

Abrams, Joseph (publishers) High-street
Aldan, Henry (printer) Queen-street
Bellamy, M. (binder) High-street
Blackwell, Benjamin, High-street
Boddington, Thomas, Oriel-street
Carde, John B. High-street
Dewe, John, Ship-street
Gill, M. St. Aldates-street
Goodden, Charles, Speedwell-street
Graham, William, High-street
Haines, John, Turl-street
Harris, Thomas, Broad-street
Holder, Henry, (printer) St. Aldates-street
Ladd, Henry, High-street
Laycock, Thomas, High-street
Lenthall, John, Oriel-street
Parker, John Henry (publisher) Broad-street
Parker, Jno. Hen. & Jas.
Plowman, Joseph, St. Aldates-street
Richards, Charles, High-street
Shrimpton, Thomas (printer) St. Aldates-st
Slatter, Henry (publisher) High-street
Spiers, Thomas Edward, High-street
Taylor, Henry, Pembroke-street
Taylor, Thomas, 119 High-street
Thornton, James, 51 High-street
Vincent, Joseph, 20 High-street
Wheeler, James L. (publisher) 106 High-street

Musicsellers, &c.

Aldan, Henry, Queen-street
Barratt, M., St. Aldates-street
Frost, Edward, High-street
Russell, James, High-street

Libraries.

Harris, Thomas, Broad-street
Holder, Henry, St. Aldates-street
Plowman, Joseph, St. Aldates-street
Spiers, Thomas Edward, High-street

Printers.

Baxter, William, St. Aldates-street
Cooke & Westbrooke, High-street
Hall, Henry, Holywell-street
Hall, Thomas, New-road
Ham, Joseph, St. Aldates-street
Morris, E. W., High-street
Summersford, Henry, Corn-market
Coombe, Thomas, University-press
Vincent, Joseph, High-street

THAME.
From Paddington. Pop. 2869.
Bradford, Henry (printer)
Robson, Edward A.
Scadding, William

WATLINGTON.
From Paddington. Pop. 1884.
Pearce, R. Couching-street
Spiers, W. G. (printer) Market-place

WITNEY.
From Paddington. Pop. 3099.
Bomford, Esau (stationer) High-street
Laurence, James N., High-street
Shayler, James (printer) Market-place

WOODSTOCK.
From Paddington 71 miles. Pop. 7983.
Eccles, William (printer)
Miles, Thomas

RUTLANDSHIRE.

UPPINGHAM.
From Euston-square 112½ miles. Pop. 2068.
Broughton, Thomas, High-street
Oliver, Charles William (library) High-street

OAKHAM.
From Euston-square. Pop. 2800.
Cunnington, G. S. (printer) High-street
Keeling, William (stationer & printer) High-st
Scotney, S. (library) High-street

SHROPSHIRE.

BISHOP'S CASTLE.
Pop. 1961.
Dubber, William, Corn-market
Griffiths, Edward, Market-cross

BRIDGNORTH.
Pop. 7610.
Edkins and Son
Gittin, G. R. (printer) High-street
Rowley, W. J. (music) High-street

BROSELEY.
Pop. 4739.
Slater, Joseph, Ironbridge

Smith, G. M., Ironbridge
Nevatt, Enoch, Broseley
Munday, Thomas, Madeley

DRAYTON.
Pop. 4163.
Bennion, Thomas P., High-street
Silvester and Co., High-street

ELLESMERE.
Pop. 2087.
Thompson, Thomas, High-street

HALES OWEN.
From Euston-sq. 119½ miles. Pop. 2412.
Mitchell, T. G. P., High-street
Roden, John, Church-street
Salt, Samuel, Cornbrow

LUDLOW.
From Euston-square 189 miles. Pop. 10,067.
Cross, V., King-street
Evans, John (music and library) New-buildings
Griffiths, T., Bull-ring
Griffiths, T., The Narrows
Jones, Richard, Broad-street
Partridge, E. J., Broad-street

NEWPORT.
From Euston-sq. 143¾ miles. Pop. 2906.
Shaw, A. P. (library) High-street
Silvester, H. P. and C., High-street

OSWESTRY.
From Euston-square to Shrewsbury 161¼ miles,
thence by Chester line. Pop. 4817.
Bayley, Charles George, The Cross
Cowdell, John, The Cross
Jackson and Salter, Church-street
Morgan, John, Church-street
Roberts, J. A., Willow-street
Roberts, Samuel (publisher) Bailey-head

SHIFFNAL.
From Euston-square to Wolverhampton 125½
miles. Pop. 1958.
Beddow, B. L., New-street
Edmonds, A. (library and music) Market-place

SHREWSBURY.
From Euston-sq. 161½ miles. Pop. 19,681.
Cadwallader, John, High-street
Davies, John, High-street
Davies, Richard, High-street
Drayton, George (printer) Mardol
Harrison and Rutland, Princes-street
Jones, F. A. (printer) Wyle-cop
Leake, J. H., Market-square
Sandford, J. O., High-street
Tibnam, William, Wyle-cop
Wardle, William, Mardol
Wall, John, Mardol

WELLINGTON.
From Euston sq. viâ Stafford, 151¼ miles.
Pop. 11,554.
Hobson, Robert, Market-place

Keay, James, New-street
Leake, Thomas (library) New-street
Smith, Benjamin, New-street

WEM.

Pop. 3747.

Cooke, William, Noble-street
Franklin, George (printer) High-street

WENLOCK.

Pop. 20,588.

Lawley, Thomas, William-street
Smith, G. M., Spittle-street

WHITCHURCH.

From Euston-sq. Pop. 3619.

Jones, R. B., High-street
Newling, Henry, High-street

SOMERSETSHIRE.

AXBRIDGE.

Trew, John B. (printer)

BATH.

From Paddington 106¾ *miles.   Pop.* 54,240.

Binns and Goodwin (printers) 19 Cheap-st.
Chaffin, E., 10 Old Bond-street
Collings, Edward, 1 Saville-row
Cook, Henry, 7 Green-street
Coombs, J. W., 24 Milsom-street
Copestick, Brothers, 13 Stall-street
Fryer, James (binder & printer) 6 York-bldngs
Gardner, E. F. (stationer) 15 Cheap-street
Gibbs, Sam. (stationer & printer) 5 Union-st
Gregory, William, 14 York-street
Hayward, Samuel (library) Abbey-churchyard
Hood, Francis, 17 Walcot-street
Hyams, Henry, Piccadilly
Jennings, Henry T., 4 Princes-buildings
Large, Joseph, 6 Union-street
Mabury, Frederick, 6 Cheap-street
Mendham, Mark, 14 Union-passage
Meyler, M., & Son (printers) St. Michael's-place
Nash, James, 23 St. Michael's-place
Noble, Samuel, 10 Fountain-passage
Noyes, T. & Son, Bladud's-passage
Peach, R. E. (printer & publisher) 8 Bridge-st
Pearson, Benjamin, 13 Milsom-street
Pittman, Parsonage-place
Rottle, John, Brook-street
Russell, C. P., 6 Terrace-walk
Sims & Son (stationers) George-street
Sidwell, Richard, Union-passage
Sidwell, M. A. & E., 25 Union-passage
Vivian, Samuel (printer) 41 Broad-street
Williams, E., Milsom-street
Wood, Brothers (printers & stationers) Old
    Bond-street

Bookbinders only.

Dyke, Brothers, Bartleet-street
Farrant, Thomas, St. Michael's-place
Gregory, William, York-street
Hoskins, George, St. James's-parade
Lambert, S., London-street
Taylor, Edmund, Beaufort-square

Taylor, William, Trim-street
White, Charles, Green-street
Woolf, Samuel, Orchard-street

Printers.

Brown, John, Barton-street
Browning, W., Walcot-street
Clarke, Charles, Argyll-street
Cogsnell, John, King's-mead
Dawson, W. & F. (stationers) High-street
Edgcumbe, James (stationer) Orange-grove
Keene, J. & J. (stationer) King's-mead
Ley, William, Chapel-row
Martin, Thomas, St. James's-parade

Stationers.

Bligh, Thomas, Pulteney-bridge
Everett, William, Pulteney-bridge
Hall, G., Abbey-street
Paulding, T., King's-mead
Pearson, Benjamin, Argyll-street
Purchase, J. J., George-street

BRIDGEWATER.

From Paddington 151¼ *miles.   Pop.* 10,317.

•Dowty, F. G. (music) Cornhill
Waymouth, J. (fancy) Fore-street
West, J. B., Fore-street
Whitby, John, Cornhill

BRUTON.

From Paddington.   Pop. 1885.

Bord, J. G., High-street
Green, W. (printer) High-street

BURNHAM.

Pop. 1701.

Petherick, P. F.

CASTLE CARY.

Pop. 1860.

More, Samuel, High-street

CHARD.

Pop. 2291.

Nowlen, Jas., Fore-street
Russell, Jos., High-street
Thoms, Jno., Market-place

CLEVEDON.

From Paddington 134½ *miles.   Pop.* 1905.

Copeland, Thos. (library)
Ransford, Sam. (library)

CREWKERNE.

Pop. 3303.

Clarke, T. F., Sheep-market
Pulman, G. P. R., Market-place

FROME.

From Paddington 115¼ *miles.   Pop.* 10,148.

Allen, J. T. (printer) Bath-street
Jones, J. S., Market-place
Langford, J. S., Market-place
Penny, Mrs., Market-place
Prior, S. T., Market-place
Tuck, S., Church-slope

GLASTONBURY.
Pop. 3125.
Cottle, Ann, High-street
Rees, William, High-street
Welch, William (binder) High-street

HENTSRIDGE.
Pop. 1136.
Rogers, Robert

ILCHESTER.
Handover, Philip (stationer)

ILMINSTER.
Pop. 3299.
Moore, Chas., Cornhill
Stoodley, Eliza, East-street

LANGPORT.
Pop. 1117.
Bennett, A., North-street
Blake, Geo., Bow-street
Moreton, J. S., Bow-street

MINEHEAD.
From Paddington.   Pop. 1542.
Dunn, R. J.

PETHERTON.
Barnett, Edwin (stationer)

SHEPTON MALLET.
Pop. 3835.
A'Court, Thos. (printer) Paul-street
Byrt, Albt., High-street
Thorn, Jno., High-street
Wason, Jno., High-street

SOMERTON.
Pop. 2140.
Flower, J. B., Broad-street
Woodward, Wm. (stationer) Broad-street

TAUNTON.
From Paddington 163 miles.   Pop. 14,176.
Abraham, Hy., Cheapside
Barnicott, Jas. (binder) Fore-street
Bragg, W., and Co. (binders) Fore-street
Court, Wm. (binder) Fore-street
Dyer, E. and C., High-street
Hiscocke, Thos., Cheapside
May, Fred., High-street
Marriott, J. W. (printer) East-street
Pile, Alex. (printer, binder, and news) North-town
Small, Chas., North-street
Sutton, Hy., North-street
Turle, Jno., North-street
Warren, Wm., High-street
Woodley, W. (printer) Tangiers
Webber, W. (printer) East-street

WELLINGTON.
From Paddington 170 miles.   Pop. 3296.
Cutler, J. (stationer)
Corner, Rd., South-street
Greedy, Jno (library) Fore-street

WELLS.
Pop. 4736.
Backhouse, Samuel, High-street
Beauchamp and Serel, Saddler-street
George, W. and R., Saddler-street
Green, Thos., High-street

WESTON-SUPER-MARE.
From Paddington 138¼ miles. Pop. 4034.
Bawden, Jos., High-street
Brown, Alex. (printer) Regent-street
Whearat, Jos. (reading rooms) Rodney-street

WINCANTON.
Pop. 2488.
Corben, Hy. W., High-street
Davis, Jno., High-street
Phillips, Thos., High-street

WIVELISCOMBE.
Pop. 2861.
Davy, Henry, Market-place
Wood, Jas. (printer) Market-place

YEOVIL.
From Paddington 176¼ miles.   Pop. 5985.
Custard, Henry M.
Wood, Jas. (printer)

SOUTH WALES.

ABERYSTWITH, ETC.
From Paddington to Hereford 144 miles, thence by coach through Kington. Pop. 5231.
Cox, John (publisher) Pier-street
Evans, Thomas, Church-street
Jenkins, David, Darkgate-street
Jones, Evan, Princes-street
Meddins, Richard, Northgate-street
Williams, E., and Son, Bridge-street

BRECON.
From Paddington to Abergavenny by rail, and thence by coach to Brecon, 170 miles. Pop. 5673.
Burgess, Samuel, Castle-street
Humpage, Samuel (library) High-street
Jones, John, High-street
Shaw, Henry (library) High-street
Wheeler, John (binder) High-street
Williams, John, Bulwark

BRIDGEND.
From Paddington to Monmouth. Pop. 9417.
Bird, George
Leyshon, William

BRYN-MAWR.
From Paddington.
Davis, John (binder)
Rogers, Ann
Stephenson, David (printer)

BUILTH.
From Brecon about 12 miles. Pop. 1158.
Prichard, T. and S. (library) High-street

CARDIFF.
From Paddington. Pop. 22,000.
Arnold, James F., Bute-street

Bird, William, and Son, Duke-street
Evans, David, High-street
Clarke, James Henry, High-street
Owen, William, Duke-street
Webber, Henry, Duke-street
Woodman, David, St. Mary-street
Williams, William, St. Mary-street

CARDIGAN.
From Paddington. Pop. 3876.
Clougher, Joseph (music) High-street
Lewis, A. E. and E., High-street
James, James Richard, High-street

CARMARTHEN.
From London 210 miles. Pop. 10,524.
Bookbinders.
Evans, John, King-street
Laurence, John, Chapel-street
Lewis, David, Guildhall-square
Pritchard, Thomas, Queen-street
Spurrell, William (publisher) King-street
Thomas, John, Priory-street
White, H., and Sons (library and wholesale stationery warehouse) Guildhall-square
Booksellers, &c.
Brigstocke, John L., Lammas-street
Evans, Eleanor, Market-street
Jones, Josiah Thomas, Blue-street
Shackell, Edward W., Guildhall-square
Thomas, John, Priory-street
White, H., and Sons, Guildhall-square

COWBRIDGE.
From Paddington.
Davis and Son
Morris, E. and M. A.
Griffiths, John

CRICKHOWELL.
Pop. 1403.
Williams, Thomas (printer)

FISHGUARD.
Pop. 1757.
Davis, Thomas
Vaughan, William

HAVERFORDWEST.
From London 257 miles. Pop. 6580.
Perkins, William (printer) Market-street
Potter, J. (printer) High-street
Young, Edmond, Victoria-place

HAY.
From Paddington to Monmouth. Pop. 1238.
Davies, James (library) High-town
Harris, William (printer, binder, and library) Castle-street
Watkins, Benjamin, Church-street

KNIGHTON.
From Paddington to Hereford.
Edwards, William, Broad-street
Morris, John, High-street

LAMPETER.
Williams, William, (reading-room)
George, William (reading-room)

LLANDILOFAWR.
From London 196 miles. Pop. 1300.
James, Thomas, King-street
Thomas, D. M. Rhosoman-street

LLANDOVERY.
Pop. 1927.
Rees, William (publisher) Market-street
Morris, Elizabeth (printer) King's-road

LLANELLY.
From London 217 miles. Pop. 8710.
Brown, George, Market-street
Rees and Williams, Water-street

MERTHYR TYDVIL.
From Paddington. Pop. 6380.
Church, William, High-street
Davis, John, Nant-street
Evans, Thomas, Aberdare
Jones, David, High-street
Jones, John, Pont Morias
Lewis, Rees, High-street
Sims, Joseph, Hirwain
Thomas, David (binder) Dowlais
White, Henry W., High-street
Wilkins, William, High-street
Williams, Peter, High-street

MILFORD HAVEN.
From Paddington.
Stribling, M.

NARBETH.
From London 230 miles. Pop. 1390.
Howell, John (printer)

NEATH.
From Paddington 200 miles. Pop. 5701.
Hayman, Alfred (printer) High-street
Hewitt, Samuel (binder) Church-street
Hibbert, Walter, New-street
Maber, Thomas (binder & printer) Church-st.
Thomas, Thomas (printer) New-street
Whittington, Mary, Wind-street

NEWCASTLE EMLYN.
From Paddington.
Jones, Joseph (binder)
Davis, John R. (printer)

PEMBROKE.
From Paddington. Pop. 10,107.
Barclay, James, High-street Dock
Barrett, Henry, High-street Dock
Clougher, Thomas, Commercial-road
Powell, William, Pembroke
Treweeks, Richard C., Pembroke

PONT-Y-PRID.
From Paddington.
Bassett, Charles
Jones, William (printer)

PRESTEIGN.
From Paddington. Pop. 1617.
Fawcett, William (library) High-street
Jones, Henry M. (printer)

RHAYADER.
From Paddington. Pop. 1017.
Wilding, Richard (stationer)

SWANSEA.
From Paddington. Pop. 216.
Adams, Edward, Castle Bailey-street
Baker, Henry, Castle-square
Bluett, George, Goat-street
Brader, John (musicseller) Wind-street
Brewster, William M., Wind-street
Davis, Thomas R., Castle Bailey-street
Dryden, Thomas (printer) Mount-street
Griffiths, Evan, High-street
Jenkins, Eliza and G. (music) Wind-street
Jones, Herbert, Oxford-street
Jones, Henry (printer) Welcome-street
Madel, Frederick (music) Western-terrace
Morris, M. High-street
Norton, John (binder and printer) Calvert-st.
Pearce, Ebenezer (printer) Wind-street
Price, Herbert (binder and printer) College-st.
Towsend, Robert (binder) Oxford-street
Williams, J., & Co. (printers) Cambrian-office

TENBY.
Mason, Richard, High-street
Rolland, Felix William, High-street

STAFFORDSHIRE.

BARTON-UNDER-NEEDWOOD,
Pop. 1561.
Batkin, Edwin (stationer) Yoxhall
Blackhall, Geo., Barton

BILSTON.
From Euston-square 123½ *miles, from Paddington* 139¾ *miles. Pop.* 23,527.
Etheridge, Jno., Church-street
Hackett, Wm., Church-street
Kemp, Jno., Oxford-street
Seliman, Samuel (binder) Church-street
Webb, Samuel, Oxford-street

BURTON-ON-TRENT.
From Euston-square 122½ *miles. Pop.* 6734.
Bellamy, R. R., Bridge-street
Darley, W. B. (printer) High-street
Goodman, Caleb (news) High-street
Whitehurst, Jno., Post-office

CHEADLE.
From Euston-square. Pop. 2728.
Horn, Thos., High-street
Thompson, Jas., (binder) High-street
Farnell, Geo., High-street

DARLASTON.
From Euston-square. Pop. 10,590.
Slater, Jas., King-street

ECCLESHALL.
Pop. 1427.
Durrad, Wm. (printer) High-street

LEEK.
Pop. 8877.
Clowes, Jas., High-street
Hilliard, W. M., Market

LICHFIELD.
From Euston-square 115¾ *miles. Pop.* 7012.
Caunter, J. S. (music) Bird-street
Egginton, F. (music) Bird-street
Lomax, T. G. (publisher) Bird-street
Meacham, Jno., Market-place

NEWCASTLE-UNDER-LYME.
Pop. 10,569.
Bayley, Thos., Iron-market
Crewe, Fredk., High-street
Dilworth, D., High-street
Moore, J. and J., Iron-market

POTTERIES.
From Euston-square to Stoke. Pop. 84,027.
Adams, Samuel (binder) Tunstall
Allbut and Son (binders) Hanley
Bate, Edwin (binder) Shelton
Barker, T., Market-lane, Longton
Brown, J., High-street, Longton
Birch, Jas., Shelton
Brougham, Henry (music) Burslem
Cyples, W., Longton
Dean, W. (binder) Stoke
Dean, Jas. (binder) Burslem
Gallimore, A., Stoke
Heames, Jas. (binder) Tunstall
Harrison, W., Burslem
Machin, L., Tunstall
Moore, Chas., Stoke
Shaw, Longton
Sutton, Longton
Thompson, John (binder) Stoke
Tomkinson, Brothers (binders) Tunstall
Timmins, Rd., Burslem
Turner, Geo., Stoke
Watts, Chas., Market, Longton
Webb, High-street, Longton

RUGELEY.
From Euston-square 123½ *miles. Pop.* 3054.
James, Thos., Market-place
Simpson, Jno., Brook-street

STAFFORD.
From Euston-square 132½ *miles. Pop.* 11,829.
Drewry, Jno. and W. (binders) Eastgate-street
Dawson, Edw. (printer) Market-place
Hill and Halden (publishers) Foregate-street
Wright, R. and W. (printers) Greengate-street

TAMWORTH.
From Euston-square 109½ *miles. Pop.* 8655.
Beard, Chas., Market-street
Jones, M., Lichfield-street
Lakin, Wm., Market-street
Thompson, Jno., Market-street

TIPTON.
From Euston-square 120½ *miles. Pop.* 24,872
Blake, Jno., Great-bridge

Constable, Jas., Princes-end
Davis, J., Princes-street
Danks, Thos., Owen-street
Greenfield, Peter, Brierley-hill
James, J. S., Upper-green
Marsh, J. W., Owen-street
Miller, Jas., Owen-street
Millichip, Thos., Hill-top
Russam, Thos., Great-bridge
Scambler, Jno., Horsley-heath
Smith, Thos., Great-bridge
Warren, Jno., Great-bridge

UTTOXETER.
From Euston-square to Burton or Derby.
Pop. 3468.

Kelly, J. R., High-street
Norris and Son, Market-place

WALSALL.
From Euston-square 120 miles. Pop. 25,680.

Griffin, Wm., Digbeth
Lerry, Wm., George-street
Simpson and Gilbert, High-street
Wilkes, E. and J., High-street

WEDNESBURY.
From Euston-square 122 miles. Pop. 11,914.

Boath and Wrenford, Market-place
Ellis, E., and Co., Market-place
Fairbank, W. (stationer) High-street

WEST BROMWICH.
From Euston-square 118½ miles. Pop. 34,591.

Tawdry, Geo., High-street
Murray, Wm., High-street
Salter, Wm., New-street

WILLENHALL.
From Euston-square 124½ miles. Pop. 11,931

Hackett, Stephen (stationer) Cross-street

WOLVERHAMPTON.
From Euston-square 126 miles. Pop. 49,985.

Bridgen, Joseph (printer & binder) Darlington-street
Beddowes, John, Worcester-street
Caldicott, A. J. (binder) Dudley-street
Fullwood, J., Snow-hill
Giusani, James (music) Market-place
Hunter, Snow-hill
Hinde, Alfred, Snow-hill
Hildreth, J. (printer) St. John-street
Mackenzie, W., High-street
Parkes, W., High-street
Quinn, John & Son (printers) Summer-hill
Richards, John, Queen-street
Simpson, Thomas, Market--place
Sully, High-street
Smith, Henry (music) Bilston-street
Vincent, High-stre t
Williams, George (printer) Queen-street
Wilcox, Queen-street

SUFFOLK.

BECCLES.
Pop. 4398.

Arnold, William, Smallgate-street
Crickmay, John (library) Market-place
Cattermole, H. & S. (binders, printers, & library) Market-place
Gaze, Edward, Sheepgate-street
Grimwade, William (library) Market-place
Loyns, R. (printer) Market-place

BOTESDALE.

Larter, Alfred
Taylor, Benjamin

BRANDON.
Pop. 2022.

Clarke, John, High-street
Kemp, Charles, High-street

BUNGAY.
Pop. 3841.

Ashby, J. S. & R., Olland-street
Child, John, & Son (printers) Broad-street
Morris, J. M., Broad-street
Reeve, J., Market-place
Williams, M. E. (music) Market-place

BURY ST. EDMUNDS.
Pop. 13,900.

Banyard, J. J., Crown-street
Birchinall, F. (printer) Crown-street
Brame, J. H., Crown-street
Buck, C. (printer & music) Angel-hill
Cole, John (printer) Butter-market
Cole, Alfred (printer) Butter-market
Fuller, William, Abbeygate-street
Fenton, G., Abbeygate-street
George, J., Abbeygate-street
Jackson & Frost (printers) Chequers-square
Lankaster, F. (library & music) Abbeygate-st
Middleditch, F., Corn-market
Robinson, John (library & printer) Corn-market
Thompson, George, Abbeygate-street

CLARE.
Pop. 1769.

Challice, John
King, William (printer)

DEBENHAM.
Pop. 1653.

Beecroft, L. (stationer)

EYE.
From Shoreditch to Mellis 91 miles.
Pop. 2587.

Bishop, Rt., Broad-street
Nurse, Rd., Broad-street

FRAMLINGHAM.
Pop. 2450.

Freeman, W. D.
Green, Rd.

HADLEIGH.
From Shoreditch 69¼ *miles.* *Pop.* 3338.
Hardacre, Hy., High-street
Piper, J. D. (library) High-street

HALESWORTH.
Pop. 2529.
Roper, Samuel
Tippell, Thos.

IPSWICH.
From Shoreditch 68 *miles.* *Pop.* 32,914.
Burton, J. M. and Co. (publishers & printers)
　Tavern-street
Cook, Jno. (library) Upper Orwell-street
Cowell, S. H. (printer) Old Butter-market
Dallinger, W. H. (library) Tucket-street
Deck, Rt. (printer and library) Cornhill
Dorking, Ant. (printer) Upper Brook-street
Haddock, T. (printer) Old Butter-market
Hunt, Edward, & Son (printers and publishers)
　Tavern-street
Morley, Dd. (fine art repository) Upper Brook-st
Nunn, Jas., Upper Orwell-street
Pannifer, N. J., Fore-street
Read, Jas., Cornhill
Scogging, Jno. (printer) Orwell-place
Shalders, Jas., Westgate-street
Talbot, Jno., Westgate-street

Bookbinders.
Brook, Jas., Princes-street
Garewood, Gdw., Falcon-street
Parker, Jos., Stephen's-lane

Musicsellers.
Ball, E. and Sons, Brook-street
Ball, Jno., Upper Brook-street
Forster, R. W., Tavern-street
Haddock, T., Old Butter-market
Hunt, Edw., & Sons, Tavern-street
Milnes, B. G., St. Matthew-street

LAVENHAM.
Pop. 1811.
Holdich, Edw.

LONG MELFORD.
Pop. 2587.
Lorking, Thos. (printer)

LOWESTOFT.
From Shoreditch 149¼ *miles.* *Pop.* 6580.
Abbott, S. F., High-street
Crisp, Geo., High-street
Crowe, Thos., High-street
Oliver, Wm. Hy., High-street

MILDENHALL.
From Shoreditch 79¼ *miles.* *Pop.* 1760.
Martin, Chas. J., Mill-street
Pope, W. T., High-street

NEEDHAM MARKET.
From Shoreditch 76¾ *miles.* *Pop.* 1367.
Quinton, John

SAXMUNDHAM.
From Shoreditch. *Pop.* 1180.
Brightley

SOUTHWOLD.
Pop. 2109.
Bye, E., Queen-street
Jones, J., High-street
Page, A., Earl-street
Debney, R. J. (library) South-grove

STOWMARKET.
Pop. 3161.
Bennington, S., Market-place
Backham, Geo. (printer) Ipswich-street
Woolby, Thos. B. (library) Ipswich-street

SUDBURY.
From Shoreditch 67¾ *miles.* *Pop.* 6043.
Berry, Jas., North-street
Chaplin, Chas. (printer) Borehamgate
Fulcher, G. W. (printer) Market-hill
Hill, Wm. (printer) Ballingdon
King, Thos. M., North-street
Woolby, Wm. (stationer) Friar-street
Wright, Jas. (printer) Market-hill

SURREY.
BARNES.
From Waterloo *miles.* *Pop.* 1879.
Whitbread, Edward (library) High-street

BATTERSEA.
Berham, Mrs. C. (fancy) Farnboro-place
Chapman, Mrs. A. (printer) High-street
Russell, D. (stationer) High-street
Titchener, Mrs. M. (stationer) Culmstock-place
Vedy, L. G. (stationer) High-street

BRIXTON.
Arnott, D. J., 18 Commercial-place
Alvey, Isaac John, 23 Commercial-place
Bowker, Henry (stationer) Tulse-hill
Bowditch, Stephen (fancy) 1 Manor-rise
Edmonds, Mrs. E., 6 Manor-rise
Fenton, John (printer) Loughboro'-place
Guntrippe Miss A., (fancy) Tulse-hill
Hatfield, Miss M. (fancy & library) Alfred-pl
Hayward, Mrs. L., 1 Woodall-place
Larney, Mrs. E. (fancy) Atkinson-place
Martin, James F. (binder) New Park-road
Pearce, Mrs. S., St. John's-villas
Wildey, Miss E. (fancy) Brighton-place
Wilson, Mrs. M. (fancy) Brixton-rise

CAMBERWELL.
Alvey, J. J. (fancy) the Green
Barnes, John, Bowyer-place
Chandler, William G. (library) High-street
Errington, Frederick (news) 15 St. George's-pl
Elm, Miss E., 7 John's-place
Finley, Miss M. L. (news) York-terrace
Haywood, John (stationer) South-place
Livick, Lewis (stationer) 3 Garden-row
Morris, Robert B. (stationer) the Green
Pyefinch, Edward (fancy) the Green

Skinner, Mrs. G. (fancy) the Green
Turner, Thomas (news) 7 John's-place
Williams, Mrs. S. (stationer) the Green
Ward, Philip, Bloxham-place
Wesson, J. N. (fancy) Mansion-house-place
Yarnton, Samuel (reading-rooms) Albion-place

CARSHALTON.
From London-bridge 13 miles. Pop. 3785.
Muggeridge, John (paper-maker) and Queen-
   street, City, London
Norman, George (stationer) Post-office
Rotherham, Miss S. (stationer)
Smitherman, Henry (manager of the paper-mill)

CHERTSEY, ETC.
From Waterloo 21¼ miles. Pop. 6029.
Kempson, William (printer) Windsor-street
Knight, Miss Sarah (stationer) Bridge-road
Lamb, Henry (printer & news) Guildford-street
Lipscombe, Misses S. & J. (fancy) Guildford-st
   Reading Room, Town-hall; Henry Lamb,
   Secretary

CHILWORTH, ETC., NEAR GUILDFORD.
From London 34¾ miles by rail. Pop. 142.
Allnutt, Henry (paper-maker)
Spencer, Alfred, Portford-mills

CHOBHAM.
From Waterloo 26 miles. Pop. 2069.
Medhurst, Thomas (printer)
   Reading Rooms and Mechanics' Institute; T.
   Medhurst, *Sec.* W. Gosling, *Librarian.*

CLAPHAM.
Batten, Jno., Clapham
Beal, William (fancy) Oxford-terrace
Coutes, Henry, Park-road
Edmunds, Thomas (news) Polygon
Evans, Charles, Old-town
Gregory, Mrs. R. (fancy) 10 Farm-terrace
Grey, Charles (fancy) Foster-place
Hands, Ebenezer, Farm-terrace
Meaden, George P. (printer) Farm-terrace
Morris, William Henry (fancy) Old-town
Morley, Mrs. M. A. (music) 10 Stockwell-ter
Prewett, Alfred (fancy) Cavendish-street
Riche, George L., Dudley-place
Ward, William R. (printer) Upper Dorset-pl

CRAWLEY.
From London-bridge 38 miles. Pop. 1474.
Herington, Joseph (printer)

CROYDON.
From London-bridge 9 miles. Pop. 10,000.
Baldiston, Frederick (printer) 8 North-end
Clarke, Henry, 76 Church-street
Collison, Miss M. (fancy) 43 North-end
Frane, Samuel (fancy) 33 High-street
Gray & Warren, (printers) 131 High-street
Hobbs, Thomas (news) 109 Church-street
Messenger, Henry (stationer) 24 High-street
Newton, Charles (binder & news) Post-office
Penson, Thomas (fancy) 62 North-end
Smith, George (fancy) 102 North-end
Wright, James S. (printer) 22 Park-street
   Literary Institution and Reading Rooms,
   Town-hall

DENMARK HILL.
Sabine, Edward (stationer) Beckenham-place
Taylor, Miss M. (wood-engraver) Beckenham-pl
Maskall, Edward (stationer) Beckenham-place

DITTON (THAMES).
From Waterloo 14¼ miles. Pop. 2351.
Middleton, Thomas (printer)
Howliston, John (printer) Weston-green
Seeley, Leonard (printer, &c.) the Elms

DORKING.
From Waterloo 29 miles. Pop. 5996.
Bowen, Thomas (news) High-street
Bowen, Tamerlane (Surrey Standard-office)
   South-street
Churchyard, Isaac, High-street
Clarke, William S. (printer) High-street
Isard, Mrs. Mary, High-street
   Library and Reading Rooms, South street

DULWICH.
Pop. 1632.
Maddison, John (stationer)

EGHAM, ETC.
*From Waterloo to Staines 19¼ miles, and from
there 2 miles. Pop. 4482.*
Byrne, Miss Elizabeth (stationer) High-street
Cock, Wm. Thomas (reading rooms) High-st
   Literary Institution; T. M. Harvey, Esq.,
   Hon. Sec., H. L. Nightingale, *Treasurer*

EPSOM.
From London-bridge 18¼ miles. Pop. 4129.
Collingwood, John N. (binder)
Dorling, Henry (printer)
Miller, William Henry (stationer)
Snashall, George (fancy)

ESHER.
From London-bridge 15 miles. Pop. 1441.
Blatch, Thomas William
M'Murray, William (paper-maker) Royal-mills
Woods, John (printer)

EWELL.
From London-bridge 14 miles. Pop. 1918.
Sawyer, James (stationer)

FARNHAM.
From Waterloo 40¼ miles. Pop. 7264.
Nichols, Robert & John (printers & binders)
   Borough
Nichols, Robert (printer) West-street
   Mechanic's Institution, Borough; Henry
   Poppleton
   Library and Reading Rooms, Downing-st
   Young Men's Association, Library, and
   Reading Room, West-street

FRENSHAM.
Pop. 1559.
Simmonds, James (paper-maker) Pilfold

FRIMLEY.

From London 34 *miles, near Farnborough.*
Pop. 1791.

Drew, Robert, York-town
Randall Henry, York-town

GODALMING.

From Waterloo 34 *miles. Pop.* 4657.

Chennell Theophilus (news) High-street
Hackman, George, & Sons (news) High-street
Lemare, Frederick, & Son (printers) High-street
Stedman, Mrs. C. S. (music & library) High-st
Sweetapple, Thos. (paper-maker) Catteshall-st
   Reading Rooms, Town-hall
   Depository of the Christian Knowledge So-
   ciety, High-street

GUILDFORD.

From London-bridge 30¾ *miles. Pop.* 8084.

Andrews, Edw. (and printer and pub. and
   proprietor of the Surrey Gazette, 61
   High-street
Freakes, Jas., 151 High-street
Gardner and Stent (printers and binders)
   32 High-street
King, Thos. Edw. (printer) 77 High-street
Norton, Jno. (printseller) 116 High-street
Pewtress and Co. (paper-makers) Stoke-mills
Richardson, B. A. (fancy) 144 High-street
Skitter, S. J. (fancy) 2 Chertsey-street
   Mechanics' Institution, North-street ; E.W.
   Martin and Jno. Gardner, *Secs.*
   Reading-rooms, 32 High-street

HASLEMERE.

From London 42 *miles,* 9 *from Godalming*
Station. Pop. 955.

Lambert, Thomas, Post-office
Simmons, James, (paper-maker) Sickle-market

KEW.

From Waterloo 6 *miles. Pop.* 1009.

Searles, George

KINGSTON-ON-THAMES.

From Waterloo 12 *miles. Pop.* 6,279.

Brydon, William (news) Canbury-field
Cunningham, Charles (news) Church-street
Diamond, John (binder) Church-street
Duffell W. J. (music) Church-street
Fricker, Henry John (printer & library) Mar-
   ket-place
Gillis, Miss Sarah (stationer) 6 Victoria-road
Hewitt, John (music) Clarence-street
Howe, Misses, Market-place
Lindsey, William (news) Thames-street
Phillipson, Geo. & Thos. (library) Market-pl
Philpott (printer) Brighton-road
Thruman, Richard W. (news) Surbiton-hill
Were, William (fancy) West-by-Thames

LEATHERHEAD.

From London 19 *miles;* 4 *from Epsom Station.*
Pop. 2041.

Hill, Thomas (stationer)
Parker, Robert (stationer)

MITCHAM.

From Westminster 9 *miles. Pop.* 4641.

Church, Samuel, Lower Mitcham
Wade, John (library)
Weight, George (news) Upper-green

MORTLAKE.

From Waterloo 5 *miles. Pop.* 3110.

Morse, George (stationer) Post-office
Whitfield, John

NEWCROSS.

From Londonb-ridge.

Astle, George, Crystal Palace library
Jowell, E., Post-office, near Tollgate

NORWOOD.

From London-bridge 6 *miles. Pop.* 77,978.

Chapman, Samuel (binder) Prospect-place
Mansell, Edward (fancy) Belvidere-road
Mountier, Thomas (stationer) High-street
Robson, Robert (fancy) 5 Thomas's-terrace
Young, Richard Henry (news) Weston-street

PECKHAM.

From the City 3 *miles. Pop.* 19,455.

Allan, Mrs. Sarah (fancy) High-street
Arless, Edw. (printer) Hill-street
Bemister, Jno. jun. (binder) 6 Rye-lane
Clubb, Wm. Eb., Rye-lane
Field, Mrs. Eliza (stationer) Queen's-road
Hussey, Wm., High-street
Jones, Mrs. M. A. (fancy) High-street
Parsons, Mrs. A. (stationer) High-street
Smith, Mrs. A. (stationer) High-street
Stowell, Mrs. R (fancy) The Rye
Wheatherley, W. E. (stationer) High-street

PUTNEY.

From Hyde-park-corner 4½ *miles. Pop.* 5280.

Christinet, Mrs. S. (stationer) High-street
Hulme, Miss H. (fancy) High-street
Patching, Samuel (fancy) High-street
Robinson, Jno. (news) High-street

RED HILL.

From London 20¾ *miles. Pop.* 2450.

Thornton, Richard (stationer)
   Mechanics' Institution ; W. A. Rees, *Sec.*

REIGATE.

From Waterloo 23 *miles. Pop.* 1640.

Allingham, Wm. (printer) Market-place
Apted, Jas. H. (news) Bell-street
Brewer, Miss S. (stationer) High-street
Drewett, Ellen (stationer) Park-lane
Packer, Mary A. (fancy library) Market-place
   Mechanics'Institution, John Payne, *Sec.*

RICHMOND.

From Waterloo 8 *miles. Pop.* 9255.

Clarke, Samuel (fancy) George-street
Darnill, Jas. (library and reading rooms)Hill-st
Darnill, Jas. (printer) King-street
Deane, Wm. (printer) George-street
Hiscoke, Jno. G. (printer, stationer, librarian,
   and news agent) 1 Castle-terrace

Patterson, Mrs. Jane (stationer and library) 7 Royal-terrace
Smith, Jos. (fancy and library) King-street
Woodcock, Jas. (printer) New-road

SHEEN (EAST) NEAR MORTLAKE.

Cordrey, Charles (stationer)
Manderson, Wm. (bookbinder)

STREATHAM.

From London-bridge 6½ *miles. Pop.* 6,901.

Bailey, Sam. Fredk. (library) Streatham-place
Straw, George (library) Bedford-row

SUTTON.

From London-bridge 14¾ *miles. Pop.* 1387.

Robinson, Mrs. G. (stationer)

TOOTING.

From London-bridge 6¼ *miles. Pop.* 2122.

Sanders, Thos. (library)
Lock, Hy. Chas. (library) High-street
Oyston, Wm. (stationer) High-street

WALTON-ON-THAMES.

From Waterloo 17 *miles. Pop.* 2881.

Pink, Frederick (stationer)
Watts, Miss Frances

WANDSWORTH.

From Waterloo 5 *miles. Pop.* 9611.

Bradbury, Wm. (stationer) High-street
Callender, Mrs. E. (library) High-street
Linfield, Wm. (bookbinder) West-hill
Marriage, Wm. (fancy) West-hill
Nugent, Mrs. M. (stationer) High-street
Polley, Wm. (printer) High-street
Thorn, Jno., High-street
Upcher, J. L. (printer) High-street

WEYBRIDGE.

From Waterloo 19 *miles. Pop.* 1225.

Akehurst, Mrs. (stationer) Post-office

WIMBLEDON.

From Waterloo 7¼ *miles. Pop.* 2,693.

Hillman, Thos.
Richards, Wm. (fancy)

WOKING.

From Waterloo 25¼ *miles. Pop.* 2837.

Bayley, Hy. V., & Co. (paper-makers) Newark-mill
Billing, Jos. (printer)
Manuell, Jno. (stationer)

SUSSEX.

ARUNDEL.

From London-bridge 71 *miles*; 2⅓ *miles from Leominster station, on the London, Brighton, and South Coast Railway. Pop.* 2748.

Dudding, John (stationer) Tarrant-street
Mason, Frederick (printer) High-street
Mitchell, William (printer and publisher of West Sussex Advertiser) High-street
Sturt, George (fancy) High-street

BATTLE.

From London 56 *miles*; 8 *from Hastings. Pop.* 3847.

Burgess, John (stationer) 75 High-street
Ticehurst, F. William, Post-office
Mechanics Institution, Alfred Slatter, *Sec.*

BILLINGSHURST.

From London 41 *miles. Pop.* 1458.

Freeland, Samuel

BOGNOR.

From London-bridge 69 *miles. Pop.* 2695.

Binstead, Miss A. (marine library, reading-room, & fancy repository) Waterloo-square
Osborn, John (music & library, reading-rooms, &c.) Post-office, High-street

BRIGHTON.

From London-bridge 50½ *miles. Pop.* 70,328.

Austin, Henry (law stationer) 47 High-street
Barrell, William (law stationer) 53 Middle-st
Bell, George (bookseller to the College) 80 St. George's-road
Beves, John M. (printer) 31 Portland-street
Bishop, Mrs. E. (fancy repository) 75 North-st
Blissett, Richard (news) 174 Eastern-road
Bonner, George, 51 Preston-street
Boore, John (binder)
Booty, Charles (library & news) 66 King's-road
Brighton Examiner Office, 77 North-street
Brighton Gazette Office, 168 North-street; Charles Curtis, *Proprietor*
Brighton Guardian Office, 34 North-street; L. E. Cohen, *Proprietor*
Brighton Herald, William Fleet & Sons, Prince's-place
Brook, Charles, 109 Western-road
Burn, Edmund (binder) 23 North-street
Burn, Edward John (news) 36 Ship-street
Chadwick, Richard (news) 3 Edward-street
Champion, Jonah (stationer) 125 London-st
Chapman, George (law stationer) 45 Middle-st
Chassereau, Miss C. (fancy warehouse) 40 King-st
Cheate, Stephen (binder) 54 East-street
Cohen, L. E. (printer & publisher of Guardian, and newspaper-office) 34 North-street
Coppard, Mrs. E. (library) 1 Norfolk-street
Corbin, William (news) 3 Union-street
Corney, John (stationer) 143 London-road
Cowdrey, William (news) 18 Church-street
Cox, (Samuel (wholesale stationer & bookseller) 55 & 56 Queen's-road
Cripps, Charles, Chain-pier
Crowhurst, Mrs. H. (fancy repository) 23 East-st
Cullis, H. H. (second-hand) 43 North-street
Curd, Charles (musical instrument seller) 87 Trafalgar-street
Darling, Robert (music seller) 45 Western-road
David, Josh., Pool-valley
Dollman, John Charles (library and reading-rooms) 7 Western-road, Hove
Duke, William (fancy repository) 17 Preston-st
Eyles, John F. (printer and publisher of Examiner) 77 North-street
Farr, William (news) 32 Trafalgar-street

4

Fisk, David (news) 169 Western-road
Fleet, William, & Sons (printers) Prince's-place
Fogden, Miss Ellen (news) 20 Sillwood-street
Folthorpe, Robert (royal library and reading-rooms) 170 North-street
Funnell, Frederick (library) 117 Edward-street
Gancia, G. (foreign & English) 73 King's-road
Gardner, Edwin (printer) 105 Church-street
Gardner, Peter (printer) 16, 17 & 20 George-st
Godard, Stradwick (news) 134 Queen's-road
Goldsmith, Mrs. E. (library) 6 Upper St. James's-street
Grant, William (foreign news, library, and Pavilion reading-rooms) 15 Castle-square, 72 Queen's-road, and 28 Edward-street
Greenin, D. H. (fancy repository) 20 & 21 East-st
Hamlet, Mrs. E. (binder) 40 Upper Bedford-st
Hawkins, Henry (printseller) 35 West-street
Haynes, Robert (news) 30 Preston-street
Hilton, John, jun. 20 Western-road
Hindley, Chas., 10 and 11 Meeting-houseslane
Hindley, Chas. (second-hand and binder) 105 St. James's-street
Hughes, Thomas (stationer) 44 John-street
Johnson, Charles A. (publisher and stationer) 31 King's-road
Jorden, William, 4 Kensington-gardens
Kilner, Stephen (library) 74 Up. Glo'ster-lane
King and Budd, 1 North-street
King and Co., 44 East-street
King, James S. (stationer) 7 Belgrave-terrace, Kemp-town
Langworthy, Wm. (fancy repos) 66 East-st.
Lavender, Alex. W. (music) 2 Castle-square
Lock, Miss H. (stationer) 44 North-gardens
Lomas, Frederick (binder) 13 Duke-street
Mc Carroll, Alex. (music) 171 North street
Manderson, Wm. (binder) 19 Trafalgar-street
Mason, W. H. (repository arts) 108 King's-rd.
Measor, James (news) 53 Ship-street
Miall, Mrs. S. (chapel library) Union-street
Moon, Wm. (book embosser for the blind) 46 Kensington-place
Patching, Wm. (stationer and repository of arts) 190 Western-road
Peek, Wm. (fancy repos.) 115 North-street
Pell, Christopher (printer) 2 Pool-valley
Philip, Henry (binder, &c.) 47 Western-road
Powell, Wm. (stationer) 5 Victoria-road
Prudden, Wm. (binder) 14 Spring-gardens
Ripley, John (fancy repos.) 9 Western-road
Roe, Miss E. (musicseller and stationer) 36 Western-road
Rotheram, George (map and print colourer) 28 Edward-street
Saunders, Edward (fancy) 3 Western-rd. Hove
Saunders, Wm. (library) 112 St. James's-street
Shackelford, Thomas, 29 Cifton-hill
Shelly, Mrs. H. (artists' repos.) 73   estern-rd.
Sicklemore (printer) 45 and 46 High street
Smith, John (printer and pub.) 8 Pool-valley
Stedman, George (dealer in periodicals) 68 St. James's-road
Steverson, John (news) 35 Glo'ster-lane
Stride, J. W., 61 Buckingham-place

Sugg, H. H. (news & library) 11 St. James's-st
Taylor, Elias (stationer, &c.) 63 Western-road
Taylor, Jno. (news) 27 North-lane
Taylor, Wm. Jno. (binder and library) 160 East-street
Tourbe, Chas. (news) 146 Edward-street
Toye, Mrs. E. (stationer) 26 Upper St. James's-street
Trowbridge, Hugh (fancy repository) 39 Sydney-street
Tucker, Jno. (music) Western-road
Venner, Miss Mary (news and stationer) 22 Duke-street
Verrall, Chas. (printer) 98 Queen's-row
Wallis, Arthur (lith., printer, stationer, &c.) 5 Bartholomew
Walsh, L. (Catholic) 77 St. James's-street
White, Alfred, 79 Western-road
Wigney, Fred. (printer and stationer) 14 Queen's-road
Wood and Co. (news) 207 Western-road
Woodward, Wm. (news) 98 St. James's-street
Wright, Fred. (music) 106 King's-road, 173 North-street
Brighton Athenæum and Young Men's Literary Union, Pavilion-buildings ; R. B. Bessant, *Secretary.*
Brighton College, Eastern-road ; Rev. Henry Cotterill, *Principal* ; Michael Turner, Esq. *Secretary.*
Brighton Mechanics' Institute, Ship-street ; Joseph Bell, *Librarian.*
Brighton Royal Literary Institution, Albion-rooms, Old-steine ; Mr. J. C. Burrows and Mr. Andrews, *Hon. Secretaries.*
Public Libraries and Reading-rooms ; Robert Solthorpe (Royal) 170 North-street
Wm. Grant, Foreign Newspaper Reading-room, 5 and 6 Castle-square
All Souls' Lending Library, 31 Eastern-rd
Chas. A. Johnson (religious) 31 King's-rd
Brighton Bible Association Depôt, 17 Prince Allen-street
Brighton and East Sussex Religious Tract Society ; C. A. Johnson, depository, 31 King's-road
Naval and Military Bible Society ; Lieut. C. R. Malden, R.N., *Sec.*
Trinitarian Bible Society, 31 King's-road
Young Men's Christian Association, 25 Middle-street ; Mr. R. J. Elliott and Mr. W. J. Tindall, *Secretaries.*

CHICHESTER.

From London-bridge 79¼ *miles.*   *Pop.* 8662.

Angel, Chas. (binder) North-street
Bennett (music library) North-street
Child, Mrs. M. (fancy repository) East-street
Farr, Miss E. M. (stamp-office) 11 East-street
Freemantle, Hy. Jno. (music) East-street
Glover, George, North-street
Heather, James (news) West-street
Hurlock, Mrs. E. (music & fancy) St. Pancras
Jardine, Mrs. M. A. (library) South-street
Knight, K. (binder) 33 East-street

Lefeaux, Jas. (binder) Close
Light, Jas. (stationer) Eastgate
Mason, Wm. H. (printer) Eastgate
Peat, Hy. (news & binder) South-street
Pullinger, Geo. (printer) North-street
Underdown, Jno. (fancy) East-street
　Chichester Literary Society, &c., South-st ;
　　Francis Smart, *Librarian*
　Depository of Christian Knowledge ; Henry
　　Greenfields, East-street

CUCKFIELD.

From London-bridge 39 miles.　Pop. 3196.

Albery, Mrs. E (stationer)

EASTBOURNE.

From London 65 miles.　Pop. 3433.

Griffin, Hy. Thos. (stationer & news) Seaside-rd
Hall, Samuel, Sea-houses
Hopkins, Misses Elizabeth & Emma (library
　and reading-rooms) Sea-houses
Mott, Wm. (printer) Seaside-road

EAST GRINSTEAD.

From London 30 miles.　Pop. 3820

Beard, Miss Jane (bookseller and stationer)
Gravett, Thomas (stationer)
Palmer, Thos. J. (bookseller and stationer)
　Literary Institution ; Thos. Cramp, *Sec.*

HAILSHAM.

*From London 64¼ miles, 3 miles from Polesgate
　Station.　Pop. 1825.*

Breads, Stephen (printer)

HASTINGS, &c.

From London-bridge 74 miles.　Pop. 17,011.

Ayles, C. C. (library and reading rooms) 35
　Robertson-street
Bacon, Geo. P. (printer, publisher, and pro-
　prietor of the Hastings Chronicle) 28 Ro-
　bertson-street
Bowner, Edw., 24½ George-street
Breeds, B. (pub. of the Hastings, &c. Fashion-
　able Express) 67, 68, and 69 George-street
Diplock, Wm. (music, printer, and library)
　29 George-street
Grimes, Jas. (news) 19 George-street
Holt, Ann (fancy and library) 24 Whitelock-
　place
More, Hy. (news) 73 High-street
Osborne, Mrs. C. (stationer) 27 Castle-street
Osborne, Hy., 56, George-street
Paine, Alex. (artists' colourman) 9 Wellington-
　place
Pierce, Edw. (library) 9 Robertson-street
Pollard, Wm. (binder) 11 High-street
Ransom, Wm. (pub. of the Hastings and St.
　Leonard's News) 42 George-street
Reid, Wm. (print, music, library, and reading
　rooms) 11 Pelham-arcade
Winter, Hy. (printer) 59 George-street
Wood, Ben. (music) 54 High-street
Wood, Mrs. C. (stationer) 37 George-street
Woods, Jno. (stationer and repository) 2 Wel-
　lington-place

Libraries and Reading-rooms.

Ayles, C. C., 35 Robertson-street
Diplock, Wm., Marine-parade
Pierce, Edw., 9 Robertson-street
Reid, Wm., 11, Pelham-place
　Literary Institution, George-street ; Wm.
　　Ransom, *Librarian*
　Mechanics' Institution, High-street ; Wm.
　　Gallop, *Librarian*

ST. LEONARD'S-ON-SEA.

Brett, Thos. B. (stationer) 28 Norman-rd West
Butler and Beagley (library and reading rooms)
　2 Eversfield-place
Cope, Chas. (stationer) 5 Norman-road East
Smith, Miss E. (stationer) 13 South-colonnade
Southall, Charles H. (Royal Victoria library
　and reading rooms by appointment) Marina
Standen, Miss E. (fancy repository) East-
　ascent
Walter, Wm. (printer) Norman-road West
Wellstead, Wm. (news) 9 East-ascent

HENFIELD.

From Brighton 9¾ miles.　Pop. 1664.

Bright, James (stationer)
　Mechanics' Institute ; Henry Longley, *Sec.*

HORSHAM.

From London-bridge 37½ miles.　Pop. 5947.

Albery, Mark (news and advertising agent, &c.)
　Market-square
Ireland, Miss A. (fancy repository) West-street
Laker, Richard (printer) Middle-street
Price, Sidney (printer) West-street
　Literary Institution ; M. R. Cragg, *Sec.*

LEWES.

From London-bridge 54¼ miles.

Bacon, George (printer) 64 High-street (Sussex
　Advertiser)
Baxter, Jno., & Son, 35 High-street (Sussex
　Express)
Berry, Mrs. Lydia (fancy) 26 High-street
Butland, Jas. (binder) 96 High-street
Davey, Thos. (printer) 180 High-street
Lower, R. W. (stationer) 43 High-street
Morris, A. (stationer) 44 High-street
Page, William (stationer) 84 High-street
Savage, Solomon (stationer) 18 Fisher-street
Solomon, Misses F. & S. (fancy repository) 4A
　High-street, Cliffe.
Verrall, Edwin (news-agent) Market-street
　Mechanics' Institution ; Geo. Adams, *Sec.*

LINDFIELD.

Pop. 1814.

Davey, Thos. (stationer and printer)

LITTLEHAMPTON.

From London 59 miles.　Pop. 2436.

Dudding, Mrs. (stationer and library)
Smart, Nevil

NEWICK.

From London 44 miles.　Pop. 966.

Taylor, James (stationer)

PETWORTH.

From London-bridge 49 miles.   Pop. 3439.

Ovenden, William (stationer)

PULBOROUGH.

From London 46 miles.   Pop. 1825.

Hews, Rich. Figg (stationer)

ROGATE.

Pop. 1117.

White, Mrs. M. (stationer and postmistress)

RYE.

From London-bridge 83 miles.   Pop. 4593.

Clark, Henry (printer) High-street
Lightfoot, Mrs. H. (stationer) Red Lion-street
Parsons, Isaac (stationer) High-street
Taylor, David (stationer) High-street

SHOREHAM.

From London-bridge 56¾ miles.   Pop. 1077.

Butler, Robert (stationer)

SLAUGHAM.

Pop. 1418.

Errey, B. J., Hand-cross.

STORRINGTON.

From London-bridge 50 miles.   Pop. 1038.

Foxwell, Geo. (stationer and reading rooms)

UCKFIELD.

From London 43 miles.   Pop. 1590.

Foster, Jno. (stationer)

WORTHING.

From London-bridge 61¼ miles.   Pop. 5370.

Barke, Miss E. (library and newsagent) 53 Montague-street
Botting, Thos. (newsagent) Chapel-street
Carter, Mrs. A., Warwick-street.
Clarke, Sam. (fancy repository) Esplanade
Davies, J. W. (fancy repository) 33 Warwick-st.
Hewitt, Miss S., 1 South-street
Palmer, Rich., Warwick-street
Phillips, Jno., 22 South-street
   Literary Institution; Wm. Verrall, *Sec.*

WARWICKSHIRE.

ALCESTER.

Pop. 2027.

Booksellers, Stationers, and Printers.

Hance, John W., High-street
Williams, Eliza, High-street
Wright, Edwd. M., Stafford-road

ATHERSTONE.

From Euston-square 101¾ miles.   Pop. 3743.

Davis, Sophia, Long-street
Holland, Wm. Chaplain (music) Market-place

BIRMINGHAM.

From Euston-square 112 miles.   Pop. 232,841.

Bookbinders.

Aldritt, Wm., Suffolk-street
Allen, Joseph, 11 Cannon-street

Beilby, Jas. Hy., New-street
Brierley, J., 11½ New-street
Corus, George, 71½ High-street
Dewson & Co., 107 New-street
Footherape, John, 84 Edmund-street
Hunt, Benj., & Sons, 75 High-street
Ingo, John D., 2 Ann-street
Pearcy & Wood, 23 Holloway-head
Peart, R., & Son, 38 Bull-street
Pratt, Wm., 82 Digbeth
Radclyffe, Thos., & Son, 108 New-street
Sheldon, John, jun., 150 Moor-street
Tomkinson, R. C., jun., 39 Snow-hill
Watt, Robt., 25 Ann-street

Booksellers and Stationers.

Anderson, James, Suffolk-street
Beilby, Jas. Hy., New-street
Bell, James, 8 New-street
Berryman, J. H., 17 High-street
Brierley, J. L. (musicseller) Dale-end
Brough, Wm., 22 Paradise-street
Buckton, Charles, Soho
Cornish, Brothers, 57 New-street
Collins, —, Summer-lane
Cornish, Wm., 108 New-street
Davidson, Alfred, 65 Broad-street
Davies, Rd., 40 Temple-row
Devonshire, Hy., 57 Dale-end
Field, R. J., 24 Balsall-street
Fisher, Alfred, 9 Moat-row
Grew, Wm., & Son, 5 High-street
Groom, John, 185 Broad-street
Guest, James, 52 Bull-street
Hall, Benj., High-street
Haswell, J. P., New-street
Hodson, Edward, Parade
Hudson, Benj., 18 Bull-street
Jackson, Wm., & Son, Digbeth
Holyoake, —, Smallbrook-street
Hubbard, J., Dale-end
Harris, W., Deritend
Joesbury, Wm. (printer) Ashton-street
Kelly, Daniel, Bath-street
Lander, Powell, & Co., 108 New-street
Langbridge, Hy. C., 11 Bull-street
Maher, Michael, Congreve-street
Matthison, Rd., Edgbaston-street
Menon, John G., & Co., High-street
Osborne, E. C., 29 Bennett's-hill
Peart, R., & Son, 38 Bull-street
Plastans, Wm., Dale-end
Pratt, William, Digbeth
Redfern, G., Bull-street
Ragg, Thomas, High-street
Showell, J. W., Upper Temple-street
Sackett, W. J., Union-passage
Taylor, Glover, & Co., 31 Union-street
Watts, Thomas, 14 Snow-hill
Tonks, John (printer) New-street
Wilcox, —, Balsall-street
White & Pike, 14 Bull-street
Winnall, Henry, 78 High-street

Music and Instrument Sellers.

Brierley, Joshua L., 104 Dale-end

Davidson, Alfred, 65 Broad-street
Elliott, Ann, 23 Ann-street
Flavell, Samuel, Bennett's-hill
Harrison, Thos., 30 Colmore-row
Sabin, F. & W. H., 23 Bull-street
Shargool, Henry, Union-street
Tolkien, J. B., 70 New-street
Turner, Frederick, Snow-hill

Printers.

Allen & Son, 3 Colmore-row
Allen, Joseph, 11 Cannon-street
Allen, Joseph, jun., Livery-street
Barr, Solomon, 142 Cherry-street
Bell, James, 8 New-street
Bennett, G. B., 86 Aston-street
Billing, M., 75 New Hall-street
Bolton, John, Brittle-street
Brierley, J. L., 104 Dale-end
Brown & Moor, Great Hampton-street
Caldicott, John, High-street
Chatwin & Co., Sherbourne-street
Davies, Rd., 40 Temple-row
Dewson & Son, 107 New-street
Edwards, Richard, 189 Broad-street
Grew, Wm., & Son, 5 High-street
Grove, James, 20 Great Charles-street
Guest, James, Bull-street
Hall & Taylor, 32 Lionel-street
Hall, Benj., 71 High-street
Haswell, John P., 52 New-street
Hudson, Benjamin, 18 Bull-street
Hunt, Benj., & Son, 75 High-street
Hunt, Geo., Union-passage
Jackson, Wm., & Son, 69 Digbeth
Joesbury, Wm., Aston-street
Kirby, Thos. & Hy., Great Hampton-street
Maher, M., Congreve-street
Moore, John, 74½ High-street
Osborne, E. C., Bennett's-hill
Pearce & Johnson, 19 Ann-street
Peart, R., & Son, 38 Bull-street
Perry, M., 110 Hockley
Radclyffe, Thos., & Son, 108 New-street
Ragg, Thomas, 90 High-street
Showell, John W., Upper Temple-street
Smith, W. B., 110 New-street
Swan, Brothers, New Hall-street
Taylor, Glover, & Co., Union-street
Tomkinson, R. C., Snow-hill
Turner, Frederick, Snow-hill
Vale, Thos., Moor-street
Watt, R., Ann-street
Watson, Geo., Warwick-passage
Watton & Co., 90 Hill-street
White & Pike, 14 Bull-street
Winnall, Henry, 78 High-street
Wright & Dain, 11 Union-street
Wright, Wm., Lichfield-street
  Old Library, Union-street; Wm. Alldritt, *Lib.*
  Aris's Birmingham Gazette, Monday ; John
    Caldicott, *Publisher*, High-street
  Mldland Counties Herald, Thurs. ; Wright
    & Dain, Union-street
  Birmingham Journal, Saturday
  Birmingham Mercury, Saturday

COLESHILL.
From Euston-square.   Pop. 1980.
Tite, William, Market-place

COVENTRY.
From Euston-square 94 miles.   Pop. 36,208.
Band, William, High-street
Goode, Edward, Smithford-street
Goode, Edward, jun., Hill-fields
Horsfall, H. L., Hertford-street
Harris, Geo., Hertford-street
Hickling, Wm., East-street
Iliffe, Wm. (printer) Smithford-street
Jacombs, T., Smithford-street
Jepper, W. Cross, Cheaping
King, Brothers, Fleet-street
Lewis, E. C. (printer) Herald-office
Lewin, David (printer) Hertford-street
Pegg, G. G., Standard-office
Rotherham, Wm. (printer) Fleet-street
Stringer, J., Burgess
Tomkinson, Joseph (printer) High-street

Printers only.
Astill, Robt., Hertford-street
Beamish, J. S., & Co., Hertford-street
Rollason, C. A., High-street
  Coventry Herald
  Coventry Standard

HENLEY-IN-ARDEN.
From Paddington to Warwick 107¾ miles.
Pop. 1143.
Endall, William (printer)
Hannett, John (binder)

KENILWORTH.
From Euston-square.   Pop. 3140.
Claremont, C. C., Castle-end

LEAMINGTON.
From Euston-square 97¾ miles.   Pop. 15,692.
Booksellers, &c.
Anderson, Thomas, 122 Warwick-street
Beck, John (publisher, binder, and printer)
  8 Upper-parade
Bishop, Thos., 80 Regent-street
Cox, Chas., Hy. (binder) 24 Upper-parade
Dark, John (printer & binder) 11 Upper-parade
Davis, Thos. (binder & printer) Windsor-street
Elston, Sarah (musicseller) 58 Regent-street
Enoch, Wm., 32 Bath-street
Glover, Joseph, 1 Victoria-terrace
Goode, E. & Hy., 22 Bath-street
Goold, Ebenezer, 35 Wellington-street
Greaves, Thos., 40 Regent-street
Green, James, 39 Windsor-street
Hewett, John, 1 Lower-parade
Knibb, Thos., 6 Upper-parade
Magoschis, Samuel, 19 Regent-street
McMahon, James, 3 Church-terrace
Poulton, Geo., 9 Victoria-terrace
Robinson, G. H. (binder) 21 Regent-street
Rosewarne, Wm., 35 Regent-street
Russell, Richd. (printer) Spencer-street
Silversides, Fredk., 13 Warwick-street

Musicsellers, &c.
Bernard, Chas., 27 Bath-street
Hughes, David, 7 Victoria-terrace
McCarroll, Alex., 9 Lower-parade
Silvani, V., Victoria-terrace

NUNEATON.
From Euston-square 96½ *miles.*   *Pop.* 8133.
Attleborough, J. S.
Barraclough, John, Abbey-street
Hubbard, Thomas
Short, M. A., Market-place

RUGBY.
From Euston-square 82¾ *miles.*   *Pop.* 6317.
Crossley & Billington (printers) Market-place
Pepperday, Wm. (printer) St. Matthew-street
Sharpe, Saml. (printer) Market-place
Taite, Wm. J. (printer) Church-street
Warner, J. (library) School-street

SOUTHAM.
From Euston-square.   *Pop.* 1711.
Pettifer, Ann (library)
Smith, Francis (printer)

STRATFORD-ON-AVON.
From Paddington.   *Pop.* 3372.
Adams, Edward, High-street
Lapworth, Richd., High-street
Stanbridge, Chas., Chapel-street
Stephenson, Wm., High-street
Ward, F. & G., High-street
Wright, Thomas, Chapel-street

WARWICK.
From Paddington 107¾ *miles.*   *Pop.* 10,973.
Cook, H. T. & Son (music) High-st
Heathcote, T. B. (library) Corn-market
Lacey & Co., High-street
Perry, W. G. (musicseller) Old-square
Price, Samuel, Market-street
Sharpe, Henry, High-street
Squires, Joseph, Saltisford
Yeomans, Isaac, Smith-street

WESTMORELAND.

AMBLESIDE.
From London 276 *miles.*   *Pop.* 1397.
Nicholson, A., Ambleside
Troughton, Thos., Ambleside

APPLEBY.
From London 270 *miles.*   *Pop.* 1262.
Barnes, John (printer) Doomgate
Cousons, Martin (news) Low-weind
Crosby, Samuel (news) Main-street
Hutchinson, M. & N. (news) Main-street
Knapton, Jas. (printer) Bridge-street

BOWNESS.
From Ambleside 6 *miles.*
Barrow, Roger
Forrest, Robert (news-room)

KENDAL.
From Euston-square 252½ *miles.*   *Pop.* 11,829.
Atkinson, Thomas (news) Strickland-gate
Dawson, Joseph, Strickland-gate
Hargreaves, Richard, Lowther-street
Hudson, John (music) Highgate
Robinson, James, Stramongate
Simpson, John (news) Strickland-gate
Walker, A. F. (library) Highgate
   Kendal Library, Lowther-street
   Mechanics' Institute, Highgate
   News Rooms, Whitehall
   Kendal Mercury, Tinkle-street, Saturday
   Westmoreland Gazette, Saturday; Thos.
      Atkinson, Strickland-gate

KIRKBY LONSDALE.
From Kendal 13 *miles, and from Euston-sq.*
via Leeds, to the Station at Hornby, 263
miles.   *Pop.* 1675.
Bateson, John, Main-street
Forster, John (printer) Main-street
News Rooms, Main-street

KIRKBY STEPHEN.
From London 266 *miles.*   *Pop.* 1339.
Close, John (printer)
Davis, Anthony

WILTSHIRE.

BRADFORD.
From Paddington.   *Pop.* 4240.
Bubb, John, Market-place
Rawling, Joseph, Pippit-street

CALNE.
From Paddington.   *Pop.* 5195.
Bailey, Edwin, High-street
Cue, Charles, High-street
Fowler, Charles, Church-street

CHIPPENHAM.
From Paddington 93¾ *miles.*   *Pop.* 6283.
Alexander, Richard, Market-place
Noyes, James, High-street
Scott, Robert, Corsham
Sidwell, Richard, Causeway

DEVIZES.
From Paddington.   *Pop.* 6554.
Bull, Henry (music seller) St. John-street
Bush, Jane A., Brittox
Randle, Nathaniel, Market-place
Sartain, Charles Edward, Brittox.

HIGHWORTH.
From Paddington.   *Pop.* 4026.
Ricketts, Joseph (printer)

MALMESBURY.
From Paddington.   *Pop.* 6998.
Alexander, Henry W., High-street
Bridges, Fitz, Sherston
Cadby, Joseph B., High-street
Hancock, William, High-street

Hanks, James H., High-street

MARLBOROUGH.
From Paddington.　Pop. 5135.
Emberlin & Co., High-street
Lucy, William W., High-street

MELKSHAM.
From Paddington 100 miles.　Pop. 2931.
Cochrane, John (printer) Bank-street
Flooks, Thomas (stationer) Market-place

SALISBURY.
From Waterloo-bridge 95 miles. Pop. 11,657.
Bookbinders.
Clapperton, Kenneth, Catherine-street
Gilmour, Francis, Catherine-street
Goddard, Charles, St. Ann-street
Hearne, John, Silver-street
Pittman, George, Silver-street
Saunders, T. A., Winchester-street

Booksellers, &c.
Blake, F. A., Blue Boar-row
Brown, George, & Co., New Canal.
Clapperton, Kenneth, Catherine-street
Hearne, John, Silver-street
Pittman, George, Silver-street
Roe, Edward, Silver-street
Saunders, T. A., Winchester-street
Whereat, William, Winchester-street

SWINDON.
From Paddington 77 miles.　Pop. 4876.
Ann, Isaac (music) High-street
Dore, Abbott (printer) Bath-road
Morris, William (printer) Victoria-street
Prince, John H. (stationer) Wood-street

TROWBRIDGE.
From Paddington 105½ miles.　Pop. 10,157.
Diplock, John, Fore-street
Knee, Richard, Church-walk.
Noble, Samuel, Silver-street
Sweet, John, Fore-street
Walker, David, Back-street
Wilkins, Samuel, Market-place

WARMINSTER.
From Paddington.　Pop. 4220.
Tayler, William Henry, Market-place
Vardy, Richard E., Market-place

WESTBURY.
From Paddington 109½ miles.　Pop. 6308.
Dyer, James C., Market-place
Michael, William, Edward-street

WILTON.
From Waterloo.　Pop. 8607.
Chalk, Alfred, South-street

WOOTTON BASSETT.
From Paddington.　Pop. 2123.
Teagle, Henry
Watts, George

WORCESTERSHIRE.
BEWDLEY.
From Paddington.　Pop. 3124.
Bryan, Edward, Load-street
Danks, Samuel, Load-street

BROMSGROVE.
From Euston-square 127½ miles.　Pop. 4426.
Deadman, Henry, Worcester-street
Maund, Benjamin, High-street
Scroxton, J. H., High-street

DROITWICH.
From Paddington 126 miles.　Pop. 3125.
Green, Mary, St. George's-square
Smith, Edward (printer) High-street

DUDLEY.
From Paddington 148 miles.　Pop. 37,962.
Bogle, Alice, Wolverhampton-street
Danks, Thomas, Castle-street
Gibson, Isaac, Castle-street
Hutchings, Ebenezer, Castle-street
Inshull, William, Stone-street
Maurice, M. W. & E., High-street

EVESHAM.
From Paddington 106¾ miles.　Pop. 4605.
Beck, John, Bridge-street
Fuller & Co., High-street
May, George, Bridge-street
Pearce, Josiah, Bridge-street
Powell, Henry (music) Bridge-street

GREAT MALVERN.
From Paddington to Worcester 120½ miles.
Pop. 3771.
Hartley, Thomas
Lamb, H. W. (library)

KIDDERMINSTER.
From Paddington 135½ miles.　Pop. 18,462.
Bird, Robert, Wood-street
Fowler, George, High-street
Friend, George (printer & pub.) Bull-ring
Hinton, Thomas, Worcester-street
Larr, William, High-street
Mark, Thomas (library) High-street
Mason, Samuel, Blackwell-street
Roberts, Samuel, Dudley-street

OLDBURY.
From Birmingham 5 miles.　Pop. 10,155.
Lowe, Josiah (printer) Birmingham-street
Mitchell, T. G. P., Birmingham-street

PERSHORE.
From Paddington 109¾ miles.　Pop. 2717.
Conn, William
Pace, Charles James
Warner, Robert

REDDITCH, NEAR BROMSGROVE.
Pop. 4802.
Bromley, Sarah (binder) Fish-hill
Hemming, W. T. (binder) Fish-hill
Shore, Thomas

SHIPSTON-ON-STOUR.
Pop. 1835.

Sale, Henry
White, Samuel

STOURBRIDGE, ETC.
From Paddington 142¼ miles. Pop. 7847.

Bourne, Robert, Wordsley
Ford, George, Brierley-hill
Fowler, Joseph (binder), Brierley-hill
Greenfield, Peter, Brierley-hill
Hemming, James (binder) High-street
Hutchings, William, High-street
Kenrick, A. & S., High-street
Levi, Edward, High-street
Mellord, Thomas, Upper High-street
Oakley, David, Upper High-street
Prescott, T., Coventry-street
Tipper, J., New-road
Whitwell, G. F., High-street

STOURPORT.
Population taken with Stourbridge.

Green, George, High-street
Oliver, William, High-street
Wheeldon, Thomas (printer) High-street

WORCESTER.

Marked thus * are also Printers.

Baker, George, 20 Meal-cheapen-street
Beekin, Sarah, London-road
Condie, David (binder) Blackfriars
Cope, William, Friar-street
*Deighton, Ann, High-street
*Eaton, Thomas, & Son, College-street
Freeman, Edward, Broad-street
*Goodwin, Thomas (stationer) Broad-street
Grainger, John, Foregate
Gosling, F. N., Foregate
Kelly, Frederick, Sidbury
Leicester, William, & Son, High-street
Lewis, Thomas, Broad-street
Marsden, James, High-street
Osborne, Francis, Cross
Pheasey, Thomas, Silver-street
*Sefton, H. F., Broad-street
*Stratford, Thomas, Cross
Tainton, Charles, Pump-street
Wood, John, & Son, Foregate-street

Music Sellers, &c.

Deighton, Ann, High-street
Goodwin, Thomas, Broad-street
Marsden, James, High-street
Sefton, Hy. F., Broad-street
Wood, John, & Son, Foregate-street'
  Worcestershire Chronicle, Wednesday; Jas.
    Knight & Co.
  Worcester Herald, Saturday; Thos. Chalk
    and Co.
  (Berrow's) Worcester Journal, Deighton
    and Co.

YORKSHIRE.
BARNSLEY.
From King's-cross 177 miles. Pop. 13,437.

Burkenshaw, G. F. (news & music) Shambles-st.
Elliott, George, Mayday-green
Hague, Benjamin, New-street
Pybus, Richard (news) Market-place
Ray and Smith (news) Market-place
Waterfield, Thomas (news) Queen-street
Lingard (news) New-street

BEDALE.
From London 223 miles. Pop. 1200.

Knowles, William, Market-place
Taylor, (Thomas) printer Market-place
  Mechanics' Institute, Market-place; James
    Arrowsmith, Librarian.

BEVERLEY.
From London 180 miles. Pop. 10,088.

Ellis, Michael, Tollgavel
Everson, James, Market
Green, John (library) Market-place
Johnson, William B. (library) Market-place
Kemp, John, Market-place
Muff, Samuel, Eastgate
Shaw, James, 6 Landress-lane
Ward, John, Butcher-row
  Mechanics' Institute, Minster-yard; Wil-
    liam Thirsk, Secretary.
  News Rooms, North Bar-street Within;
    J. T. Machell, Secretary.

BINGLEY.
From London 206 miles. Pop. 5019.

Bailey, Jonas (music) Main-street
Dobson, John, Main-street
Harrison, John, and Son, Myrtle-place
Hodgson, Thomas, Main-street

Paper-makers.

Clapham, William, and Brothers, Morton
Smith, John, Morton
  Mechanics' Hall, Russell-street; John
    Hustler, Secretary.

BOROUGHBRIDGE.
From London 202 miles. Pop. 1095.

Horsfield, Henry, Borobridge
Mitchell, John, Borobridge
Turner, Thomas S., Borobridge

BOSTON SPA.

Nichols, Thos. (library and news) Boston Spa

BRADFORD.
From London 196 miles. Pop. 149,543.

Anderson, Robert (news) 30 Wakefield-road
Barker, Benjamin, 52 White Abbey
Bentley, Mary (news) Market-street
Blackburn, William H., Market-street
Boulton, Samuel, Lumb-lane
Brown & Blackburn (binders) Manchester-rd.
Brown, Jacob, John-street
Byles, Henry B. (printer) 17 Kirkgate
Cooke, William (news) Vicar-lane

Coultons, John, Low-lane
Curtis, William (binder, &c.) Bermondsey
Dale, John (printer) 15 Bridge-street
Drake, John, Northgate
Hainsworth, Joseph, Manchester-road
Higson, James, Shipley
Hill, James, Bazaar
Holroyd, Abraham, 107 Westgate
Hudson, Edward, 36 Bolton-road
Jowett, John M., Ivegate
Knight, James G., Queensgate
Laycock, George (news) 51 High-street
Lumley, Joseph (binder) 5 Leeds-road
Lund, Joseph, 82 Westgate
Mawson, Henry Ogle (printer) 43 Kirkgate
Moorhouse, John (news) Wakefield-road
Morgan, John (news) 113 Wakefield-road
Nelson, Michael, Hustler-gate
O'Leary, Arthur, 18 Bridge-street
Parkinson, John (printer) Mount-street
Parry, Robert, Chapel-court
Stanfield, Charles (printer) 5 Westgate
Spencer, R. and T. (binders) Bolton-road
Tetley, William (news) 3 Bedford-street
Umpelby, Thomas, 2 Lumley-street
Waddington, Joseph, 12 Wells-street
Walker, Benjamin (printer) 6 Market-street
Waterhouse, Thomas, 13 Darley-street
Wignal, Elizabeth (news) 1 Wapping-road
Wilkinson, Christopher (news) Tyrrel-street

Musicsellers, &c.
Blackburn, Wm. H. (printer) 15 Market-st.
Clayton, Solomon, Piccadilly
Dale, John, 15, Bridge-street
Jackson and Winn, 4 Cheapside
Leach, John, Ivegate
Marchbank, John, 136 Westgate
Misdale and Co., Cheapside
Rhodes, James, 10 Darley-street
Walker, Benjamin, 6 Market-street

Printers.
Anty, Squire, Kirkgate
Dendon, John, & Co., 4 Sunbridge
Pawson, Richard, Dale-street
Scarlett, Samuel W., 68 Northgate
Vint, John, Lowwell, Shipley
Walmsley, Robert, 92 Thornton-road
Wardman, Henry, Chapel-lane
White, Walton, Nag's Head-yard
Bradford Observer, Thursday ; Wm. Byles, Kirkgate
Commercial News-room, Darley-street
Mechanics' Institute, Leeds-road ; William Bell, *Librarian*
Mechanics' Institute, Shipley ; Henry Farrar, *Secretary*
Exchange News-room, Kirkgate ; William Fawcett, *Secretary.*
Conservative News-room, Albion-court ; Wm. Greenwood, *Secretary*
Oddfellows' Room and Library, Darley-st.

BRIDLINGTON WITH FLAMBOROUGH.
From London 203 *miles.* *Pop.* 8143.
Baron, Wm., Garrison-street-quay

Cape, James, High-street
Furlby, John, High-street
Hickson, Rachael, High-street
Smith, Robert, King-street-quay
Thornton, William, Market-place
Varley, John, Queen-street-quay
Wilson & Aldridge (music) Prince-st.-quay
Wood, John (tract depôt) Flamborough

CLECKHEATON, ETC.
From Bradford 6 *miles.* *Pop.* 5170.
Firth, Squire and John
Siddall, John

DEWSBURY, ETC.
From London 184 *miles.* *Pop.* 5033.
Brook, Thomas M. (news) Market-place
Crossley, John, Bridge-end
Cullingworth, Henry (news) Market-place
Dawson, Samuel, Market-place
Ellis, Joseph (stationer) Ossett
Fearnsides, James, Batley
Ward, Joseph (binder and news) Church-st.
Wilkinson, John H. (news) Market-place
Literary Institution, Batley ; William J. R. Fox, *Secretary.*
Mechanics' Institution, King-street ; John Buckley, *Secretary.*
Subscription Library, Ossett ; David Phillips, *Librarian.*

DONCASTER.
From London 161 *miles.* *Pop.* 12,312.
Atock, William, Baxtergate
Brook, George and Thomas, High-street
Bisat, Eleph. (binder and news) Baxtergate
Drury, Edward J., Baxter-gate
Hartley, Robert, High-street
Robinson, Elizabeth, French-gate
White, Charles, Baxter-gate
Mechanics Institution, High-street ; C. J. Fox & E. Easterfield, *Secretaries.*

Musicsellers, &c.
Lyon, Sherwood, Baxter-gate
Marsh, John, High-street
Doncaster Chronicle, Friday ; Robt. Hartley, High-street
Doncastsr, &c., Gazette, Friday ; Messrs. Brook, White, & Hadfield, High-street

DRIFFIELD.
From London 193 *miles.* *Pop.* 3963.
Blakeston, Jas. C. (music & library) Middle-st
Holderness, Thomas, New-road
Turner, William, jun., Market-place

EASINGWOLD.
From London 208 *miles.* *Pop.* 2717.
Gill, Thomas, Market-place
Todd, James, Long-street

GOOLE, ETC.
From London 175 *miles.* *Pop.* 4722.
Kay, John (stationer) Bridge-street
Small, Alfred, Aire-street
Literary Institution ; Mary Platt, *Librarian*

HALIFAX.

From London 194 *miles.   Pop.* 33,582.

Baildon, John, 1 Bull-green
Bayldon, George, Upper George-yard
Birtwhistle, Thomas & William, North-gate
Burrows, Norcross (printer) Waterhouse-st
Farrar, Joseph, Union-street
Holts, Charles (news) Shelf
Jacobs, Joshua, Garden-st
Jagger, William, Cripplegate
Leyland & Son (library & printers) Corn-mrkt
Lord, James (news) North-gate
M'Arthur, Mary (library) 28 Waterhouse-st
Midgley, William, 20 Russell-street
Milner & Sowerby (wholesale, & publisher)
    Upper George-yard
Milner, Susannah, Causeway
Nicholson, Joseph (library & printer) 3 King's
    Cross-street
Nicholson, William (printer) 3 Cheapside
Scholefield, John W., Old Market
Whitley & Booth (printers) 3 Crown-street
Wilson, Daniel, North-gate
Wilson, Henry, 27 Broad-street
Wood, Caroline (library) 6 Union-street
    Mechanics Institute, Swan Copps ; William
        Corke, *Secretary*
    News Room, 17 George-street ; Geo. Baines,
        Secretary
    Subscription Library, Harrison-road ; John
        Crowder, *Librarian*
    Halifax Courier, Saturday ; W. R. Phelps &
        T. T. Latimer, Square-road
    Halifax Guardian, Saturday ; Jas. U. Walker,
        George-street

Law Stationers.

Highley, James S., 2 George-street
Longbottom, John W., 5 West-gate

Printers.

Crabtree & Son, Upper George-street
Farrar, R. F., Russell-street
Martin, Henry, Upper George-yard
Nicholson, John, Russell-street

Paper Makers.

Bracken, Jonathan, & Son, Old Cock-yard
Broadbent, Joseph (dealer) Old Cock-yard
Whiteley & Co., Stainland

HARROGATE.

From London 200 *miles.   Pop.* 3434.

Dawson, Wm. (library & news room) Lower
    Harrogate
Langdale, William, High-street
Palliser, P., High-street
    Literary Institute ; R. Hawksworth, *Sec.*
    Harrogate Advertiser, Saturday ; P. Palliser,
        High Harrogate
    Harrogate Herald, Thursday ; Wm. Daw-
        son, Lower Harrogate

HAWES.

From London 252 *miles.   Pop.* 1708.

Braithwaite, John
Hunter, John (printer)

HECKMONDWIKE.

From Halifax 8 *miles.   Pop.* 4848.

Watts, James (printer, binder, & news agent)

HOLMFIRTH, &C.

From Huddersfield 6 *miles.   Pop.* 5767.

Crossland, Joseph (binder) Upper-bridge
Jenkinson, Alfred, Thurstonland
M'Clellan, Alex., Hollow-gate
    Mechanics' Institute & News Room, Victoria-
        street ; J. Moorhouse, *Secretary*

HOWDEN.

From London 175 *miles.   Pop.* 2235

Pratt, William F., Bridge-gate
Small, William, Market-place.
Spink, Mary, Churchyard
Furlay, William C., Bridge-gate

HUDDERSFIELD.

From London 189 *miles.   Pop.* 30,880.

Bairston, Joseph (library & news) 12 Cross
    Church-street
Brook, J. & G. (library & news) Westgate-st
Brown, Benjamin, 1 New-street
Chapman, William, Mold-green
Clayton, Edw. (library & news) Kirk-gate
Crossley, John (music) Buxton-road
Hardy, Waters (news) 6 Market-place
Kaye, William, Taylor-hill
Kemp, Elizabeth, 18 New-street
Ogden, George John, William-street
Palmer, Alfred, 61 New-street
Pilter, Robert (music & news) 5 New-street
Quamby, Arch. (news) Lockwood
Richardson, John, 19 Castle-gate
Roebuck, Henry, 16 King-street
Shaw, Joseph, Beast-market
Thompson, James, 71 New-street
Whitehead, George (news) Lockwood
Woodcock, Wm. H., & Co., 67 King-street

Law Stationer.

Priestley, Ezra, Upperhead-row
    Law Library, Kirkgate ; Thomas H. Battye.
        Librarian
Moore, Jonathan (library) Buxton-road
    Philosophical Library, Ramsden ; William
        Nelson, *Librarian*
    Subscription Library, Westgate ; Joseph
        Brook, *Librarian*

Musicsellers, &c.

Gledhill, William, 51 Ramsden-street
Mellor, Richard, 24 Cross Church-street
Moore, Jonathan, Buxton-road
Naylor, Thomas, Lockwood
Parratt, Thomas, Ramsden-street
Sturge, Henry, 4 Stable-street
Wood, Joseph, 8 High-street

Paper Makers.

Hastings & Mellor, 1 Victoria-street
Lancashire, George, & Co., New-street
Whiteley, John, & Son, Stainland, near Halifax

Printers.

Atkinson, William, New-street
Bairston, Joseph, Cross Church-street

Brook, J. & G., West-gate
Brook, Joseph, 1 West-gate
Brown, Benjamin, 1 New-street
Hardy, Waters, 6 Market-place
Kemp, Elizabeth, 18 New-street
Pilter, Robert, 5 New-street
Pratt, William, New-street
Roebuck, Henry, 16 King-street
Whitehead, George, Lockwood
　　Huddersfield Examiner, Saturday; Joseph
　　Woodhead, Ramsden-street
　　Huddersfield Chronicle, Saturday; John
　　James Skyrme, 18 Kirkgate

HULL.

From London 171 miles.　Pop. 84,690.
Bookbinders.

Adams, James, 9 George-yard
Cherry, Septimius, 25 Bishop's-lane
Eddon, Jabez (printer) Market-place
Hudson, William, Witham
Oglesby, William, 18 Scale-lane
Screeton & Crompton, 16 Bishop's-lane
Simpson & Oglesby, White Horse-yard
Smith, Charles, 5 Medley-street
Wadsworth, William M., 12 Collier--street

Booksellers, &c.

Coatsworth, John (printer & binder) Saville-row
Cussons, Richard T. (printer) 62 Whitefriars
Escritt, Thomas, 42 Saville-street
Farrell, James, 5 Castle-street
Firth, Thomas, St. John-street
Forster, William L., New Charles-street
Gale, Thomas B. (printer) Mytton-gate
Goddard & Lancaster (printers and binders)
　　15 Silver-street
Goodwill & Lawson (printers) 22 Silver-street
Harland, Mary (printer and binder) 13 Car-
　　lisle-street
Harper, John, 9 Carr-lane
Hill & Holder (printers) 180 High-street
Holdich, Charles William, 14 Queen-street
Jackson, John (printer) 28 Mytton-gate
Jubb, Thomas, 80 Queen-street
Long, Joseph William (printer and binder) 15
　　Saville-street
M'Innes, John (printer) 58 Whitefriars-street
Nicholson & Rayner (printers) 48 Lowgate
Noble, Mary (printer) 23 Market-place
Parkinson, John, 47 Spencer-street
Peck, Michael Charles (printer and binder) 43
　　Lowgate
Pulleyn, Jonathan (printer) 20 Silver-street
Rollitt, Christiana & Matilda, 11 Carlisle-street
Shillito, Edward (printer) 154 Porter-street
Simpson, Mary, 2 Queen-street
Stark, John M. (printer) 64 Market-place
Stephenson, Plaxton, & Co. (printers) 51
　　Lowgate
Tanock, Jacob, 51 Sykes-street
Ward, Grace (library) 10 Junction-street

Musicsellers, &c.

Atkinson, Mary Ann, 29 George-street
Tagg, John, 5 George-street

Holder, John W., Whitefriars-gate
Hemping, H. & W., 6 Carlisle-street
Levett, William, 1 Fish-street
Retalic, George, 14 Bishop's-lane
Tarvey, William, 28 Adelaide-street
　　Eastern Counties Herald, Thursday; Wil-
　　liam Stephenson, 51 Lowgate
　　Hull Advertiser, Friday; Edward F. Col-
　　lins, 26 Lowgate
　　Hull News, Saturday; William Stephenson,
　　51 Lowgate
　　Hull Packet, Friday; Edward Sidebottom,
　　22 Whitefriars-gate

Printers.

Anderson, Wm. Lee, Old Excise-office-buildings
Chapman, Thomas, 49 Carr-lane
Collins, John, Lowgate
Dimbleby, Jabez, White Horse-yard
Graham, John, 6 George-yard
Jubb, Thomas, 80 Queen-street
Kirk, William, 161 High-street
Montgomery, John, 35 Scale-lane
Oliver, John, 17½ Lowgate
Sprent, William (publisher) Reed-street
Stather, John, 8 Dock-street
Whiting, Henry, Whitefriars'-gate

Paper-makers.

Allison & Co., 5 St. John-street
Hesk, George, 23 Spencer-street
Smithson & Mayfield, 47 High-street

Libraries, Circulating.

Benson, John, 33 Chariot-street
Brewis, William Henry, 85 Potter-street
Clark, William, 22 Cogan-street
Cookman, Lucy, 11 Carlisle-street
Crompton, Benjamin, 35 Scale-lane
Forster, William L., New Charles-street
Lucas, James, 43 West-street
Lucas, Joseph, 34 Wincomlee
M'Gennis, John, 21 Sykes-street
Penrose, Henry, 66 Osborne-street
Prissick, Harriet, 4 Waterhouse-lane
Reeves, William K., Great Union-street
Robinson, William, 5 St. James's-street
　　Hull Subscription Library, 15 Parliament-
　　street; John R. Clarke, *Librarian*
　　Law Library, 8 Parliament-street; John
　　Charlesworth, *Librarian*
　　Lycæum Subscription, St. John-street; John
　　Jarratt, *Librarian*
　　Mechanics' Institute, 2 George-street; James
　　Young, *Librarian*
　　Operative News Room, 78 Lowgate; Jere-
　　miah Faulkner, *Manager*

KEIGHLEY.

From London 202 miles　Pop. 18,259.

Aked, Robert, Low-street
Balshaw, John, Church-street
Crabtree, Jas. L., Change-gate
Craven, Elijah, Church-street
Dineen, Thomas (library) Market-place
Hudson, Thomas D., 32 High-street
Rhodes, John, Market-place

Musicsellers, &c.

Midgley, John, High-street
Sunderland, A. S., High-street

Paper-makers.

Bracken, Jonathan, & Co., Ingrow-mills
Town, John, Goose Eye-mill

KNARESBOROUGH.

From London 197 miles. Pop. 5536.

Hannam, John D., High-street
Langdale, William, High-street
Parr, William (Bible) High-street
  Literary Institution, Market-place ; Richard
  Marshall, *Librarian*

KNOTTINGLEY, ETC.

*From Pontefract 3 miles, and 17 miles from
the Port of Goole. Pop. 4540.*

Dobson, Thomas, Brotherton
Hepworth, William S., Aire-street

LEEDS.

From Kings-cross 205 miles. Pop. 172,270.

Bookbinders.

Button, Jonathan Andrew, 93 Church-street
Duthie, John, 17 Albion-street-
Dyson, William, Meadow-lane
Gaines, Jeremiah (bookseller) 10 Fleet-street
Gamble, George, 6 Heaton-court
Green, Aaron, Central-market
Hopps, John, 144 North-street
Machell, Mary A., 27 Newsome-yard
Mills, John, 1 Guildford-street
Pickard, Anthony (printer & publisher) Cross-
  court, Briggate
Prince, Thomas (bookseller) Newsome-yard
Reynard, John, White Horse-yard
Sans & Charnock (printers) Rose & Crown-yard
Shute, Thomas & William Henry, 3 Fleet-st
Slocombe, Rd. (bookseller) 18 Commercial-st
Tanfield, William, Rose and Crown-yard
Utley, John, 51 Briggate
Ward, James, 52 Lads'-lane
Wood John, St. John's-square

Booksellers, &c.

Andrews, Henry (library) 23 St. Peter's--street
Ashworth, Thomas, 64 Albion-street
Barr, Richard (library &printer) 18 Marsh-lane
Bean, James Wm. (printer) Lowerhead-row
Beecroft, Michael, 9 Basinghall-street
Blackie & Son, 7 Park-row ; Alexander Blackie,
  Agent
Booth, Nathan, 32 Boar-lane
Buckley, Henry (library) 91 Wellington-st.
Buckton, Joseph (printer) 50 Briggate
Bulwer, Thomas (library) 32 George-street
Child, Thomas, 18 North-street
Cooke, John (library) 67 Meadow-lane
Cross, John (printseller) Commercial-street
Cullingworth, G. (law) 75 Briggate
Fenteman, Thomas, & Son (picture) 15 Boar-
  lane
Fisher, Samuel (library) 93 West-street
Green, David, 38 Boar-lane
Harrison, Thomas (printer) 55 Briggate

Heaton, John (library) 7 Briggate
Hicks, Abraham R., Lowerhead-row
Holdsworth, Israel, Central-market
Hustwaite, John (old) Kirkgate-market
Inchbold, Henry (printer) 62 Briggate
Ingle, James M., 48 Briggate
Jefferson, John, 93 North-street
Johnson, Jos. (library) Rotation-office-yard
Jones, William (library) Burmantoft
Knight, James Y., & Co., 39 Briggate
Lishman, Matt. (library) 62 Bridge-street
Longbottom, Charles, 4 West-street
M'Ilveen, Joseph, Burley-street
Mann, Alice, 12, Duncan-street
Martin, Alex., 34 Bridge-end
Masser, John, 5 Guildford-street
Mills, John (Catholic) 1 Guildford-street
Newsome, Reid (printer & pub.) 149 Briggate
Newton, Thos. (library) 98 Woodhouse-lane
Ramsden, George, 13 Vicar-lane
Robinson, Henry, 42 Woodhouse-lane
Slade, William, 7 Bond-street
Slocombe, Richard (printer) 18 Commercial-rd.
Sykes, Joseph, 64 Marshall-street
Walker, Hy. W. (binder) 26 Briggate
Webb, Millington, & Co. (binders and printers,
  wholesale) 2 Bond-street
Wood, Wm. H. (old and new) 17 Market-st.

Libraries.

Catholic, Upper Albion-street
Glover, Jane, 34 Woodhouse-lane
Harrison, William, Meanwood-road
Hatfield, William, 68 Park-lane
Holbeck and New Wortley, Whitehall-road ;
  Joseph Tetterington, *Secretary*
Holbeck Subscription, Water-lane ; Joseph T.
  Merrington, *Secretary*
Hunslet Subscription, Low-road ; John Brook,
  Librarian
Law Library, 4 Park-lane ; Arthur Holland,
  Librarian
Leeds Mechanic & Literary Institution, South-
  parade
Leeds Old Library, 20 Commercial-street
  Thomas Milner, *Librarian*
Medical Library, 1 East-parade
Methodist Library, Brunswick Chapel
Miller, William, 42 Duke-street
Peacock, William B., 19 Hunslet-road
Skilbeck, George, 49 Kirkgate

Musicsellers, &c.

Binks, Charles, & Co., Commercial-street
Booth, William, 2 Wade-street
Dearlove, M. W., 4 Nelson-street
Heaps, John K., 10 Meadow-lane
Hopkinson, John & James, 6 Commercial-st.
Leggott, Thomas, 68 Upperhead-row
Longley, Thomas, 48 Merrion-street
Mellor, Richard, Commercial-street
Smith and Winkup, 168 Woodhouse-lane
Sykes, John, 30 Boar-lane
Wilson, C. A., & Co., Sherwood's-yard, Briggate

Newspapers.

Leeds Intelligencer, Saturday ; Christopher Kemplay (printer) 19 Commercial-street
Leeds Mercury, Saturday ; Edward Baines and Sons, 149 Briggate
Leeds Times, Saturday ; Frederick Hobson (ptinter) Briggate

Paper-makers.

Bentley, Samuel, and Son, 67 Water-lane
Booth, Nathaniel, 32, Boar-lane
Dyson, John J., 68 Nile-street
Falkner, Alex. (printer) 7 Greek-street
Hastings & Mellor, 5 Call-lane
Jackson & Asquith (printer) Mill-hill
Kirk, John, 116 Meadow-lane
Martin, Alexander O., Bridge-end
Martin, James, Bishopsgate-street
Mawson, William, 42 Lady-lane
Neill, John, & Co., 14 Dock-street
Smith, John, 24 Bond-street
Stocks, Benjamin, Sovereign-street
Town, Joseph, Trinity-street

Printers.

Baines, Edward, & Sons, 149, Briggate
Barr, John, Cheapside
Button, J. A., Waterloo-road
Cooke & Clarke, Boar-lane
Crawshaw, George, George and Dragon-yard
Goodall, John, 16 Wade-lane
Jowett, Samuel, 31 Boar-lane
Marshall, John, 44 Albion-street
Mills, John, 1 Guildford-street
Moorish, Mary, 31 Fleet-street
Moxon & Walker, 4 Queen's-court
Parrott, John, 3 Fleet-street
Roebuck, David J., 24 Bank-street
Sharp & Middleton, 65 Basinghall-street
Slater, Henry, 4 Lydgate
Swallow, John (music) 16 Corn Exchange
Topham, Samuel, & Son, 5 West-bar
Ward, James, 52 Land's-lane
Wray, Thomas, White Cross-yard
Wilson, Mrs., Glasshouse-street

Stationers, Wholesale.

Booth, Nathaniel, Boar-lane
Martin, Alexander, 3 Briggate
Masser, Joseph F., Albion-buildings
Mawson, William, 42 Lady-lane
Town, Joseph, 35 Trinity-street
Ward, James, 10 Land's-lane
Webb, Millington, & Co., 2 Bond-street

LEYBURN.

From London 235 miles.　Pop. 800.

Fall, Thomas
Plews, William

MALTON.

From London 214 miles.　Pop. 7661.

Barnby, George, Wheelgate
Harrison, George, Market-street
Smithson, Henry (library, and publisher of the Malton Messenger) Yorkers-gate

Mechanics' Institute, Yorkersgate ; Thomas Banks, *Librarian*
News Rooms, Yorkersgate ; William Flint, *Secretary*
Tradesman's Subscription, Finkle-street ; Matthew Bankes, *Secretary*

MARKET WEIGHTON.

From London 190 miles.　Pop. 2001.

Coates, Thomas, Market-place
Crowther, Henry, Market-place

MIDDLESBOROUH-ON-TEES.

From London 246 miles.　Pop. 7431.

Richardson, Joseph (library) Commercial-st.
Windross, James, Market-place

MIRFIELD, NEAR PONTEFRACT.

Rogers, Thomas (printer & library) Easthorpe-lane

MORLEY.

From Leeds 4 miles.　Pop. 4821.

Pickles, Samuel
Stead, Samuel (printer)
Mechanics' Institute, Churwell ; Charles Smith, *Librarian*

NORTHALLERTON.

From London 221 miles.　Pop. 4995.

Metcalf, John
Warrior, William
Mechanics' Institute, Golden Lion-yard ; M. Brown, *Librarian*

OTLEY.

From London 196 miles.　Pop. 4522.

Hodgson, Thomas, Market-place
Walker, William, (wholesale & pub.) Kirkgate
Webb, Millington, & Co. (wholesale & pub.) Boroughgate
Wilcock, Abraham (news) Burley

Paper Makers.

Nicholson, Michael, Poole
Garnett, Peter, & Son, Otley Mills

PATELEY BRIDGE, NEAR RIPON.

From London 224 miles.　Pop. 1862.

Mechanics' Institute, Pateley-bridge ; Wm. Neesome, *Librarian*

PICKERING.

From London 222 miles.　Pop. 3112.

Boak, William (printer) Market-place
Webster, William, Potter-hill

POCKLINGTON.

From London 195 miles.　Pop. 2546.

Abbey, Thomas, Market-place
Easton, Robert, Church-lane
Forth, John (library and news) Market-place
Haggard, John, Market-place

PONTEFRACT, ETC.

From London 173 miles.　Pop. 10,675.

Bownas, Wm. Edward (music and printer) Market-place

Copley, G. Fox (music & printer) Market-pl.
Kidd, Wm. (music) Shoe-market
Linney, George F., High Ackworth
Nelstrop, George, High Ackworth
Waite, Hy. John (printer) Castleford
Public News-room, Market-place ; John Scholefield

Printers.
Forster, Hy., Church-lane
Richardson, Rd., Cross-lane

RICHMOND.
From London 229 miles. Pop. 4106.
Bell, John, Finkle-street
Bowman, Thos. & Ann, Market-place
Mechanics' Institute, Theatre ; John Bowe, *Secretary*

RIPON.
From London 208 miles. Pop. 6080.
Fairburn, James, Market-place
Harrison, Wm., Market-place
Hill, Samuel S., Westgate
Judson, Wm. (library) Market-place
Thirlway, Hy., & Son, Market-place
Mechanics' Institute, Low Skelgate ; Mr. Hawksworth, *Librarian*
News-room and Library, Low Skelgate ; Thomas Jackson, *Librarian*

ROTHERHAM.
From London 168 miles. Pop. 6325.
Barras, Catherine (music & library) High-st.
Carr, Joseph, Bridge-gate
Easton, Samuel (stationer) College-street
Gilling, Abraham (stationer) Church-street
Hinchliffe, Ann, High-street
Mechanics' Institute, Howard-street ; John Guest and John Barras, *Secretaries*
Subscription Library, College-street ; Elizabeth Turner, *Librarian*
Subscription News-room, College-street

SADDLEWORTH, NEAR ROCHDALE.
From London 196 miles. Pop. 17,799.
Brook, Wm. Taylor, Delph
Chadwick, Jonathan (stationer) Mossley
Chapman, Moses (stationer) Upper-mill
Hutchinson and Backhouse, Upper-mill
Robinson, Joseph Mayall, Mossley
Mechanics' Institution, Mossley ; Jonathan Lawton, *Secretary*
Mechanics' Institution, Upper Mill ; John Schofield, *Secretary*

SCARBOROUGH.
From London 216 miles. Pop. 12,158.
Ainsworth, James (library) 24 Newborough-st
Beeforth, George (library) 3 St. Nicholas-street
Crosby, George (library) 82 Newborough-street
Greasley, James, Without the Bar
Greasley, William (periodical) Bedford-street
Grice, John, 79 Newborough-street
Theakston, Solomon William (library) 31 St. Nicholas-street
Agricultural Library and News-Room, King-street ; Ann Wrigley, *Librarian*

Musicsellers.
Ainsworth, James (printer & music) 24 Newborough-street
Beeforth, George L. (printer & music) 3 St. Nicholas-street
Crosby, George (printer & music) 82 Newborough-street
Theakston, S.W. (printer & music) St. Nicholas-street
Wilson, Mary (music) 28 Hunter's-row
Scarborough Gazette, Saturday ; S. W. Theakston, *Proprietor*
Subscription News-Room, King-street ; Thos. Weddell, *Secretary*

Printers.
Russell, Archibald, 19 Newborough-street
Todd, Christopher, 12 George Inn-yard
Mechanics' Institute, Vernon-place ; Samuel Bailey and John Edmonds, *Secretaries*

SELBY.
From London 212½ miles. Pop. 5109.
Booth, John, Finkle-street
Harkiss, George, Churchyard
Hutchinson, Francis (library) Crescent
Mechanics' Institute, Churchyard ; William Liversidge, *Librarian*

SETTLE.
From Euston-square 247¾ miles. Pop. 1976.
Ellison, James (binder) Settle
Forster, Josh., Settle
Wildman, John (printer) Settle
Wildman, Stephen, Stainforth

SHEFFIELD.
From King's-cross 162½ miles. Pop. 135,310.
Bookbinders.
Moore, Thomas, Watson's-walk
Stevenson, Thomas, Pye-bank
Townsend, William (stationer) 12 Surrey-street

Booksellers, &c.
Algar, Brothers (printers) 23 Church-street
Allison, James, 87 Scotland-street
Barraclough, William, 40 Fargate
Binks, William, 92 Trippet-lane
Blythe, John, 93 Scotland-street
Brown, George (binder) 72 Eyre-street
Bullivant & Priest (binders) 60 Orchard-street
Cavill, George, 33 Queen-street
Forbes, Daniel, 30 Union-street
Ford, William (library) 6 York-street
Fowler, William H., 1 Bow-street
Hall, Elizabeth (binder) 10 Bank-street
Harrison, Samuel (binder & printer) 5 High-st
Hopkins, Joseph, 159 West-street
Horrax, John David, Norfolk-row
Ingham, Daniel T. (printer) 43 South-street
Innocent, John, 7 Campo-lane
Jarvis, Charles K., 2 Division-street
Johnson, Josh., 30 Fargate
King, John W. (library) 47 Broomhall-street
Leader, Robert, jun. (printer) 2 Bank-street
Leonard, Christopher (binder) 32 Waingate
Metham, John W., 116 Pond-street

New, Stephen (binder & printer) 14 Waingate
Otley, Richard, 4 South-street
Parkin, Mark, 180 West-street
Pearce, Henry (printer) 188 Gibraltar-street
Pearce, Josh., jun. (binder) 24 High-street
Pearson, J. (library & printer) 189 Gibraltar-st
Pye, Mary (news) 52 West-street
Ridge & Jackson (stationers) 5 King-street
Ridgeway, Thomas, Watson's-walk
Rodgers, Thomas, 26, Norfolk-market
Stephenson, Richard P., 124 Barker-pool
Sutton, John, 123 South-street
Thomas, James, 29 Pinstone-street
Thomson, Christopher, 83 Division-street
Turner, Thomas, 62 Silver-street
Wade, Sarah (library) 83 West-street
Welch, William, 36 Orchard-street
Whittaker, Anthony (library & music) 22 Far-gate
White, William, Collegiate-crescent
Widdowson, Aaron, Little Sheffield

Libraries.

Appleton, Joseph F. (library) Attercliffe
Athenæum, George-street; William Smith, jun., *Secretary*
Church of England, Carver-street; Henry Wild, *Librarian*
Law Library, 1 Hartshead; John Fairburn, *Librarian*
Mechanics' Institution, Surrey-street; Michael Beal, *Librarian*
Mechanics' Library, Watson's-walk; Alfred Smith, *Librarian*
Sheffield Library, Surrey-street; Ann Wells, *Librarian*
Wade, Sarah (library) West-strest
Welsh, John (library) 3 New Church-street

Musicsellers, &c.

Butterworth, Edwin, 196 West-street
Dawson, George (printer) 51 Norfolk-street
Fitzpatrick, Henry, 88 Far-gate
Frith, George, 14 West-hill
Harvey, John, 118 Barker pave
Hobson, William, 115 Portobello-street
Jones, Francis, Westfield-terrace
Law, Henry, 12 Bow-street
Millward, James, 124 West-street
Rogers, Mary E. & D., 4 Norfolk-row
Saunders, George L., 21 High-street
Smith, Joseph, 10 Dixon-lane
Stacey, William, 101 West-street
Wood, Charles, 25 Division-street
Free Press, Saturday; Eaton, Blenkin, & Co., 23 Angel-street
Independent, Saturday; Robert Leader, jun., Bank-street
Sheffield Examiner, Saturday; J. H. Greaves, Prior-court, High-street
Sheffield Times, Saturday; Samuel Harrison & Henry Pawson, High-street

Printers.

Bell & Tompkin, Watson's-walk
Blurton, John, 30 Castle-street
Burgin, George, & Son, 26 Chapel-walk

Eaton, Blenkin, & Co., Angel-street
Fisher, Edward, 38 Scotland-street
Ford, William, 6 York-street
Gladwin, John, Bank-street
Greaves, James H., High-street
Hides, William, 24 York-street
Mountain, James, 99 Far-gate
Parkin, William, 22½ Far-gate
Pearce, Joseph, 118 Gibralta-street
Pearce, Joseph, jun., 24 High-street
Richardson, John A., 8 Silver-street
Ridge & Jackson, 5 King-street
Walker, Charles, 25 North Church-street
Youdan, Thomas, 2 Mulberry-street
Literary Society, Surrey-street; John Holland, *Actuary*

SKIPTON.

From London 211 miles. Pop. 4926.
Garnet, John (library, publisher of the Skipton Advertiser) High-street
Tasker, John, & Son, High-street
Winterbottom, John, Sheep-street
Mechanics' Institution, Market-place; Geo. Kendall, *Secretary.*

SOWERBY BRIDGE, NEAR HALIFAX.

Pop. 4365.
Gill, William (printer)
Scott, Martin
Sugden, James, Stainland

Paper-makers.

Hastings & Mellor, Bradley-mills
Shepherd, Jno. & William, Rushworth
Whiteley, Jno., & Co., Frith-house-mills
Mechanics' Institution, Elland; Thomas Turner, *Sec.*

STAMFORD BRIDGE.

From York 8 miles. Pop. 1075.
Gray, John (library)

STOKESLEY.

From London 238 miles. Pop. 2040.
Brown, William J. (news) Market-place
Pratt, John Slater (wholesale & pub.) West-end
Mechanics' Institute, Town-hall
Parochial Lending Library; John Thompson, *Librarian*

THIRSK.

From London 217 miles. Pop. 5319.
Masterman, Henry, jun., Market-place
Peat, Robert, Market-place

THORNE.

From London 165 miles. Pop. 2820.
Mason, Ann, Market-place
Mason, Joseph (printer) Market-place
Thorpe, George (library) Market-place

TICKHILL, ETC.

From London 156 miles. Pop. 2087.
Baines, William L. (printer) High-street
Bee, John (printer) Northgate
Ellis, John, High-street
Lye, Mary, Sunderland-street
Wilson, Martha (printer) High-street, Bawtry

WAKEFIELD.

From King's-cross 181 *miles.* *Pop.* 22,057.

Cryer, John (old and news) Bread-street
Hicks, Matthew B. (printer and news) 57 Westgate
Hicks, Charles (printer) Market-place
Hurst, Rowland (news and printer) Westgate
Lamb & Heald (news and printers) 19 Westgate
Micklethwaite, Thos. (news and printer) Westgate
Robinson, John (news and printer) Southgate
Robinson, John (printer) Westgate
Stanfield, John (binder) Market-place
Tyas, George (printer) 17 Northgate
    Wakefield Journal, Saturday; Thos. Micklethwaite, Exchange.
    Wakefield Express, Saturday; John Robinson, Southgate
    Mechanics' Institution, Wood-street; W. S. Banks, *Sec.*

WATH ON DEARNE.

From Rotherham 5½ *miles.* *Pop.* 1495.

John Sykes (library)

WHITBY.

From King's-cross 254 *miles.* *Pop.* 10,989.

Allison, Joseph, Flower-gate
Newton, William, Baxter-gate
Horne, Ralph (library) Bridge-street
Kirby, Robert, Church-street
Reed, Silvester (library) Old Market-place
Richardson, John, Flower-gate
    Institute of Science and Literature, Church-street; John Taylerson, *Sec.*
    News Rooms at Custom-house Coffee-house and Haggerstone
    Subscription Library, Pier; Robert Kirby, *Librarian*

WORTLEY.

From Leeds 3 *miles.* *Pop.* 7896.

Best, George (news) Wortley
Bond, William (news) New Wortley

YARM.

From London 235 *miles.* *Pop.* 1647.

Forster, Robert, Library

YORK.

From King's Cross 190¼ *miles.* *Pop.* 40,359.

Bookbinders.

Brassington, Richard, Waterloo-place
Dickenson, Edward, 104 High Peter-street
Gill, Robert, 11 Walmgate
Hope, George, 3 Castle-gate
Lyon, Joseph, Lord Mayor's-walk
Lyth, George, Townend-street
Pawson, George, 6 Coney-street
Pickering, George, Lockey's-court, Fossgate
Sumner, Oliver, 23 Ogleforth
Teasdale, John, Gazette-office-court
Walton, Thomas, Whiteley's-court, Saint Saviour's-gate

Booksellers.

Allom, John, 16 New Bridge-street

Bellerby, Henry & Son, 13 Stonegate; and paper manufacturers and printers, Thornton-mills, near Pickering
Blyth & Moore (printers) St. Helen's-square
Brown, John, 4 Collier-gate
Burdekin, Richard (printer) 16 High Ousegate and 2 Parliament-street
Chapman, William, 103 Mickle-gate
Joseph Cockle, 2 Finkle-street
Croshaw, Cornelius (printer) 35 Stonegate
Dunn, George, 20 Church-street
Fairburn, Henry, 2 Stonegate, and 19½ Little Stonegate
Glaisby, John, 9 Coney-street
Hanger, John, 13 Railway-street
Hargett, Thomas, 22 High Peter-gate
Hope, George (printer) 8 Castle-gate
Humphrey, David, 24 Fossgate
Hunter, James, 15 Low Ousegate
Kendrew, John, 23 Collier-gate
Lambert, George, 12 Collier-gate
Lyth, William R., 21 Davy-gate
Marsh, Thomas, Minster-gate
Nicholson, Henry, Blossom-street
Pickering, Thomas, 8 Spurrier-gate
Rennie, John, Stowboro-lane
Sampson, John, 52 Coney-street
Shillito, Joseph, 17 Spurrier-gate
Sotheran, Henry, 44 Coney-street
Stutter, William E., 7 Little Blake-street
Sunter, Rob. (to the Queen) 23 Stonegate
Veres, William, 33 Trinity-lane
Whiteman, Thomas, 44, Goodram-gate

Libraries.

Bellerly, Henry and Son, 13 Stonegate
Blyth and Moore, St. Helen's-square
Dalton, William, 96 Walmgate
Dean and Chapter's, Minster-yard
Dickenson, Edward, 104 High Peter-gate
Dunn, George, 20 Church-street
Glaisby, John, 9 Coney-street
Marsh, Thomas (Law) Peter-gate
Sampson, John, 52 Coney-street
    Select Subscription, 16 Blake-street; Ann Ellison, *Librarian*
    York Subscription, 1 St. St. Leonard's-place; John Swinbank, *Librarian*

Music Sellers, &c.

Clarkson, Richard, 41 Coney-street
Clarkson, Thos. Fenn, Coney-street
Hardman, William, 36 Coney-street
Hood, Mark, 19 Great Shambles
Marsh, James, 34 Coney-street
Robinson, John, 39 Stonegate
Waddington, William Alfred, Stonegate

Newspapers.

York Farmers' Friend, Saturday; Henry Fairburn, Stonegate
York Herald, Saturday; William Hargrove, 9 Coney-street
Yorkshire Gazette, Saturday; James F. Lancelot, 13, Stonegate
Yorkshireman, Saturday; Wm. Geo. Dove, Parliament-street

Printers.

Allerston, William, 35 Saint Saviour's-gate
Coultas, John, 19 Low Ousegate
Hargrove, William, Pavement
Hill, John, 4 Mary-gate
Kendren, Nathaniel, 22 Collier-gate
Johnson, Robert, 47 Coney-street
Monkhouse, Wm. (lith.) Lendal
Moore, Samuel R., 44 Stonegate
Pickering, Richard, 8 Spurrier-gate
Pickwell, William, High Jubber-gate
Sotheran, Henry, 44 Coney-street
Sotheran, William, 38 Low Peter-gate
Sunter, Robert, 23 Stonegate
Whiteman, Thomas, 44 Goodram-gate
    York Institute of Science and Literature;
        William Bell, *Librarian*
    News-rooms, Blake-street
    News-rooms, St. Helen's-square

MISCELLANEOUS LIST OF IRELAND,
SCOTLAND, &c.,

AND THOSE FORWARDED TOO LATE FOR INSER-
TION IN THEIR PROPER PLACES.

Booksellers, &c.

Adams, J., Arbroath
Anderson, Ebenezer, Loanhead
Anderson, J. B., High-street, Dundee
Anderson, John (binder) High-st., Edinburgh
Andrew, John, Ochiltree
Annandale, Alexander (paper-maker) Lassuade
Baird, R. A., Greenock
Banks, Alexander J., North-bridge, Edinburgh
Barbet, Stephen, High-street, Guernsey
Ballantyne, J., Bernard-street, Leith
Bell & Co., Bank-street, Edinburgh
Bell, Archibald (binder) Rose-st., Edinburgh
Bell, Robert, Dundee
Bertram, J. G., Hanover-street, Edinburgh
Black, A. & C., North-bridge, Edinburgh
Blackie & Son, College-street, Edinburgh
Blackwood, W., & Sons, George-street, Edinb.
Bowack, N., Leith-street, Edinburgh
Bullock & Co. (binders) St. David's-st., Edinb.
Bradwell, T., Miller-street, Manchester
Braidwood, James, George-street, Edinburgh
Brown, A., College-street, Edinburgh
Brown, Alex., & Son, Union-street, Aberdeen
Brown, R. L., Glasgow
Brown, Henry, High-street, Dundee
Burkett, Richard, Westport, Edinburgh
Burns, D., Brechin
Byce, David, Glasgow
Bryson, Kirkaldy
Cadell, R., St. Andrew-square, Edinburgh
Caldwell & Co., Waterloo-place, Edinburgh
Caldwell, R., Hanover-street, Edinburgh
Cambell, Argyle-street, Glasgow
Cameron, G. & J., Glasgow
Cameron & Co. (stationers) Steads-place, Edinb.
Catherall, Thomas, Bangor
Cay & Black (news) George-street, Edinburgh

Cavill, Richard, Swinefleet
Chambers, W. & R., High-street, Edinburgh
Chambers, James, Castle-street, Dundee
Chadderton, Grafton-street, Dublin
Church, Zachariah (news) Mitcham
Christie, A., Nicolson-street, Edinburgh
Clarke, T. & T., George-street, Edinburgh
Clarke, George, & Son, Broad-street, Aberdeen
Clarke. T., Dunfermline
Colquhoun, W. D., College-street, Edinburgh
Cole, E. W., Stonehouse
Constable, Thos., & Co., Edinburgh
Cornish, James, Lord-street, Liverpool
Cornish, James, Grafton-street, Dublin
Corns, W., & Co., Waterloo-place, Edinburgh
Coulson, J., Cheshunt, Hertfordshire
Courage, A., George-street, Aberdeen
Crawford, A. (stationer & binder) Edinburgh
Currrie & Co. (stationers & binders) Hunter's-
    square, Edinburgh
Craig, D., & Co. (paper-makers) Portobello
Cumberland, Luton, Bedfordshire
Cuthbertson, William, Anan
Curry, W., & Co., Sackville-street, Dublin
Davidson, R. D., North-street, Edinburgh
Davidson, George, King-street, Aberdeen
Dewar, T., Dale-street, Liverpool
Donald, A., Adelphi-street, Glasgow
Drummond, C., Kirkgate, Edinburgh
Dillon, P., Greenock
Duffy, James, Wellington-quay, Dublin
Dunbar, J., Galashiels
Durden, J., Landport
Durham & Thomson, High-street, Dundee
Edmiston & Douglas, Princes-st., Edinburgh
Elgin, W., St. Andrew-street, Edinburgh
Ewin, Kinross
Fannin & Co., Dublin
Ferguson, W., Bank-street, Edinburgh
Ferguson, John, Stewartson
Ferrier, D., Leith-street, Edinburgh
Forbes, Charles, Edinburgh
Fletcher, A., Armagh
Fraser, W., New Market-street, Aberdeen
Fraser & Co., George-street, Edinburgh
Fullarton & Co., Lothian-street, Edinburgh
Gall & Co., North-bridge, Edinburgh
Gardner, Alexander, Paisley
Garrie, Perth
Gellately, Arbroath
Glass & Duncan, Glasgow
Grant, Thomas, George-street, Edinburgh
Gray, Alexander, St. Michael's-st., Aberdeen
Grant, R., & Son, Prince's-street, Edinburgh
Greig & Son, Edinburgh
Greenhill, John, Bank-street, Edinburgh
Griffin, R., & Co., Glasgow
Guthrie, D., & Co., Ayr
Harthill, J., & Son, Waterloo-pl, Edinburgh
Hadden, John, High-street, Glasgow
Hay, David, Leith-street, Edinburgh
Henderson, John, Belfast
Henry, Geo., Broad-street, Aberdeen
Hempden, John, Londonderry
Humphrey, G., Bangor

Herbert, George, Dublin
Hery & Co., Dublin
Hodges & Smith, Dublin
House, Wm. (news) Uxbridge
Hudson, R., Westport, Edinburgh
Hogg, J., Nicolson-street, Edinburgh
Inglis, W. & C., Hanover-street, Aberdeen
Innes, William, Edinburgh
Innis, William, Greenock
Jackson, J., Ulverstone
Jackson, P., Dublin
Jerdan, David, South-street, Dalkeith
Johnstone, W. & A. K., St. Andrew's-sq, Edinb
Johnstone, W. F., Dumfries
Johnstone, J., Bathgate
Johnstone & Hunter, Prince's-st, Edinburgh
Johstone, J., Greenock
Kay, Joseph, Broughton-st, Edinburgh
Keith, —, Inverness
Kelly, W. B., Grafton-street, Dublin
Kerr, James, Nicolson-street, Edinburgh
Kennedy, W. P., South-street, Edinburgh
Killahin, John, Kilmarnock
King, Robt. & Geo., St. Nicholas-st, Aberdeen
King, —, George-street, Aberdeen
Laird, Geo. W., Montrose
Laing, C., High-street, Forfar
Laing, A., Greenock
Laurie, Wm., Union-street, Aberdeen
Lewis, George, Selkirk
Lennox & Co., Greenock
Leslie, John, Grey-street, Edinburgh
Lindsey, W., Gallowgate, Aberdeen
Lindsey, James, Edinburgh
Love, Wm., St. Enoch-square, Glasgow
Lowe, J. D., George-street, Edinburgh
McDowell, T. & W., North-bridge, Edinburgh
Macdonald, John, Crown-street, Aberdeen
Maclean, Samuel, Union-street, Aberdeen
Maclaren, John, Prince's-street, Edinburgh
Macleod, James, Glasgow
Maclachlan & Co., South-bridge, Edinburgh
Mackenzie, Wm., Glasgow
McCoid, —, Stranraer
McGlashan, Sackville-street, Dublin
McKean, —, Creetown
McKelvie, —, Greenock
McMillan, —, Kirkintilloch
McMillan, W. D., Gatehouse
Macphail, M., St. David-street, Edinburgh
McPherson, W., Broad-street, Aberdeen
McPhun, W. R., Glasgow
Madden & Hare, Dublin
Marshall, J. & J., Leith-street, Edinburgh
Marsh & Beattie, Edinburgh
Martin, Robt., Brown-street, Edinburgh
Martin, A. R., Bangor
Margey, Henry, Glasgow
Marrison, J., & Sons, Greenock
Mathers, D., Nicholson-street, Edinburgh
Mather, W. F., Rose-street, Edinburgh
Mason, —, Dublin
Maurice, Ogle, & Son, Glasgow
Mayne, —, Donegal-square, Belfast
Melville, H. & J., Greenock

Menzies, John, Prince's-street, Edinburgh
Messenger, H. High-street, Croydon
Middleton, Wm., Dundee
Mitchell, Wm., Union-street, Aberdeen
Miller, —, Oban
Miller, John, Bank-street, Edinburgh
Miller, John, Tolbooth, Edinburgh
Miller, John, Haddington
Milne, J. & W., Hanover-street, Edinburgh
Milne, A. & R., Union-buildings, Aberdeen
Morris, R., Register-street, Edinburgh
Morgan, Thomas, Cork
Moodie & Co., Edinburgh
Murdoch, Abraham, St. Nicholas-st., Aberdeen
Muirhead, J. & A., Nicholson-street, Edinburgh
Murray & Stuart, Edinburgh
Murray, T., & Son, Glasgow
Murray, W. J., Cork
Murray, M., & Co., Newcastleton
McWhirter, George (paper-maker) Colinton
Nelson, Thomas, Hope-park, Edinburgh
Nicholson, —, Kirkcudbright
Nichol, James, 40 George-street, Edinburgh
Nimmo, William, Kirkgate, Edinburgh
Ogilvie, John, Upper Kirkgate, Edinburgh
Ogle & Murray, South-bridge, Edinburgh
Oliphant & Sons, South-bridge, Edinburgh
Orr, F.,and Sons, Glasgow
Oliver and Boyd, High-street, Edinburgh
Padon, Alexander, Dundas-street,-Edinburgh
Painter, Charles, St. Nicholas-street, Aberdeen
Parlane, J. and R., Paisley
Paterson, M., Catherine-street, Edinburgh
Paton and Ritchie, Hanover-street, Edinburgh
Petrie, J., Lothian-street, Edinburgh
Phillip, B., Warriston-place, Edinburgh
Polson, R. J., Enniskellen
Ponsonby, T., Dublin
Porter, J., Dublin
Powell, T., Westmoreland-street, Dublin
Redpath, Alexander, High-street, Edinburgh
Redruth, J. (news) Uxbridge
Rechley, William, Ballinasloe
Reid and Son, Shore, Leith
Rice, William, Belfast
Robertson, John, Dublin
Robertson, William, Sackville-street, Dublin
Robinson, W., Greenside, Edinburgh
Robinson, John, Grafton-street, Dublin
Rogers, Alexander, Montrose
Rome, T. Z., Langholme
Ross and Son, High-street, Blairgowrie
Russell, William, Broad-street, Aberdeen
Sarney, D. (news) Windsor-st., Leamington
Shand, R., Dundas-street, Edinburgh
Shaw, Frederick, High-street, Dundee
Shepherd, George, Broad-street, Aberdeen
Shepherd, W. Castle-street, Forfar
Shepherd and Aitcheson, High-street, Belfast
Sims and McIntyre, Donegal-street, Belfast
Sime, John, Murray-gate, Dundee
Sime, William, Over-gate, Dundee
Simpson, J., Dundee
Sinclair, Robert, Tolbooth-wynd, Leith
Smellie, J., Langholme

Smith, J. L., Antigua-street, Edinburgh
Smith, T., Ferryport
Smith, Alexander, Thornton-place, Aberdeen
Smith, John, Union-street, Aberdeen
Smith, L. and J., Nether Kirk-gate, Aberdeen
Stevenson, T. G., Prince's-street, Edinburgh
Stevenson, W., St. Nicholas-street, Aberdeen
Stewart, R., Greenock
Stewart, Charles, Union-street, Aberdeen
Stronger, C., Wall-gate, Wigan
Stillie, James, Prince's-street, Edinburgh
Sutherland and Co., George-street, Edinburgh
Sutherland, D. R., Hanover-street, Edinburgh
Sutherland, A., Leith-street, Edinburgh
Sutherland, J. & Co., Calton-street, Edinburgh
Sutherland, R. P., Heriot's-buildings, Edinb.
Sweeten, W., Penrith
Sydenham, Richard, High-street, Poole, Dorset
Tallis, John, and Co., Roxburgh-st., Edinburgh
Taylor, James, 21 George-street, Edinburgh
Taylor, W. L., Peterhead
Thin, James, Infirmary-street, Edinburgh
Thompson, —, Manchester
Thompson, —, Armagh
Thompson, G., Liverpool
Todd, A., St. Patrick's-square, Edinburgh
Tully, C., Roscommon

Turner, J., Bridge-street, Manchester
Turner, H., Piccadilly, Manchester
Vair, James, Bristol-street, Edinburgh
Veith, Thomas, St. Andrew's-square, Edinburgh
Vessie, J. and S., Gallowgate, Aberdeen
Virtue, George, Lothian-street, Edinburgh
Walker, James, Kirk-gate, Aberdeen
Walker, John, High-street, Musselburgh
Wallbrook, M., Wellington-quay, Dublin
Watt, James, Montrose
Waterston and Co., Bernard-street, Leith
Watson, W. F., Prince's-street, Edinburgh
Whedale, —, Luton, Bedfordshire
Wilson, Thomas, Stewartson
Wilson, William, George-street, Edinburgh
Wilson, Robert, School-hill, Aberdeen
Wilson, J. A., Upper Kirkgate-street
Wiseheart, —, Dublin
Wilkins, W., Abbey-street, Derby
Weston, J., Lothian-street, Edinburgh
Whitehead, J., Appleby
Whitehead and Burns, Cupar
Whyte, W., and Co., George-street, Edinburgh
Wood, James, Prince's-street, Edinburgh
Woollard, —, Castle-street, Liverpool
Wright, David, Broad-street, Aberdeen
Young, R., North Bank-street, Edinburgh

LONDON.

BOOKSELLERS, &c.

Marked *l*, are also libraries ; *pu*, publishers ;
pr, printers ; *s*, stationers ; *n*, newsvenders ;
a, account book makers ; *b*, bookbinders ; *m.pu*,
musicsellers & publishers
Abington, George, 76 Fetter-lane, *pu*
Abraham, J. 13 London-street, Paddington
Ackermann, R., & Co., 96 Strand, *pu s*
Adams, W. J., 59 Fleet-street, *pu*
Addey & Co., 21 Old Bond street, *pu*
Adams, R., 3 Cumberland-pl. Old Kent-rd., *s.pr*
Alexander, 207 High-street, Hoxton
Algar, J., 2, Little Turnstile, Holborn
Allan, W. (for.) 13 Paternoster-row, *pu*
Allen, W. H., & Co., 7 Leadenhall-street, *pu*
Allen, R. W., 30 Ebury-street, Eaton-sq., *s*
Allen, F., 19 St. Martin's-le-Grand, *n*
Allen, J., 20 Warwick-lane, City, *pu*
Allen, Thos., 9 Osnaburgh-place, New-road
Allman, T. & Son, 42 Holborn-hill, *pu*
Ambridge, J., 1 Lower-street, Islington, *s*
Andrews, John, 167 New Bond-street, *pu*
Andrews, Miss, 13 Duke-st., West Smithfield
Ansell, J. K., 7 Russell-pl., Old Kent-rd., *s*
Appleton, D., & Co., 16 Little Britain
Appleyard, E., & Co., 4 Shoe-la., Fleet-st., *pu*
Appleyard, Henry, 1 Duke-street, Adelphi, and
      Fleet-lane, *s*
Appleyard, Miss, Newington-causeway

Archer, W., 88 Berwick-street, Soho, *s*
Armsby, A., 28 Liverpool-ter., Islington, *s.pr*
Arpthorpe, W., 22 Bishopsgate-street, *pu*
Atchley & Co., 106 Gt. Russell-street, Blooms-
      bury, *pu*
Ashbee & Dangerfield, Bedford-st., Strand, *pu*
Aylott & Co., 8 Paternoster-row, *pu*
Bagster, S., & Sons, 15 Paternoster-row, *pu*
Bailey, O., 22 Newman-street, Oxford-st., *pu*
Bailliere, H. (for.) 219 Regent-street
Bailey, Brothers, Royal Exchange, *pu*
Bain, James, 1 Haymarket
Baisler, J., 124 Oxford-street
Baker, Thomas, 19 Goswell-road
Baldock, Robert, 85 High Holborn
Baldwin, R., 47 Paternoster-row, *pu*
Banister, J. E., 1A Leadenhall-street
Banks, G. J. & R., Bermondsey New-rd., *pr.pu*
Banks, Jas., 59 Marchmont-st., Brunswick-sq
Barham, T., & Co., 24 Albion-street, Hyde-pk
Barker, James, 19 Throgmorton-street, *n*
Barker, Robert, Church-street, Hackney, *s*
Barlow, G., 32 Jewin-street, City, *n*
Baron, F., King William-street, Strand, *pu*
Barnard, T., 85 Charlotte-street, Fitzroy-sq
Barratt, W., 21 Portugal-st., Lincoln's-inn, *b*
Barrett, E., Bishopsgate-st. Without, *n*
Barritt & Co. (Bible) 173 Fleet-street, *pu*
Barther & Sowell (for.) 14 Gt. Marlboro'-st

Bartlett & Co., 10 Bloomsbury-square, *pu*
Bartlett, C. A., 32 Paternoster-row, *pu*
Bateman, T., Tottenham-street, Tottenham-court-road, *b*
Bateman, J. A., 1 Ivy-lane, *pr.pu*
Bath, H., 29 Russell-ct., Drury-lane, *n*
Batsford, B. T., 52A, High Holborn
Batt, B., 32 Rotherhithe-street
Batty, J. H., 159 Fleet-street, *pr.pu*
Bayley, E. E. & M., Church-street, Hackney
Baynes, H., 2 Clement's-lane, City, *s.a.pr*
Bebbington, W. A., 426 Strand, *s*
Bedford, Chris., 23 Bartholomew-close
Bean, Charles, James-terrace, New North-rd
Beeson, W., 3 Mile-end-road, *s*
Beaton, S. O., 18 Bouverie-street, *p.pu*
Bell & Daldy, 186 Fleet-street, *pu*
Bell, J. R., 19 Exeter-street, Strand, *pu*
Bell, R. J., Bedford-street, Strand, *pu*
Bellamy, B., 2 Maiden-lane, Strand
Benbroke, A., York-buildings, Bloomsbury, *l*
Bender, H., 23 Newport-street, Long-acre, *s*
Benham, G., 10 Water-street, Blackfriars, *s*
Beniouski, Major, Bow-street, Covent-garden
Bentley, J., 13 Paternoster-row, *pu*
Bentley, R. S., New Burlington-street, *pu*
Berger, Geo., 19 Holywell-street, Strand, *pu*
Betts, John, 115 Strand, *s*
Bickers & Bush, 1 Leicester-square, *pu*
Biggs, G., 421 Strand, *pu*
Biggs, J., & Son, 53 Parliament-street
Bignell, F. W., 1 Bishop's-place, Dorset-squre
Bingham, C. E., 84 Mount-street, Grosvenor-square, *n.s.pr*
Birch, W., High-street, Kensington
Bird, J. C., Blenheim-terrace, St. John's-wood, *s*
Blackburn, J., 11 Park-terrace, Kennington, *s*
Blackie & Son, 11 Warwick square, *pu*
Blackwell, H., 16 King's-row, Pentonville
Blackwood, W., & Sons, 37 Paternoster-row, *pu*
Blackwood, J., 8 Lovell's-court, Paternoster-row, *pu*
Blencowe, C., York-place, Kensington-road
Blight, G., 168 Fenchurch-street, *s*
Bogue, D., 86 Fleet-street, *pu*
Bohn, H. G., York-street, Covent-garden, *pu*
Bollen, C., 47 Lambeth-walk, *pr. s*
Bond, W. H., 8 Bell-yard, Temple-bar
Boone, T. & W., 29, New Bond-street, *pu*
Booth, L., Duke-street, Portland-place, *s*
Boosey & Sons, 23 Holles-st., Oxford-st. *m. pu*
Borman, 5 Britannia-row, Hoxton
Bosworth, T., 215 Regent-street, *pu*
Boulter & Co., 143 Strand, *s. pu.*
Bowering, T. K., 211 Blackfriars-road, *pr.n.s*
Bowles, James, 224 High Holborn, *s.pr.a*
Boyles, Court Guide-office, 120 Pall-mall
Bradbury & Evans, 11 Bouverie-street, *pr. pu*
Bradshaw's Guide-office, 59, Fleet-street
Brand, E., 2 Charlotte-st., Portland-square
Brand, E. C., 35 Jewin-street, City
Brassington, J., 27 High-street, Kensington, *s*
Brewer & Co., 23 Bishopsgate-street, *m.pu*
Brewer, M., 160 Fenchurch-street
Brien, W., 13 Eagle-street, City-road, *pu*

Briggs, L., 116 London-rd, Southwark, *l*
Brinkman, E., Eliza-place, Sadler's-wells
Bromley, P., Great Ormond-st, Queen-square
Brooks, R. J., Torrington-place, Bloomsbury
Broom, W. H., Althorpe-place, New-road, *s*
Brown, A. S., & Co., Parsonage-row, Newington-butts, *pr*
Brown, C. R., 193 Bishopsgate Within, *s*
Brown, D., 51 Holywell-street, Strand, *n*
Brown, J., Charlotte-court, Tottenham-court-road, *pu*
Brown, G., Charlotte-place, Goodge-st, *pu*
Brown, James, High Holborn
Brown, J. W., 8 Maud-place, Mile-end
Brown, W., Old-street, St. Luke's
Brown, W. (for) 124, High Holborn
Brickhill, W., Newington-butts, *pr*
Bryce, D., 48 Paternoster-row, *pu*
Buck & Wootton, 33 Mount-st, Lambeth, *pr.s*
Buck, R., 4 & 5 Black Horse-alley, Fleet-st
Bucknell, J., 28 Carnaby-street, Golden-sq
Bull, Huuton, & Co., 19 Holles-st, Cavendish-square, *l.pu*
Bullman, R., Aldine-chambers, *pu*
Bumpus, John, 158 Oxford-street
Bumpus, Thomas, 6 Holborn-bars
Bumpus, T. B., 1 Birchin-lane, City, *pu*
Bumstead, George, 205 High Holborn
Bunney, J. C., 40 Fleet-street, *pr. pu*
Burbidge, C. S., 2 Grove-terrace, Bayswater
Burley, J., 4 Blackwall-street
Burdett, J. T., St. John's-st, Smithfield, *s.pu.*
Burn, James, 11 Kennington-grove, *s*
Burns & Lambert, 63 Paternoster-row, *pu*
Burrup & Son, 12 Royal Exchange, *s*
Butler, R., 6 Hand-court, Holborn, *m.pu*
Butt, Edward, 6 Paternoster-row
Butterworth, H., & Co., 7 Fleet-street, *pu*
Bye, William, 40 Leonard-street, St. Luke's
Byfield, Hawkesworth, & Co., 20 Charing-Cross, *s. pu*
Calder, F. W., 199 Oxford-street
Calder, G. A., 1 Bathurst-street, Hyde-park, *s*
Callaway, H. E., 39 Clerkenwell-green
Camus, M. P. (for) 10 Charles-st, Middlesex Hospital
Canton, R., 49 Watling-street, *pr.pu*
Carline, T., 12 Catherine-street, Strand
Carr, Robert, 14 Houndsditch
Carter, D., 257 Poplar High-street, *n*
Cash, W. & F. G., 5 Bishopsgate-street, *pu*
Castle & Lamb, Bull's Head-court, Newgate-street, *n*
Caulfield, W., 6 Gray's-inn
Causton, H. K., 3 Nag's Head-court, *pr*
Cawthorn & Hutt, 24 Cockspur-street
Chalmers, J., 50 New Globe-road, Hoxton
Chalmers, W. & R., Paternoster-row, *pu*
Chandler, W. G., 3 High-street, Camberwell
Channon, T. S., 5, Brompton-place, Knightsbridge, *s*
Chapman & Hall, 193 Piccadilly, *pu*
Chapman, John, 8 King Wm.-st, Strand, *pu*
Charlton & Wright, Newgate-street, *pu*
Chatto, Thomas, 25 Museum-st, Bloomsbury

Chisman, J., 42, Albany-st, Regent's-pk, *s*
Churchill, John (med.) New Burlington-st, *pu*
Churton, Edw., 26 Holles-st. Oxford-st. *l.pu*
Claret, S., 28 Upper Clifton-st., Finsbury
Clarke, Andrew (for.) 4 City-road
Clarke, E., 20 Gt. Guildford-street, Borough
Clarke, Wm., 1 Holywell-street, Strand
Clarke, W. M., Warwick-lane, City, *pu*
Clarke, H. G., & Co., 252 Strand, *pu*
Clarke, Jno. O., 38½ New Bridge-st., Blackfriars, *pr.pu.s*
Clarke, R. (for.) Finch-lane, Cornhill, *n*
Cleaver, H., 46 Piccadilly, *pu.s.n*
Clemence, Jno., 29 City-terrace, City-road, *n*
Clements, J., 21 & 22 Little Pulteney-street, *pu*
Clowes, W., & Son, 14 Charing-cross, *pr.pu*
Clyde, Jas. (for.) Newman-st., Oxford-st., *b*
Cobbett, A., 137 Strand, *pu*
Coe, C. E., 20 Gt. James-st., Bedford-row, *b.pr*
Cogan, R., 49 Red Cross-street, Barbican, *l*
Cole, T., 15 Great Turnstile, Holborn
Cole, W., 17 Bedford-street, Commercial-road
Cockshaw, A., Horshoe-ct., Ludgate-hill, *pr.pu*
Collins & Ponsford, 300 Strand, *pu*
Collins, S. Y., 7 Barrett-street, Lambeth, *n*
Collins, W., Lovell's-ct., Paternoster-row, *pu.s*
Colnaghi, P. & D., Pall-mall, *pu*
Contencin, J., 13, Dean-street, Westminster
Cook, Jas., Holywell-street, Strand
Coomes, M., 141 Regent-street
Cope, R. J., 16 St. Chads-row, Gray's-inn.
Cope, T., Buckingham-street, Strand, *pu*
Corbett, T., 218 Tottenham-court-road, *l*
Corcoran, D., 47 Duke-street, Lincoln's-inn, *s*
Cornish, E., 11 Red Lion-street, Holborn *pr*
Cornish, Jas., 297 High Holborn, *pu*
Cotes, N. H., 139 Cheapside, *s.l*
Cottrill, Miss, 8 Robert-st., Grosvenor-sq., *n*
Courtier, Chas., 8 Bouverie-street
Cowan & Standring, 8 Finsbury-street, *pu*
Cowie, J., & Son (for.) 2 St. Ann's-lane, City
Cowie, Jolland, & Co., 2 Chapel-pl., Poultry, *pu*
Cocks, R., & Co., New Burlington-street, *m.pu*
Cox, C., 8 King William-street, Strand, *pu*
Cox, Jno., Drury-lane, *n*
Cox, Geo., 18 King-street, Covent-garden, *pu*
Craddock & Co., 48 Paternoster-row, *pu*
Crantz, J. P., 2 Shoe-lane, *pu*
Cramer, Beale, & Co., 201 Regent-street, *m.pu*
Crawley, C. F., 19 Devonshire-street
Cresswell, C., Crawford-street, *s*
Croager, T., Craven-place, Paddington, *s*
Crockford, J., Essex-street, Strand, *pr.pu*
Crossland, Jno., Fenchurch-street, *pr.s*
Cross, R., St. Mary's-terrace, Walworth
Crouch, G. W., Priest's-place, Blackfriars, *b*
Crouch, W., Queen-street, Cheapside, *pu*
Crozier, J., 5 New Turnstile
Cruse, D., 5 Compton-street, Clerkenwell
Cundall J., New Bond-street, *pu*
Curry, J. & J., 203 Sloane-street, *s*
Curtis, A., Union-street, Bishopsgate
Cuthbertson, J., Brompton-road, *s*
Daker, J. O., 5 St. George's-st, Old Kent-rd.
Dalley, E., 22 Queen-street, Seven-dials, *n*

Dalton, W. H., 28 Cockspur-street, *pu*
Daly, C., Greville-street, Hatton-garden, *pu*
Daniel, R., 2 King-street, Covent-garden, *n*
Daniel, E., Mortimer-street, Cavendish-sq, *pu*
Daniels, T. W., 20 Baker's-row, Whitechapel-rd
Darby, Chas. 2 Inverness-terr, Bayswater, *pr.s*
Darling, Jas., 20 Little Queen-street
Darton, J. M., & Co., Holborn-hill, *pu*
Davidson, J., Peter's-hill, Doctors' Com. *m.pu*
Davies, F. P., 162 Fleet-street, *pu*
Davies, H. G., 35 Portman-st, Edgware-rd, *s*
Davies, W., Murray-street, Hoxton, *l*
Davis, Chas. Racquet-court, Fleet-street, *pu*
Davis, Reuben T., 17 Carey-street
Davis, F., 2 Mile-end-road, *m*
Dawson & Sons, Cannon-street, City, *s.pr.n*
Dawson, N., High-street, Poplar, *pr.s*
Day, J. H., 44 Holywell-street, Strand, *pu*
Day, T. F., 13 Carey-street, Lincoln's-inn
Day & Son, Gate-street, Lincoln's-inn, *pu*
Dean, T., & Son, Ludgate-hill, *pu*
Death, H., Beckford-row, Walworth, *s*
Deighton, J. H., Walworth-place, *n*
Detkins, E., 8 Davies-street, Berkeley-square
Dewar, Jno., 3 Mile-end-road
Diprose, J., Wine-office-court, Fleet-street, *pu*
Dodson, D., Holywell-street
Dolman, Chas., 24 Paternoster-row, *pu*
Donovan, J., 2 Alexander-place, Borough
Downes, R., 53 Paternoster-row
Downie, John, 30 Greek-street, Soho, *l.n*
Drewett, W., 265 Borough, *s*
Drummond, L., Symon's-street, Chelsea, *b*
Drysdale, J., 168 Goswell-street
Duff & Hodson, 65 Oxford-steret, *m.pu*
Dugdale, J., 50 Holywell-street
Dugdale, W., 16 Holywell-street
Duggan, Thos., Seacoal-lane, Snow-hill, *pu*
Dugwell, R., 218 Whitechapel
Dulau A. B., & Co., Soho-square, *pu*
Dunn, Joseph, 5 Barnsbury-place, Islington
Dunn, W., 32 Beach-street, Barbican
Dunster, H., 6 Princes-terr. Caledonian-road, *s*
Dyce, F. G., 1 King's-road, Bedford-row
Earl, Geo., 67 Castle-street, Oxford-street
Ebers, Mrs. E. S., 27 Old Bond-street, *l*
Eckett, R., 5 Horseshoe-court, Ludgate-hill, *pu.*
Edmunds, T., 2 Little Bell-alley, City, *n*
Edsall, H., 1, Crown-street East, Walworth
Edwards and Jones, 161, Regent-street, *s*
Edwards, Henry, 3 Pitt's-place, Old Kent-rd.
Edwards, J., Mason's-alley, Basinghall-street
Edwards, Mrs. C., 42 Waterloo-road, *s*
Edell, Edward, 16 Duke-street, Lincoln's-inn
Edle, John, 16 Bear-street, Leicester-square
Egley, Thomas, 58 George-st. Portman-sq., *s*
Eglington, Goswell-road, *pu*
Elkins, W. H., 47 Lombard-street, City
Ellis, H., 8 Walsingham-place, Kensington, *s.m*
Elliott, H., New Oxford-street, *s.pu*
Elsworth, F., 39 Chancery-lane
Elt, C. H., 18 Hedge-row, Islington, *s*
Elwin, G., 3, Seymour-street, Euston-square
Emanuel, Mrs. E., 4 Astley-terr. Cadogan-st.
Evans, A. E., & Sons, 403 Strand, *pr.pu*

Evans, W., & Co., 22 Warwick-square, *pn*
Evans, Mrs. & Miss, 43 Tachbrook-street, *s*
Evans, C., 6 Wellington-street, Strand, *pu*
Evans, Mrs. E., 28 Camomile-street, *s*
Evans, J., 20 King's-road East, Chelsea, *s*
Evans, J., 9 Portugal-street, Lincoln's-inn, *pu*
Evans, John E., 4 Snow-hill, *s*
Evans, W. T., 12 & 13, Patriot-row, Camden-rd.
Everett, W., & Son, 17 Royal Exchange, *n*
Ewins, S. D., 9 Ave-Maria-lane
Eyre and Spottiswoode, 189 Fleet-street, *pu*
Eyre and Williams, 19 Bouverie-street, *pu*
Fairburn, Mrs., 10 Billiter-street, City, *pu*
Farrington, E., 2 Bath-street, City, *pu.n*
Faze, Hy., 1 Edward-terrace, Kensington, *s*
Faulkner, C., 10 Portsmouth-st. Lincoln's-inn
Faulkner, E., 10 St. Alban's-pl. Edgware-rd. *s*
Fellowes, B., 39 Ludgate-street, City
Fernandez, J., 77 York-street, Westminster, *pu*
Featherstone, F. M., 31 Duke-st. Lincoln's-inn
Field, John, 65 Regent-street, *pu.s*
Fisher & Son, Kingsland-road, *pu*
Fisher, T., 239 High-street, Borough
Fletcher, T., 12a Charterhouse-square
Flaxman, W. J., 60 Ebury-street, Pimlico, *s*
Flude, J. W., 2 Postern-row, City, *pr*
Ford, E., Islington-green
Ford, K. J., 11 Barnsbury-place, Islington, *s*
Ford, W. S., 18a Holywell-street, *pr.pu*
Fores, H. P., 42 South Audley-street, *s*
Fortin, P., 97 Dean-street, Soho
Foster, W., 114 Fenchurch-street, *s.pu*
Fox, Charles, 67 Paternoster-row, *pu*
Francis, D., 21 Mile-end-road, *pr.pu*
Francis, J., 4 Wellington-street, Strand, *pr.pu*
Francis, T. H., 57 Brudenell-pl, Mile-end-rd, *s*
Franks, Mrs. M. A., 114 Gray's-inn-lane
Fraser, H., 44 College-street, Camden-town
Frederick, S. B., 8 Melville-terrace, Camden-town, *pr.pu*
Freeman, W., 69 Fleet-street, *pu*
Frego, Thos., 6 Charlotte-st, Fitzroy-sq, *s.n*
French, B., 3 St. Mary's-terrace, Walworth
Fryer, W., 5 Albany-street, Regent's-park
Fudge, G. F., 13 Sloane-square, *s*
Fullarton, A., & Co., Newgate-street, *pu*
Gadsby, J., 1 George-yard, Bouverie-street, *pu*
Gardiner, B. W., 10 Prince's-street, Cavendish-square, *s.pr.pu*
Gardner & Sons, 7 Paternostar-row, *pu*
Gardner, E., 44 Paddington-street, *pr.s*
Garnson, J., 19 Temple-street, Whitefriars
Gawtress, W., 161 Fleet-street, *p*
George, John, 34 Hatton-wall
George, T., 8 St. George's-road, Borough
Gibbs, Miss E., 18 Tichborne-street, *s*
Gibbs, J. W. M., 16 Southgate-ter, Islington, *n*
Gilbert, Brothers, 18 Gracechurch-street, *s.pu*
Gilbert, S. & T., 4 Copthall-buildings, City
Gilbert, J., 49 Paternoster-row, *n.pu*
Gillham & Co., 67 Haymarket, *pu*
Gibson, Samuel, Mile-end-road, *s.m*
Ginger, G. W., 21 Great College-street, *s*
Gladding, John, 20 City-road
Gladding, R., 97 & 98 Whitechapel-road

Glaisher. W., 53 Lamb's Conduit-street
Glaisher, George, 470, New Oxford-street
Goddard, W., 22 John-st, Tottenham-court-rd
Godfrey, Miss H., 47 William-st, Regent's-pk
Goff, M. J., 5 Wells-street, Islington, *s*
Golding, G., 31 Seething-lane, City
Gooch, E. F., 51 King William-street, City, *s*
Goodburn, E., Wardrobe-ter, Doctors'-commons
Goode, T., 30 Aylesbury-st, Clerkenwell, *pu.n*
Goodes G., 106 Crawford-st, & 9 Up.Montague-st, *s*
Goodinge, J. B., 21 Aldersgate-street, City, *pr*
Gordon, James, 146 Leadenhall-street, *s.n*
Gosling, G. G., 97 Westborne-street, Pimlico
Gould, G. T., 7 Ireland-row, Mile-end
Graf, Charles, 13 Paternoster-row, *pu*
Grant & Griffith, St. Paul's-churchyard, *pu*
Grattan, T. W., 6 Amen-corner, *pu*
Graves, H., & Co.. 6 Pall-mall, *pu*
Green, B. L., 62 Paternoster-row, *pu*
Green, James, 48 Gt. Queen-st, Lincoln's-inn
Green, J. W., 4 Brighton-place, Hackney-road
Gregory, J., 34 & 35 Little Queen-st, Holborn
Gridley & Co., 13 Crawley-street, St. Pancras
Griffin, R., & Co., 5 Warwick-sq, *p*
Griffith, A. F., 8 Baker-street, Portman-sq, *s*
Griffith, F., Camberwell-green, *s*
Griffith, John, 7 Hanway-street, Oxford-street
Grix, Mrs. H., 47 Featherstone-street
Groom, G. P., 4 Field-ter, Bagnigge-wells-rd, *l*
Groom, J. H., 2 Eversholt-st, Clerkenwell, *s.m*
Groombridge & Sons, 5 Paternoster-row, *pu*
Guillaume, J. J., 33 Elizabeth-street, Eaton-sq
Gurners, W., 11 Brompton-row, *s*
Gyfford, S., 35 Great Tower-street, City, *s*
Haddock, H. J., 103 High-street, Borough, *s*
Hagger, J., 67 Paternoster-row, *pu*
Hailes, J. C., 27 Leadenhall-street, *s*
Haines, W., 24 Fetter-lane, *l.pr*
Hales, W. K., 10 Bouverie-street, Fleet-st, *pu*
Hall, Virtue, & Co., 25 Paternoster-row, *pu*
Hall, Fred., 16 Paddington-street, Marylebone
Hall, Thomas, 6 Moira-place, City-road
Halsted, C., 120 High-street, Camden-town
Hamilton, Adams, & Co., Paternoster-row, *pu*
Hamilton, Charles, 10 York-place, New-road
Hammatt, Mrs. M., 13 Little Warner-street, *l*
Hance, P., 14 Upper Glo'ster-street, Chelsea, *s*
Hanson, George, 74 Regent-st, Westminster, *l*
Hardwicke, R., Duke-street, Piccadilly, *pr.pu.s*
Hardy & Co., 195 High-street, Poplar, *s*
Hardy, E. A., 4 Hungerford-street, Strand
Harris, B., 66 Hatton-garden, *s*
Harris, Chas., 25 Bow-street, Covent-garden
Harris, Chas. J., 128 Strand, *pu*
Harris, D., 2 York-ter, High-st, Portland-twn, *s*
Harris, Geo., 9 Dean-st, Holborn, *l.n*
Harris, Geo., Albany-pl, Commercial-rd East, *s*
Harris, H. W., 6 Blackfriars-road, *n.pu*
Harris, W., 39 St. John-st, Clerkenwell, *s*
Harris, W. J., 45 Grafton-street, *s*
Harrison, Thos., 59 Pall-mall, *pr. pu*
Harrison, E., 146 Kingsland-road, *pu*
Haselden, C., 21 Wigmore-st, Cavendish-sq, *pu*
Hatchard, Thos., 187 Piccadilly, *pu*
Hatton & Griesbech, 99 Chancery-lane, *s*

Hawes, W., 118 Gt. Portland-street, *n*
Hayman, W., 36 Trafalgar-sq, Stepney
Hearle, Geo., 17a Holywell-street, Strand
Hearne, John, 81 Strand, *pu*
Heath, Wm., 497 New Oxford-street
Heaton, 42 Holywell-street, *l*
Hebert, Mrs. L., 88 Cheapside, *l*
Helfrich, F., 41 Curzon-street, Mayfair, *s*
Henley, Chas., 8 Charles-street, Westminster
Henningham & Holles, 5Mount-st,Grosvenor-sq
Heylin, Alex., 28 Paternoster-row, *pu*
Hering & Remington, 137 Regent-street, *s.pu*
Highley, Samuel, 32 Fleet-street, *pu*
Hill, D. J., 96 Aldersgate-street
Hill, Chas. John, 14 King-st, Holborn, *pu*
Hill, Hy., 4 Holywell-street, Strand
Hill, W. R., 294 Oxford-street
Hilliard, Hy., 23 Basinghall-street, *s*
Hobday, S., 32 Queen-st, Cheapside, *s.pr*
Hobson, G., 17 Cromby's-row, Commercial-road East
Hoby, Jas., 123 Mount-street, Grosvenor-sq
Hoby, John, 35 Chapel-st, Belgrave-square
Hodgson, S., 6 & 9 Gt. Marylebone-st, *pu.l*
Hodgson, Thomas, Aldine-chambers, Paternoster-row, *pu*
Hodson, Jas. S., 22 Portugal-street, *pr.pu*
Hodson, W. H., 11 Lovell's-court, Paternost row(booksellers'agency&Directory-office),*pu*
Holder, W. T., 311 Strand
Holmes, Jas., 39 Hampstead-road, *s*
Holmes, Percy, 31 Newcastle-street, Strand
Holmes, T., 76 St.Paul's-churchyard, *pu*
Holmes, W., 195 Oxford-street, *s*
Holyoake, G. J., & Co., 147 Fleet-street, *pu*
Holloway, W., Hanway-street, *m.pu*
Honeysett, E. H., 137 High-st, Camden-twn, *s*
Hookham, T., & Sons, 15 Old Bond-st, *pu*
Hopcraft, W, 42 & 43 Mincing-ln, City, *pr.pu*
Hope & Co., 16 Gt. Marlborough-street, *pu*
Hopkins, F., 5 Bishopsgate-street Within, *s*
Horne, W. M., 2 Skinner-st, Somers-town, *s.n*
Horsell & Shirriffs, 492 Oxford-street, *pr.pu*
Horsman, J., Brownlow-street, Holborn, *n*
Horwood, W., 36 Ludgate-street, *s*
Houlston & Stoneman, 65 Paternoster-row, *pu*
Howard & Son, 114 Holborn-hill
Howard, J., 7 Lamb-place, Kingsland, *n.m*
Hewett, N., 37 Princes-street, Leicester-square
Hughes & Butler, St. Martins-le-Grand, *pu*
Hughes, John, Stationers'-hall-court, *pu*
Hughes, W.,Aldine-chmbrs, Paternoster-rw,*pu*
Hughes, W., 8 Park-st, Camden-town, *s*
Hunt, M., 6 Charlwood-street, Pimlico
Hunter, W., 20 Chalton-street, Somers-town
Heardle & Co., 8 Racquet-court, Fleet-st, *pr.pu*
Hurst & Blackett, 13 Gt. Marlborough-st, *pu*
Husk, F. C., 24 Haymarket
Huskisson, J., 104 High Holborn
Hutchinson & Co., 29 Newcastle-st, Strand,*pu*
Ibbett, W. H., 15 Maidenhead-ct, Aldersgate-st
Imray, Jas., & Son (nautical) 102 Minories
Inchbold, T. M., Aldine-chambers, Paternoster-row, *pu*
Inglis, John, 13 Tysoe-st, Clerkenwell

Ingram, Herbert, & Co., Milford-ln, Strand,*pu*
Ingram, Geo., 3 Britannia-st, City-road, *pu*
Jackson & Walford, 18 St. Paul's-churchyd, *pu*
Jackson, B. D., 236 High-street, Bow, *s*
Jackson, H. (medical) 30 King-st, Boro'
Jackson, Peter, Angel-steeet, St. Martin's-le-Grand, *pr.pu*
Jarrold & Sons, 47 St. Paul's-churchyard, *pu*
Jeans, C., 40 High-street, Portland-town, *s*
Jefferies, Hy., 56 King-street, Soho
Jefferies, E. T., 14 Sun-st, Bishopsgate, *s*
Jeffs, W. (foreign) 15 Burlington-arcade, *pu*
Jenkinson, W., 16 Shoe-lane, Fleet-street, *pu*
Jennings, John & R., 62 Ceeapside, *pu*
Jepps, Thos., 1 Queen's Head-pas, Newgate-st
Jerrard, P., 111 Fleet-street, *pu*
Johns, W., 35 Holywell-street, Strand
Johnson, W., Kennington-lane, *pu*
Johnson, W. S., 60 St. Martin's-lane, *pr pu*
Johnstone, W., 5 Queen-street, Cheapside
Jones, J. E., 84 Connaught-terrace, Edgware-rd
Jones, Miss L., 45 Marchmont-street
Jones, Thos. (medical) 91 Aldersgate-street
Jones, Thos., and Co., 10 Paternoster-row *pu*
Jones, T. L., 20 Drummond-street, Euston-sq, *s*
Jones, W., 2 Triangle, Kennington, *s*
Jordan, R., 25 Shaftesbury-terrace, Pimlico
Jordan, W., 169 Strand, *n*
Joy, W., 44 Paternoster-row, *pu*
Kaines, Edw., 4 Great Hermitage-street, St. George's East, *s*
Kay, Chas., 39 Bridge-place, Harrow-road, *s*
Kean, J., 20 Norwich-court, Fetter-lane
Keates, J. H., 142 Sloane-street, *s*
Keay, D., 13 Gough-square, Fleet-street, *pu*
Kebble, T. H. 162 Fleet-street, *pu*
Kelly and Co., 20 Boswell-court, *pr pu*
Kelly and Pritchett, 32 Houndsditch, *pr*
Kelly, L. A., 2 Vigo-street, Regent-street, *s*
Kelly, Thos., 16 Paternoster-row, *pu*
Kendrick, J., 27, Ludgate-street, St. Paul's
Kennedy, Thos., Fetter-lane, *pu*
Kennett, R. J., 14 York-street, Covent-garden
Kent, W., and Co., Paternoster-row, *pu*
Kerby, Chas., 118 Whitechapel-road, *n*
Kerby, Jno. and Son, 190 Oxford-street. *s n pu*
Kerr, J., 33 Duke-street, Manchester-square
Kerton, W. G., 6 Ivy-lane, City, *pu*
Kettle, Chas., 256 High Holborn
Key, T. W., 18 Westborne-place, Paddington, *s*
Kimpton, B., 43 High Holborn
Kimpton, H., 82 High Holborn
Kimpton, J. M., 68 Gt. Russell-st, Bloomsbury
Kimpton, Rd, 31 Wardour-street, Soho
King, Jno., 5 Wine-office-court, Fleet-street, *pu*
King, Henry, 8 Spring-street, Paddington, *s*
King, Thos., Church-street, Hackney, *s*
King, W. B., 3 Whitefriars-street, Fleet-st, *pu*
Kirbey, W., 79 Regent-street, Lambeth
Kissick, Jno., 10 Tottenham-court-road
Knight and Co., 313 Strand, *pr pu*
Knight, Chas., 90, Fleet-street, *pu*
Knight and Son, Clerkenwell-close, *pr pu*
Knowles, W., 16 Conduit-street, Paddington
Lacy, T. H., 17 Wellington-st N., Strand *pu*

Ladd, S. J., 10 Johnson-place, Harrow-road
Lake, S. H., 90 Lambeth-walk, *l*
Lambert, B., 17 Goswell-street, *s*
Lang and Koehler (for,) 38 Ludgate-hill, *pu*
Laughton, Jas., 23 Wells-street, Wellclose-sq
Lavars, Jas., 81 Gt. Portland-street, *s*
Law, C. H., 131 Fleet-street, *pu*
Lawless, Mrs. P., 13 Philpot-lane, City, *l*
Lawrence, Samuel, 30 Church-la, Whitechapel
Laurie, T., 17 Wells-row, Islington, *s*
Lawson, F. L., 19 Melton-street, Euston-sq., *n*
Layton, C. & E., 150 Fleet-street, *s.pr.pu*
Leader and Cocks, 63 New Bond-street, *m.pr*
Lea, Hy., 22 Warwick-lane, City, *pu*
Leath, Jas., 5 St. Paul's-churchyard, *pu*
Lee, Miss C., 24 Princes-ter, Caledonia-road, *s*
Lee, John, 440 West Strand
Lee, J., 9a Billiter-square, City, *n.s*
Lee, R. E., 127, Fleet-street, *pu*
Legg, W. J., 8 Chapman-street, St. George's E
Leighton, J. & J., 40 Brewer-street, Golden-sq
Lemare, T. T., 2 Oxford Arms-passage
Le Page, R. C. (for) 1 Whitefriars-street, *pu*
Leslie, J. (theological) 58 Gt Queen-st Holborn
Letts & Son, 8 Royal Exchange, *s*
Levy, Mrs. A., 22 Garden-row, London-road, *l*
Lewis, H. K., 15 Gower-street, Euston-sq, *pu*
Lilly, J., 19 King-street, Covent-garden
Lincoln, F., 128 Blackfriars-road
Little, Mrs. F., 34 Henrietta-st, Covent-garden
Livick, Lewis, 3 Garden-row, Camberwell
Lloyd, E., 12 Salisbury-square, *pr.pu*
Lockington, Miss C., 19 Ryder's-court, Leicester-square
Lofts, Jno., Mile-end-road, *s.m*
Lofts, Jno., 262 Strand, *pr.pu*
London Printing and Publishing Company, Blue Coat-buildings
Long, H., 18 Wellington-street N, Strand, *pu*
Longman's & Co., 39 Paternoster-row, *pu*
Loveland, Hy., 15 Essex-street, Islington, *s*
Low, S., & Son, 47 Ludgate-hill, *pu*
Low, Jno., 4 Chichester-rents, Chancery-lane
Lowe, C., 10 Elizabeth-place, Sadler's-wells
Lowry, J. R., 115a Old-street, St. Luke's, *m*
Lumley, E., 126 High Holborn, *pu*
Luntley, J., and Co., 3 New Broad-street-ct, City, *pr.pu*
McCary, H. J., 32 St. James's-street, Pall-mall
McDaniell, J., 1 Charter-house-street
McNeil and Co., 23 Moorgate-street, *s.a.e*
Macintosh, Alex., 169 Fleet-street, *pu*
Macgregor, Maclure, and Macdonald, 37 Walkrook, *pu*
Mackenzie, W., 22 Paternoster-row, *pu*
Mackie, Alex., 4 Chalton-street, Somers-town
Macmichael, J., 2 Pier-terrace, Chelsea, *l.s*
Madden, Jas. (oriental) 8 Leadenhall-st, *s.pu*
Mahon, M. J., 18 Blackman-street, Bow, *s*
Maish & Co., 2 Crane-court, Fleet-street, *pu*
Maltster, Jas., 95 East-street, Manchester-sq, *s*
Manchee, Jas., 18 Mid-row, Holborn, *pu*
Mann, Nephews, 39 Cornhill, *s.a.pu*
Mann, W., 8 Church-street, Paddington, *s*
March, J., 12 Webber-st, Blackfriars-rd, *pr.pu*

Marcus, O. C. (for) 8 Oxford-street, *s*
Marke, T., 3 Frederick-place. Hampstead-road
Marks, T., 25 Foley-street, Portland-place, *s*
Marks, J., 80 Houndsditch, *pr.pu*
Marks, J., 12 Prospect-place, Kingsland, *s*
Marks, J. L., 91 Long-lane, Smithfield, *pr.pu*
Marks, Sol., 60 Great Prescott-street, Goodman's-fields, *pu*
Markwell, J. T., 46 Great Tichfield-street, *n*
Marlborough and Co., Ave Maria-lane, *n.pu*
Marsh, E., 84 Houndsditch, *pu*
Marshall, W. W., Edgware-road, *s*
Marston, E., 4 Cullum-street, *s*
Martin, A., 11 Warwick-square, City
Martin, P. T., 35 Verulam-street, Gray's-inn
Mason, Mrs. A., 5 Upper Southwell-street
Mason, G. T., West-street, Soho
Mason, Jno., 66 Paternoster-row, *pu*
Mason, W., Clerkenwell-green
Mason, W. A., 6 Holywell-street, Strand
Massie, C., 27 Cannon-street-road, *s.*
Masters & Co., 78 New Bond-street & Aldersgate-street, *pu*
Masters, T., 2 New-bridge-st, Blackfriars, *pu*
Master, Geo., 62 Old-street, St. Luke's
Matthews, J., 5 Up Wellington-st, Strand, *pu*
Mattocks, W., 29 Poppin's-court, Fleet-st, *s.pu*
Mauris, C., 54 Goodge-street
Maxwell, W., 32 Bell-yard, Temple-bar, *pu*
Maynard, S., 8 Earl's-court, Leicester-square
Medical Directory Office, 128 Strand
Medicott, E., 13 Sumner-place, *l*
Meeke, C., 2 Crane-court, Fleet-street, *pr.pu*
Mesnard, H. A., 6 Green-street, Leicester-sq.
Middleton, G., 27 Eversholt-street, *l*
Millard, T., 70 Newgate-street
Miller, J., 43 Chandos-street, Covent-garden
Miller, J. (for) Henrietta-street, Covent-garden
Miller, J., 1 College-street, Westminster, *n*
Miller, W., Upper East Smithfield
Miller, W. H., 6 Bridge-road, Lambeth, *pr.s*
Mills, Geo., 3 Upper Seymour-street, Eustonsquare, *pu*
Minth, F., (for) Conduit-street , *pu*
Minfress, R., 13 Paternoster-row, *pu*
Mitchell, A., 16 Charles-street, Middlesex Hospital, *pu*
Mitchell, C., & Son, Red Lion-ct, Fleet-st, *pu*
Mitchell, J., 33 Old Bond-street, *l.pu*
Mitchell, W. O., 39 Charing-cross, *pr.n.s*
Mitchell, Holywell-street, Strand, *pu*
Molini, C. F. (for) 17 King William-st Strand
Moncas, Thos., 45 Holywell-street, Strand
Moore, F., 89 Lisson-grove North, *s*
Mordey, T., 126 Guildford-street, Borough, *l.n*
Morelli, C. F., 228 Hoxton, High-street
Morley, Z., 27 Park-terrace, Park-road, *n.s*
Morrison, J. A., 14 Wellington-place, Backroad, *l*
Mortimer, John, 140 Strand, *pu*
Moseley & Keele, Catherine-street, Strand, *n*
Mountcastle, G., 10 Bedford-ct, Covent-garden
Moxon, E., 44 Dover-street, Piccadilly, *pu*
Mozley, J. C., & Co., 6 Paternoster-row, *pu*
Mudie, C. E., 510 Oxford-street, *l*

Muldary, M., 9 Virginia-street, St. George's E.
Munting, J., 56 Gray's-inn-lane
Munting, R., 6 Little-turnstile, Holborn
Munting, W., 40 Gray's-inn-lane
Murcott, C., 11 Vinegar-yard, Drury-lane
Murray & Co., 179 Sloane-street, *s.b*
Murray, John, 50 Albemarle-street, *pu*
Murray, W., 57 Oxford-street, *s*
Myers, J. M., 13 Duke-street, Aldgate
Myers, A. & J. S., Leadenhall-street, *pu*
Nash, G. & J., 12 Motcombe-street, Belgrave-square, *s.n.l*
Nash, J., 23 Bowling-street, Westminster
Nash, J., 18 Parker's-row, Bermondsey
Nattali & Bond, 23 Bedford-st, Covent-gdn, *pu*
Neely, W., 1 St. Swithin's-lane, City, *s*
Neesom, C., 93 Brick-lane
Nelson, T., and Son, 29 Paternoster-row, *pu*
Newbery, W., 6 King-street, Holborn, *pu*
Newby, T. C., 30 Welbeck-street, *pu*
Newbold, G., Strand, *pu*
Newman, J. and W., 3 Bruton-street, *s*
Newman, J., 235 High Holborn
Newman, W., 6 Caroline-place, City-road
Nichols, F., 2 Milton-street, City, *s.pr*
Nichols and Sons, 46 King-st, Westminster, *pr*
Nicol, J., 54 Parker's-row, Bermondsey, *l*
Niele, W., 46 Burlington-arcade
Nisbett and Co., 20 Berners-st, Oxford-st, *pu*
Noble, J., 75 Old-street, St. Luke's
Noble, J. A., 1 Freeman's-place, Mile-end
Noble, C., 312 Strand
Noble, J. A. jun., Waterloo-place, Commercial-road East
Nock, S. and B. (med.) 16 Bloomsbury-street
Norris, J., 1 St. George's-pl, Camberwell-road
Novello, J. A., 69 Dean-street, Soho, *m.pu*
Nutt, D. (for.) 270 Strand, *pu*
Ogilvy, Mrs. P., 62 Grove-pl, Brompton, *s.n*
Oliff, J., 14 Queen's-ter, St. John's-wood, *s*
Oliver and Co., 38 Holywell-street, Strand
Ollivier, 19 Old Bond-street, *m.pu*
Onwhyn, J., 1 Catherine-street, Strand, *n.pu*
Ordish, T., and Co., Brompton-row, *s*
Orger and Co., 174, Fenchurch-street
Orr, W. S., and Co., 2 Amen-corner, *pr.pu*
Osborn, C., 16 Haberdashers'-walk, Hoxton
Osman, W., 6 Adelaide-terrace, Islington, *pr*
Ostell, W., 24 Hart-street, Bloomsbury, *pr*
Owen, H., 21 Noble-street, City, *n*
Pace, J., 19 Brecknock-place, Camden-town, *s*
Packer, G., 2 Warneford-place, Camden-town
Packer, G., 23 King-street, Portman-square, *s*
Palmer, C. and T. H., 55 Gracechurch-street, *s*
Palmer, E., and Son, 18 Paternoster-row, *pu*
Palmer, C., 31 Little Bell-alley, City
Palmer, G. J., 27 Lamb's-conduit-street
Palmer, S., 39 King-street, Holborn
Pamplin, W., 45 Frith-street, Soho
Park, P., and Son, 181 Long-lane, Southwark
Park, A. A., 46 Leonard-st, Finsbury-sq, *pr.pu*
Parker, Furnival,&Parker, 30 Charing-cross, *pu*
Parker, J. W., 445 West Strand, *pu*
Parker, P. & P. 181 Long-lane, Bermondsey, *s*
Parker, C. J., 46 Brewer-st, Golden-square, *s*

Parker, J., 7 Radnor-street, St. Luke's, *s*
Parker, J. H. and J., 377 Strand, *pu*
Parker, T., 44 Ferdinand-st, Hampstead-road
Parkins and Gotto, 24 Oxford-street, *s*
Parnell, G., 21 King-street, Bloomsbury, *s*
Parnell, J., 39 High-street, Marylebone, *s*
Partridge & Oakey, 34 Paternoster-row, *pr.pu.s*
Pateman, W., 4 Wine-office-ct, Fleet-street, *pu*
Pattie, J., 2 Queen's Head-pas, Newgate-st, *pu*
Pattie, M. A., 110 Shoe-lane, Fleet-street, *pu*
Paul, J., Chapter-house-court, St. Paul's, *pu*
Pawsey, R., 27 Exeter-street, Sloane-st, *n.pu*
Pavey, J., 47 Holywell-street, Strand, *pu*
Peacock and Son, 18 Salisbury-square, *pu*
Pearson, E., 242 Blackfriars-road
Pedder, J., 2 Bloomsbury-street, Bloomsbury
Pedder, W., 34 Caroline-place, Islington
Pedder, W., 13 Holywell-street, Strand
Pendrill, C., 110 St. Martin's-lane
Perrin, E., 2 Prospect-row, Mile-end
Perry and Co., 37 Red Lion-square, Holborn
Petheram, J. 44 Holborn, *pu*
Pettit, J., 127 Fleet-street
Pevrill, 24 Penton-row, Walworth
Peverley, T., 3 Commercial-place, Kingsland
Phelps, J. B., 44 Paternoster-row, *s*
Phillips, J., 13 Upper Tachbrook-street
Philp, R. K., 69 Fleet-street, *pu*
Pickersgill, S., 33 Great Quebec-street, *l*
Pearcy, W., 9 Shepperton-pl, New North-rd, *n*
Pilcher, W., 71 Gray's-inn-lane, *n*
Piggott, A. M., Aldine-chambers, and Kennington, *s.pu*
Pinnick, J., 50 High-street, Camden-town
Piper, Stephenson, and Spence, 23 Paternoster-row, *pu*
Pitman, F., 20 Paternoster-row, *pu*
Planer, C., 61 Cambridge-street, Pimlico
Plummer, A., 46 Theobald's-road, *n*
Plummer G. G., 42 Spicer-street, Spitalfields
Pollard, A., 9 Little Bell-alley, City
Pond, R. R., Exeter-change
Poole, J. J., 130 London-road, Southwark
Pope, H., 22 Budge-row, City, *pr.pu*
Porter, J. L., 71 Sloane-street
Potter, Thomas J., 60 Tabernacle-walk, *pr.s*
Potter, W., New Church-st, Westminster, *l*
Pottle and Son, 14 Royal Exchange, *n*
Poulton, G., 30 Kingsland-crescent
Ponten, J. B., and Co., Cannon-street, City, *n*
Pound, G. W., 9 Moreton-street, Pimlico
Pounceby, J., Leman-st, Whitechapel, *pr.pu*
Preston, G., Princes-street, Little Queen-street
Price, John, 20 Cross-st, Commercial-rd East, *n*
Purkess, Geo., 60 Dean-street, Soho, *pu*
Pyrke, T. K., 12 High-street, Notting-hill
Quaritch, B. (for.) Castle-st, Leicester-square
Quentin, H. S., 24 Bell-yard, Fleet-street, *pu*
Ramuz, M., 41 Rupert-street, Haymarket
Rastall, T., 24 Ebury-street, Pimlico, *n.s*
Ratcliffe, A., 15 Queen-street, Lincoln's-inn
Rayner, J., 169 Kingsland-road
Reece, J., 32 Clement's-lane, City
Reeves and Turner, 114 Chancery-lane
Reeve, L., 5 Henrietta-street, *pu*

Reeves, George, 2 Parkside, Knightsbridge
Reeves and Son, 113 Cheapside, *pu*
Read and Co., Johnson's-ct, Fleet-st, *pr.pu*
Reid, R. R., 15 Charing-cross, *s*
Reffell, H. H., 14 Great Portland-street, *s.b.n*
Relfe, Brothers, 15 Aldersgate-street
Religious Tract Society, Paternoster-row, *pu*
Renshaw, H. (med.) 356 Strand, *pu*
Renshaw, J., 38 Gracechurch-street
Reynolds, J., 174 Strand, *pu*
Reynolds, G. W. M., Wellington-st, Strand, *pu*
Reynolds, S. A., 11 Church-row, Aldgate
Rhind, J., 7 Little Sussex-place, Hyde-park
Rich, Brothers, (American) 12 Tavistock-row
Richardson, Brothers, 23 Cornhill, *pu*
Richardson and Son, 172 Fleet-street, *pr.pu*
Richardson, A., 8 Upper Islington-terrace
Rickford, M., 32 Lime-kiln, Limehouse
Ridgeway, J., 169 Piccadilly, *pu*
Rimell, G., 22 Frederick-place, Hampstead-rd
Rimmell, J., 401 Oxford-street
Rivington, F. and J., Waterloo-place, *pu*
Robbins, J., 45 Upper Baker-street, New-road
Roberts, A., 14 Bowling-green-la, Clerkenwell
Roberts, F., 2 New-street-square, *pu*
Roberts, J., 2 Arabella-row, Pimlico
Robertson, A., 30 Chancery-lane
Robinson, J., 109 Oxford-street
Roe, M., 16 Vere-street, Clare-merket
Rogers, E. P., 11 Thornhill-pl, Caledonian-rd
Rogers, W. J., 76 Friar-street, Blackfriars-road
Rogerson and Co., 246 Strand, *pr.pu*
Rolandi, F. (for.) 20 Berners-street
Rose, W. H., 15 Milton-street, City, *s.l*
Routledge G. and Co., 2 Farringdon-st, *pr.pu*
Rowe, S., 124 Cheapside, *pu.s*
Rowsell, J., 28 Great Queen-street
Rowsell, S. W., 31 Cheapside, *a.s*
Rowney, G., and Co., Rathbone-place, *pu*
Royle, J. 2 Blandford-street, Portman-square
Royston and Co., 40 Old Broad-st, City, *pr.s*
Ruemans, F., 2 Oxford-row, Old Kent-road
Russell, A., 15 Bridge-terrace, Harrow-road
Rutter, W., 2 Cottage-place, City-road
Ryle, A., 2 Monmouth-court, Seven-dials, *pu*
Sage, J., 4 Newman's-row, Lincoln's-inn-fields
Salter, Mrs. A., 34 Great Suffolk-st, Borough, *l*
Salter, W., 17 New-street, Dorset-spuare
Sams, W. R., 1 St. James's-street
Samuel, J., 41 Gt. Randolph-st, Camden-town
Sandell and Co., 12 Peerless-place, City-road
Sanders, J.J., 11, Paradise-row, Rotherhithe, *pr*
Sangster and Fletcher, Paternoster-row, *m*
Saunders and Ottley, 50 Conduit-street, *pu*
Saunders, W., 50 Rufford's-buildings, Islington
Scadding, J., 34 Belgrave-place, Pimlico, *s.l*
Scholefield, W. 36 Holywell-street, Strand
Scott, A., 28 Charter-house-square, *pu*
Scott, John, 5 King's-row, Walworth, *n*
Seale, A., 5 Portland-place, St. John's-wood
Sears., M., 55 Penton-street, Islington
Seeley & Co., 2 Hanover-st, Hanover-square, *pu*
Seeley, Jackson & Halliday, 54 Fleet-street, *pu*
Seeley, George, Cambridge Bible Warehouse,
    Water-lane, Whitefriars

Sedgwick, D., 81 Sun-street, Bishopsgate
Sewell, M., 8 Charterhouse-square
Shapcott, A., 54 Rathbone-place, *pu*
Sharpe and Hale, 4 Berkeley-square
Shaw, J., & Sons, 136 Fetter-la, *pr.pu*
Shaw, J. F., Southampton-row, Russell-square
    and Paternoster-row, *pu*
Sheard, A. A., 19 Charterhouse-lane
Shee, P. B., 56 Paddington-street, *m.n*
Shelton, E., 69 Fleet-street, *pu*
Sheppard, R., William-street, Blackfriars-road
Silverthorne, 47 Addison-street, *n.s.l*
Simmons, R., & Son, White Conduit-street
Simmons, G., 64 Edgware-road
Sims & McIntyre, Aldine-chambers, *pu*
Simpkin,Marshall,&Co.,4 Stationers'-hall-ct,*pu*
Skeet, C. J.,10 King William-street, Strand, *pu*
Skeffington, W., 163 Piccadilly, *pu*
Skelt, B., 17 Swan-street, Minories, *pr.pu*
Slater, J., 58 Fleet-street, *pu*
Smith, Elder, & Co., 65 Cornhill, *pu.s*
Smith, W. H., & Son, 136 Strand, *pu.n.s*
Smith, Alfred, 102 Cheapside, *l.s*
Smith, Charles, 6 Hart-street, Mark-lane, *pr.pu*
Smith, D. O., 7 Church-street, Blackfriars-road
Smith, E., 3 Godfrey-street, Chelsea
Smith, H., 4½ Edward-street, Portman-square
Smith, Brothers, & Co., King-st, Cheapside, *n*
Smith, Henry, 3 Graham-street, Islington, *n*
Smith, Henry, 16 Holywell-street, *pu*
Smith, J. R., 36 Soho-square, *pu*
Smith, S., 12 Gower-street, New-road
Smith, T., 20 Brewer-street, Golden-square
Snow, John, 35 Paternoster-row, *pu*
Soloman, S., 37 Duke-street, Aldgate
Somerfield, J., 67 Marylebone-lane, *pr.s*
Sotheran & Co., 10 Tower-street, City, *pu*
Soul, M., 3 Agar-street, Strand, *pu*
Southgate & Co., 22 Fleet-street
Sowerby, J. E., 3 Meads-place, Westminster
Spence, J. C., 3 Holywell-street, Strand
Spencer, Richard, 314 High Holborn
Spiers, W., 42 Great Prescott-street, Good-
    man's-fields, *pr*
Spokes, L., 36 Rosoman-street, Clerkenwell
Spon, E. & F., 16 Bucklersbury, *pu*
Stacey, R. S., 150 Shoreditch
Standley, R. J., 61 Brook-street
Stanford, E., 6 Charing-cross
Stanesby, J. & S. A., 13 Tachbrook-street, *pu*
Stannard & Dixon, Poland-street, *pu*
Starling, J. K.; 87 Upper-street, Islington
Staunton, M., & Son, 9 Strand
Steel, D., 2 Spring-gardens, Charing-cross, *n.s*
Stephens, S. F., 123 Albany-street
Stephens, T., 47 Skinner-street, Snow-hill, *pu*
Stephens & Norton, 26 Bell-yard, Lincoln's-inn
Stephens, G., 58 Hoxton Old Town
Stevens, S., 24 Bloomsbury-street
Stevens, W., 42 Tottenham-court-road
Stevington, 51 Charles-st, Middlesex-hospital
Stewart, C. J., 11 King William-street, Strand
Stocking, H., 2 Duke-street, Adelphi
Stockley, S. A., 2 Great Quebec-street
Stracey, R. & E., 2 Hanover-pl, Regent's-park

Straker, Mrs. A., Monkwell-street, City
Straker, W. (theological) 25 Henrietta-st, Covent-garden
Strange, W., sen., & Co., 8 Amen-corner, *pu*
Strange, W., jun., 8 Queen's Head-passage, *pu*
Stretten, B., 73 Anne's-place
Stroud, H. C., 163 Blackfriars-road
Souter, E., 2 Cheapside
Suttaby, R. & A., Stationers'-hall-court, *pu*
Swale & Wilson, 25 Gt. Russell-st, Bloomsbury
Sweet, H., 1 Chancery-lane, *pu*
Swift, J., 4 Little Queen-st, Westminster
Tacey, J. C., 18 City-road
Tallent & Allen, 21 Paternoster-row, *pu*
Tarner, G. E., 16 High-street, Marylebone, *s*
Taylor, A., 33 Gt. Castle-st, Regent-st, *pu*
Taylor, G., 101 Edgware-road, *s*
Taylor, J., 7 London-terrace, Hackney-road, *s*
Taylor, M., 1 Wellington-street, Strand
Taylor, T., 13 Pleasant-row, New-road, *s*
Taylor, J., 3 Queen's Head-passage, City, *pu*
Taylor, W. R., 200 Strand
Taylor, W. S., 40 Goodge-street, Tottenham-court-road
Tegg, W., & Co., 85 Queen-street, City, *pu*
Templeman, C., 6 Great Portland-street
Terry, P., 6 Hatton-garden, *s.n*
Tessyman, C., 78 Gt. Queen-st, Lincoln's-inn
Theobald, R., 26 Paternoster-row, *pu*
Thinn, F., 3 Brook-street, Grosvenor-sq, *pr*
Thomas, J., Catherine-street, Strand, *pu*
Thomas, W., & Co., 19 to 21 Catherine-street, Strand, *pu*
Thomason, E., 75 Red Lion-st, Clerkenwell, *s*
Thompson, E., 19 Broad-court, Bow-street
Thompson, G. J., 2 Ivy-place, Hoxton, *s*
Thomson, T. D., Up. King-st, Bloomsbury, *s*
Thomson, W. D., 138 Up-street, Islington, *s*
Thorburn, R., 2 Carthusian-street
Thorpe, J. H., 46 Gray's-inn-lane
Thredgold, J., 9 Sidney-st, Commercial-road
Thredgould, T. H., 31 Oxford-st, Mile-end, *s.n*
Tidd, J. L., 57 Goswell-road, *n*
Tilney, R., 13 Copenhagen-street, Islington
Tobin, M., 25 Lambeth-road
Tolkien, 27, King-William-street, City, *m.pu*
Tomkins, T. G., 163 Strand, *s*
Torond, H., Warwick-square, *pu*
Tovey, J., 177 Piccadilly
Trubner & Co. (foreign) 12 Paternoster-row
Truelove, E., 240 Strand, *pu*
Tucker, W., 17 Great George-st, St. George's East, *n*
Tupling, J., 320 Strand
Turner, H., 2 Drummond-street, Euston-square
Turner, W., 46 Squirries-street, Bethnal-green
Tweedie, W., 337 Strand, *pu*
Tyler, T., 164 Tottenham-court-road, *s*
Tyson, H., High-street, Newington-butts
Upham & Beet, 46 New Bond-street, *pu*
Van Voorst & Co., 1 Paternoster-row, *pu*
Varden, W. H., 154 High-street, Borough, *s*
Varty & Owen, 31 Strand, *s.pu*
Venden, E., 30 George-street, Portman-sq, *s*
Verney, G., 1 Oxford-place, Chelsea, *l.n*

Vickers, E. A., 11 Barton-st, Westminster, *s.l*
Vickers, G., 28 & 29 Holywell-street, *pu*
Virtue, G., & Co., Ivy-lane, and Cottage-place, City-road, *pu*
Virtue, J., 3 Water-street, Blackfriars
Vizettelli & Co., 3 Peterborough-ct, Fleet-st, *pu*
Wade, Thomas, 13 High-street, Kensington, *s*
Wade, T., 15 Prince's-terrace, Caledonian-road
Walker, W., 106 Newgate-street
Walker, W., 196 Strand, *s*
Wall, M., & Co., 78 Upper Seymour-street, *s*
Wall, James, 340, High-street, Wapping, *s*
Wall, S., 47, North-street, Edgware-road, *s*
Walbank, R., & Son, 7 High-street, Hoxton, *pr*
Waller, W., & Son, 188 Fleet-street
Walton & Maberley, Ivy-lane, *pu*
Ward & Co., 27 Paternoster-row
Ward & Lock, 158 Fleet-street, *pu*
Washbourne, H., & Co., 25 Ivy-lane, *pu*
Waterlow & Son, London-wall, *pr.pu.s*
Watson, J., Aldine-chambers, *pu*
Watson, W., 3 St. Ann's-lane, Aldersgate-st
Watt, E., 2 New-turnstile, Holborn
Watts, J., 96 St. George's-road, Southwark
Weale, J., 59 High Holborn, *pu*
Wetherby, C. & J., 6 Old Burlington-st, *pu*
Webb, Billington, & Co., 5 Wine-office-ct, *pu*
Webb, J., 21 Lambeth-walk, *s*
Webster & Co., 60 & 61 Piccadilly, *pu.s*
Wells, H., 3 Leigh-st, Burton-crescent,
Wertheim & Macintosh, 24 Paternoster-rw, *pu*
Wesley, John, 54 Paternoster-row, *pu*
Wesley, W., 34 Paternoster-row, *pu*
Wessel & Co., 239 Regent-street, *m.pu*
West, R., 16 Jamaica-row, Bermondsey
West, W., 57 Wych-street, Strand
Westell, J. (foreign) Tottenham-court-road
Westerton, Charles, St. George's-place, Hyde-park, *pu.l*
Wettone, H., 313 Oxford-street, *n.s*
Wheatley, B. R., 44 Bedford-st, Covent-garden
Wheeler, A., 7 Agar-street, Strand, *s*
Wheeler, F. W., 220 Strand
Wheldon, J., 4 Paternoster-row
Whittaker, T. W., 31 Oakley-st, Lambeth
Whittaker & Co., Ave Maria-lane
White, A., 31 Holywell-street, Strand
White, G., 36 Gt. Russell-st, Bloomsbury, *pr*
White, H., 337 Oxford-street, *m*
White, John, Devereux-court, Strand
White, L., 11 Silver-street, Kensington
White, Thos., 161 Fleet-street
White, F. H. 12 Cross-st, Newington-butts, *l*
White, W., 70 Piccadilly, *pu*
Whitley, T., & Co., 191 High-st, Shadwell, *s.pr.n*
Whitfield, E. T., 178 Strand, *pu*
Whiting, S., 7 Hosier-ln, West Smithfield, *s.n*
Whittome, J. R. J., 4 Mount-rw, Liverpool-rd
Wilcoxon, H., 44 Goodge-street, Tottenham-court-road
Wyld, E., 44 Marshall-street, Golden-sq, *s.n*
Wyld, J., Charing-cross, *pu*
Wildy & Sons, Carey-st. and 90 Chancery-la, *pu*
Wilkes, J. C., 47 Bridge-street, Southwark
Wilkes, R. S., 16 Craven-street, Strand

Willding, C., 15 Leigh-st, Burton-crescent, *n*
Williams & Norgate (for.) 14 Henrietta-street, Covent-garden
Williams, Ben., 11 Paternoster-row, *m.pu*
Williams, E. L., 19 Conduit-st, Paddington, *s*
Williams, E. P., 5 New Bridge-st, Blackfriars
Williams, S. T., 19 Moorgate-street, City, *s*
Williams, W. J., 1 Cross-court, Drury-lane
Willis, G., Gt. Piazza, Covent-garden, *pr*
Willis, A., 8 Newgate-street, *s*
Willoughby & Co., 22 Warwick-lane, *pu*
Willshire, —, 4 Portsdown-terrace, Kilburn
Wilson, E., 157 Leadenhall-street, *pu.s*
Wilson, E., 11 Royal Exchange, *pu*
Wilson, H., 81 Bermondsey-street, *pu*
Winn, R., 24 Holywell-street, Strand, *pu*
Winn, W., 34 Holywell-street, Strand, *pu*
Witte, D. C., 23 St. John's-road, Hoxton
Wood, J. T., 33 Holywell-street, *pu*
Wood, R. J., 139 Fleet-street, *pu*
Wood, T., 10 Felix-terrace, Islington
Wood, W., 39 Tavistock-street, Covent-garden
Woodley, J. H., 30 Fore-street, City, *s*
Woods, R. E., 20 Cumberland-row, Walworth
Worster, H., 1 James-street, Goswell-road
Wright & Simkin, 29 Newcastle-st, Strand, *pu*
Wright, E., 200 Gt. Dover-street, *l*
Wright, G. R., 60 Pall-mall, *pu*
Wright, H., 9 Stockbridge-terrace, Pimlico
Wright, W., 4 St. George's-road, Southwark
Yapp, W., 4 Old Cavendish-street
Yarranton, E., 16 Compton-street, Soho
Yates, Jas., 105 Goswell-street
Younghusband, J., Eversholt-street, *s.pu*

BOOKBINDERS, &c.

Marked *s*, are also stationers; *b*, booksellers.

Adams, Thos., 14, Little Tower-street
Adlard, Jno., 35 Villiers-street, Strand
Agg, Chas. Jas., 8 Racquet-court & 116 Fleet-st
Agg, Mrs. May, 8 Racquet-court & 116 Fleet-st
Aitken, Fred., 45 Warwick-street, Pimlico
Aked, Jos., 1 Palsgrave-place, Strand
Allen, Ed. G., 12 Tavistock-row, Covent-garden
Allen. Jno., 24 Endell-street, Long-acre
Andrews, Fred., 8 Rochester-row, Westminster
Angell, Francis Wm., 20 Cursitor-street
Anscombe, W. H., Russell-street, Chelsea
Armitage, W., 36 Threadneedle-street
Arnott, W., 39 St. Andrew's-hill, Doctors'-com.
Aston, Jas., 11 Craven-buildings, Drury-lane
Austin, E., 20 Ironmonger-lane, Cheapside
Austing, H. J., 3 Fitchett's-court, Noble-street
Axon, Jno. W., 16 Bartholomew-close
Baker, Miss Ruth, 15 Bath-st, Newgate-st.
Ball, Jas., 23 Lambeth-hill, Upper Thames-st.
Balls, H. J., 66 Albany-street, Regent's-park
Barford, W., 27 Poland-street, Oxford-street
Barker, Chas., 19 Marylebone-street
Barker, Chas., 7 Sydney-alley, Leicester-square
Barrett, W., 21 Portugal-st, Lincoln's-inn-fields
Bartlett, Philip, 2 Mountain-place, City-road
Batchelor & Martin, 107 St. Martin's-lane
Batchelor, Jos., 112 Fetter-lane

Bateman, T., 36 Tottenham-st, Fitzroy-sq.
Baxter, Hector, 49 Bartholomew-close
Beadon, Abraham, 41 Gloucester-st, Queen-sq.
Bedford, Francis, Blue Anchor-yd, Westminster
Beeton & Co., 25 Bouverie-street
Bell, Jas., 21 Lawrence Pountney-lane
Bevan, Chas., & Son, 5 Chapel-place South
Blake, S., 10 Allerton-street, Hoxton
Blumfield, Geo., 22 Well-street, Cripplegate
Bolton, Jas., 27 Graham-street, City-road.
Bones, W., & Son, 76 Fleet-street
Bowden, Jno., 2 Wilson-street, Drury-lane
Broughton, B., 2 Whitmore-place East, Hoxton
Brown, Jas., 20 Sidmouth-street, Gray's-inn-rd
Brown, Jno., 10 Elizabeth-terrace, Islington
Brown, Jos. W., 8 Maude-place, Mile-end.
Brown, Mark, 38 Britannia-st, Gray's-inn-rd.
Brown, Mrs. M., 5 Hoxton-square
Bruce, Thos., 5 Joiner-street, Westminster-rd.
Bryant, Edmund, 5 White Horse-yd, Drury-la.
Bulck, Robt., 7 Lichfield-street, Soho
Bullwinkle, Jos., 41 St. Mary Axe
Burn, Jas. F., 37 & 38 Kirby-street, and 35 Hatton-garden
Bush, Thos., 15 Jewry-street, Aldgate
Callard, Chas., 5 Shepperton-street West
Camp, John, 13 John-street, Spafields
Canham, Jas., 6 King-street, Camden-town
Carpenter, J. & T., 4 Wardrobe-terrace
Cash and Astle, 80 Coleman-street, City
Catmur, H., 98 Bethnal-green
Catmur, J. L., 3 Cherry-tree-ct, Aldersgate-st
Chubb, Thos., Pemberton-row, Gough-square
Clarke, Jno., 61 Frith-street, Soho
Clyde, Jas., 9 Newman-street, Oxford-street
Coe, C. E., 20 Gt. James-street, Bedford-row
Cole, T. W., 5 Walworth-place, Walworth-rd.
Colwell, Geo., 2 Surrey-row, Blackfriars
Cook, H. J., 84 Gray's-inn-lane
Crandal, Jno., 65 Newman-street, Oxford-st.
Crawford, Alex., 16 Peerless-row, City-road
Crawford, J. & A., 18 Peerless-row, City-road
Crews, Mrs. C., 24 Little Queen-st, Holborn
Crisp, J., & Son, 54 Newman-street, Oxford-st
Curtis, Sam., 28 Milton-street, Cripplegate
Dalton, Fred., 14A Bear-yd, Lincoln's-inn-flds
Darley, W., 3 London-terrace, Hackney-road
Davis, J. & Co., 104 Sloane-street
Davis, C. S., 18 Wilderness-row
Davis, Hy., 17 Gresse-st, Tottenham-ct.-road
Davison, Mrs. M., 11 Jewin-cres., Cripplegate
Dawson, T., 44 Devonshire-street, Queen-sqre
Day, Rt., 13 Lower Sloane-street, Chelsea
Dean, A., 35 St. Martin's-st., Leicester-square
Dean, James, 28 Villiers-street, Strand
De Knock, James, 11½ Oxford-mews, Upper Southwick-street, and 11½ Porchester-st., Edgware-road
Donkin, Henry, 17 Newcastle-street, Farringdon-street
Dow, Peter, 5 Brend-street-hill, City
Driscoll, Henry, 12 and 13 St. Clement's-lane
Ducatel, A. J., 18 Cumberland-street, Chelsea
Dunn, Alf., 14 Chandos-street, Covent-garden
Dunn, Alf., 5 Heathcock-court, 414 Strand

Edgeler, W., 7 Houghton-street, Clare-market
Eedy, Bennett, 37 Tavistock-st., Covent-gardn
Eeles, T. R., & Son, 16 and 22 Cursitor-street
Egleton, T. S., & Son, 169 Fleet-street
Egleton, A., 17 Queen-street, Clerkenwell
Ellison, William, 17 Ave Maria-lane, City
Embery, H., 19 New-st., Cloth-fair, Smithfield
Ewing, M., 3 Playhouse-yard, Blackfriars
Fellowes, W., 4 Amen-corner, Paternoster-row
Field, Edw., 15 Francis-street, Newington
Finch, William, 8 Pearson-street, Kingsland-rd
Fisher, Thos, 19 Hanway-street, Oxford-street
Fletcher, Joseph, 55 Red Cross-st:, Cripplegate
Flude, J. W., 2 Postern-row, Tower-hill
Ford, Mrs. M. A., 60 Wood-st., Cheapside
Foster, Chas. 16 Lit. Northmpn.-st.Clerkenwell
Fraser, James, 5 Castle-street, Long-acre
Furber, A. F., 19 Woburn-buildings
Gale, Henry, 34 Upper Park-street, Islington
Gardner, Edw., 45 Paddington-street
Gibbs James, 8 Gt. Newport-street, Long-acre
Gibson G. 1A Duke's-row, New-road
Gillard, William, 14 Kirby-street, Hatton-grdn
Glaisher G, sen. 23 Nassau-street, Middlssex
    Hospital
Goodwin, Ed., J, 15 Shoe-lane
Gosby, E. G., 41 George-street, Blackfriars
Gosnell, Wm., 21 Rathbone-place. Oxford-st
Gyde, Chas., 7½ Red Lion-court, Fleet-street
Haggis, Geo., 20 Cursitor-street, Chancery-la
Haggis, Wm., White Horse-yard, Fetter-lane
Hammond E., 3 Gt. Dover-street, Borough
Hart H. & Rt., 45 Crimscott-street, Bermondsey
Hatton & Griesbach, 99 Chancery-lane
Hatton, Adol. F., 24 Gt New-street, Fetter-la
Hayday, J., 31 Little Queen-street, Holborn
Herbert, C., 21 Churton-st., Vauxhall-br.-rd
Hipkins & Spon, 16 Bucklersbury
Hipkins, J., 6 Sidney-st., Commercial-rd East
Hogg, Sam., 27 Pancras-pl., Old St. Pancras-rd
Holland, George, 114 Chancery-lane
Holland, Joseph, 5 Bull & Mouth-street
Holmes, H. G., 1 New-inn-buildings, Wych-st
Holmes, Wm., 11 Bowling-green-buildings, s
Hone, Frederic, 100 Goswell-road
Honeyman, J. N., 27 Gt. Queen-street
Hood, J. H., 25 Red Lion-square, Holborn
Howe, John, 7 Upper Marylebone-st
Hunt, Henry, 24 Cullum-street
Hunter, Mrs. S., 178 High Holborn
Hyett, Alf., 11 Pearl-cres., Bagnigge-wells-rd
Inman, T. J., 12 Essex-pl., Mare-st., Hackney
Isacke, Wm., 18 Sherborne-lane, City
Jackson, Mrs. Maria, 42 Park-street, City-road,
    and 42 Gt. Chart-street, Hoxton
James, P. J., 15, Kirby-street, Hatton-garden
Jefferies, A. T., 5 Angel-court, Skinner-street
Jeffrey, John, 61 Charlotte-street, Portland-pl
Jenks, John, 14 Angel-court, Strand
Johnson, W., 13 Leicester-street, Regent-st
Jones, Jesse, 33 Cambridge-road, Mile-end
Kaines, G. F., 8 Wellclose-sq., St. George's Ea
Kaines, J., 20 New-road, St. George's East
Kelly & Sons, 7 Water-street, Strand
Kelly, John, 15 Gower-place, Euston-square

Key & Whiting, 7 and 8 Oxford Arms-passage,
    Warwick-lane
Keynton, John, 8 Regent-street, City-road
King, Robt. W., 32 Bartholomew-close
Kitcat, George & James, 50 Hatton-garden
Knapp, G. J., 10 Green-street, Blackfriars-rd
Knibb, Francis, 30 Kirby-street, Hatton-gardn
Lake, James, 9 Blackfriars-road
Lamboll, H. 17 Cloth-fair, West Smithfield
Land, John, 2 West-street, Walworth-road
Larkin, R. W., 40 Newman-street, Oxford-st
Lea, Thos., 23 Clarendon-street, Somers-town
Leighton, J. & J., 40 Brewer-st., Golden-sq., b
Leighton, Son, & Hodge, 13 Shoe-lane, and
    Harp-alley, Farringdon-street
Lewes, Henry, 33 Ranelagh-street, Pimlico
Lewis, J., & Sons, 9 Gough-square, Fleet-st
Lewis, Chris., 54 South Molton-street
Lewis W., 1 and 2 St. John's-court, St. Mar-
    tin's-le-grand
Liddon, J., & Son, 64 Bartholomew-close
Linden, G., 11 Easton-street, Clerkenwell
Lloyd, Wm., New-yard, Gt. Queen-street
Loader, J. T., 90½ Holborn Hill
Lock, Wm., 117 Borough-road, Southwark, s
Logan, R. 4 Providence-bldngs., New Kent-rd
Loring, J., 28 Clift-street, New North-rd, s
Low, John, 4 Chichester-rents, Chancery-lane
Lys M., 22 Little Trinity-lane, City
M'Culloch, John, 14 Bride-lane, Fleet-street
M'Farlane, John Y., & And. G. 10 Old Bailey
M'Murray, W., 2 Lillypott-lane, Noble-street
Mabbott, Matthews, & Co., 28 East-passage,
    Cloth-fair. b
Macefield, John, 26 Myrtle-street, Hoxton
Macefield, 72 Myddelton-street, Clerkenwell
Macomie, Brothers, 6 Percy-st., Bedford-sq
Mann, C., 4 Little Titchfield-street, Great
    Portland-street
Mansell, George, 67 & 68 King-street, Boro
Marrable, John, 21 Castle-street, Finsbury
Martin, D. W., 1 Prujean-square, Old Bailey,
    and 6 Charlton-place, Islington
Martin, George, 80 Shoe-lane, Holborn
Martin, P. T., 44 Clarendon-square, Somers-tn
Martin, Robert, 7 Princes-street, Barbican
Martin, Thomas, 14 Fetter-lane, Fleet-street
Maskell, Edward, 10 Denmark-ter, Islington, s
Mason, Wm. A., 6 Holywell-street, Strand
Massey, H., 103 Park-street, Grosvenor-square
Maton, C., 53 Myddelton-street, Clerkenwell
Miller, Peter, 14 Poland-street, Oxford-street
Moreham, E. P., 5 Bartholomew-close
Morley, J., 61 Walnut-tree-walk, Lambeth
Morris, Robt. B., Broadway, Camberwell-green
Morrison, Thos., 24 New-street, Brompton
Murray & Stainesby, 179 Sloane-street, b
Murray, F., 24 Gt. Warner-st, Clerkenwell
Napper, Henry, 13 Everett-st, Russell-square
Napper, Wm., 43 Castle-street, Holborn
Nevett, J., 1 Johnson's-court, Fleet-street
Newman, Benj., 13 Oxford-street, Whitechapel
Newton, Freeman, 90 Leadenhall-street
Norman, Mrs. A. (executors of) Leigh-place,
    Brooke's-market, Holborn

Nutt, W., 12 Craven-buildings, Drury-lane
Oldfield, A., 17 Devonshire-street, Bloomsbury
Oliver, Geo., 43 Windsor-terrace, City-road
Orrin, Joseph, 26 Marian-square, Hackney, and 26 Sekforde-street, Clerkenwell
Orriss, Eben., 1 Gt. Sutton-street, Clerkenwell
Orton, John, 1½ St. Mary Axe, Aldgate
Paine, Wm., 17 Ranelagh-grove, Pimlico
Palmer, Enoch, 313 Strand
Palmer, Henry, 14 Gloucester-st, Hoxton
Palmer, T. D., 5 Gt. Chesterfield-st, Marylebone
Parkins, John, 2 Church-st, Westminster, s
Pasmore, W., 17 Manor-place, Walworth-road
Payne, J. T., 31 Tabernacle-walk, Finsbury
Pearman, W., 4 Lincoln-st, King's-rd, Chelsea
Peck, Thos., 52 Hoxton-square
Peck, T. A. S., 8 Warwick-square, Newgate-st
Peirson, Robt., 23 Gt. Winchester-street
Perraton, W., 28 Kirby-street, Hatton-garden
Phillips, Thos., 12 Plumber-st, City-road
Piper, H., 6 King's-place, Commercial-road East, and 51 Shadwell High-street
Pittard, J., 15 Little New-street, Shoe-lane
Pocock, J., 102 Brunswick-st, Hackney-road
Polworth, R., 8 Queen's-row, Pimlico-road
Ponder, Alfred, 9 Somerset-place, Hoxton
Pool, Joseph, 26 Bartholomew-close
Pope, James, 12 Church-street, Hackney, s
Potter, T. J., 60 Tabernacle-walk, Finsbury
Power, W., 66 Drury-lane, Holborn
Pownceby, J., 277 Whitechapel-road, b
Price, James, 21 Chiswell-street, Finsbury
Proudfoot, T., 73 George-street, Euston-square
Pymm, George, 32 Villiers-street, Strand
Pymm, Mrs. S., 14 Upper Crown-st, Westm
Quick, E. J., 5 Howard's-pl, Northampton-rd
Quitstorf, G., 25½ Bouverie-street, Fleet-street
Raines, T., 24 Gt. Ormond-st, Queen's-square
Ravenscroft, W., 4 Up. James-st, Golden-sq
Ray, Stewart, 43 Duke-street, St. James's
Reffell, H. H., 14 Gt. Portland-street, b
Reynolds, W., 6 Eldon-street, Moorfields
Riach, James, 47 St. George's-rd, Southwark, b
Richards Wm. 6 High-street, Newington
Richmond G. 17 Skinner-street, Snow-hill
Riley Mrs. A. 27 Bennett-street, Stamford-st
Riley Chas. 5 Queen's-head-passage, Newgate-st
Riley G. 18 Warwick-square, Newgate-street
Riviere R. 28 Great Queen-street, Lincoln's-inn-fields
Rogers G. 1 Obelisk-buildings, Waterloo-road
Rowbotham Joseph, 70 Castle-street East, and 13 Berner's-mews, Oxford-street
Royle, John, 2 Blandford-st, Manchester-sq
Rumfitt J. W. 33 Castle-street, Leicester-sq
Russell, E. 10 Brownlow-street, Holborn
Sallis W. 5 Cross Key-square, Little Britain
Sanders J. 2 Ivy-lane, Paternoster-row
Sangster G. 2 Ball-court, Giltspur-street
Sapford N. 17 Kirby-street, Hatton-garden
Saunders Brothers, 106 London-wall, s
Sauze James, 47 Aldermanbury
Serjeant Mrs. H. 11 Staining-lane, City
Shapcott Alex. 54 Rathbone-place, s
Sharp & Hale, 4 Berkeley-square, Piccadilly

Shaw, John, 21 Bouverie-st, Fleet-street
Shaw, Stephen, 22 Old Boswell-ct, Strand
Silani, F., 23 Villiers-street, Strand
Simmons & Sons, 18 White Conduit-street
Simpson, G., 25 Bread-st.-hill, Cheapside
Sizer, Huntley, 19 Frith-street, Soho
Slate, Thomas E., 103 Hatton-garden
Smith & Collings, 5 & 19 Ivy-lane, Paternoster-row
Smith, John, and Co., 52 Long-acre, s
Smith, Mrs. T., 22 Pembroke-place, Vauxhall-bridge-road
Smith, W., 15 St. John's-lane, West Smithfield, and 47 Borough-road
Smith, William, 2 Skinner's-pl, Sise-lane
Soul, Eli, 26 Tabernacle-walk, Finsbury
Soul, Matthew, 80 Nichols-sq, Hackney-rd.
Soulsby and Regan, New-yard, Lincoln's-inn-fields
Spencer, Robert and Son, 16 Bridgewater-sq, and 10½ Bridgewater-gardens, Barbican
Stagg, R., 37 Devonshire-street, Queen-square
Stanley, Mrs. E., 11A Carburton-st, Portland-road
Stephenson, J., 37 Nichols-sq, Hackney-road
Strahan, Mrs. A., Castle-street East, Oxford-st.
Strahan, A. H., 29 Thomas-st, Stamford-st.
Strahan, D. N., 10 Winsley-street, Oxford-st, s
Straker, Mrs. Ann, 35, Monkwell-street, City
Stratford, W., 9 Hampstead-st, Fitzroy-sq.
Suttley, J., 4 Cross-street North, and New-st, Bermondsey
Symmons, E., 31 Bouverie-street, Fleet-street
Tammadge, H., 6 & 7 Margaret-st, Clerkenwell
Taylor, Charles, 37 Coldbath-square
Taylor, Mrs. S., 6 Warwick-sq, Newgate-st.
Tepper, J., 46 Southampton-buildings, Holborn
Tesseyman, Charles, 5 Broad-court, Bow-st.
Thoms, William, 8 Bache's-terrace, City-road
Thorburn, John, 3 Pleydell-street, Fleet-street
Thorn, R. T., 59 Basinghall-street, City
Todd, W., 9 Gray's Inn-terr, Gray's-inn-lane
Tree, William, 198 Blackfriar's-road
Trender, J. & J., 16½ Redcross-street, Barbican, and 23 Well-street, Jewin-street
Trickett, George T., 67a Hatfield-street
Tucker, Mrs. M. A., 7 Little Warner-street, Clerkenwell
Tuckett, Chas., 66 Gt. Russell-st, Bloomsbury
Turner, S., 2 Devonshire-street, Bishopsgate
Upfold, William. 43 Buttesland-street, Hoxton
Usher, H., 13 Acton-street, Gray's-Inn-road
Valentine, J. S., 42 Baldwin's-gardens
Walker, John, 15 William-street, Waterloo-rd
Wallwork, J. J., 42 Great Marlborough-street
Warwick, Mrs. S., 1 Rolls'-buildings, Fetter-la
Watkins, F. W., Paradise-row, Gravel-lane
Watkinson, G. W., 7 Southampton-buildings
Watson, John, 13 Ryder's-court, Leicester-sq.
Weemys, E. & Co., 1 Long-lane, Smithfield
Welch, T., 33 Gloucester-st, St. John's-st-rd
West, Mrs. Ann Frances, 52 Hatton-garden
West, Benjamin, St. James's-walk, Clerkenwell-green
Westley, W., 8 Warwick-square, Newgate-street

Westleys & Co., Friar-st, Doctors'-commons
White, Mrs. L., 13a Silver-street, Kensington
Whyte, A., 13 Blue Cross-street, Leicester-sq
Wickwar, John, 6 Poland-street, Oxford-street
Wighton, William A., 17 Lower Eaton-street, Pimlico
Williams, William, 1 Duchy-street, Strand
Wilson, W. & H., 19 Foley-place, Great Portland-street
Wilson, Joseph, 2 Eliza-place, Sadler's-wells
Wilson, W. J., 5 Gloucester-terrace, Mile-end
Wilton, Brothers, 6a Bream's-buildings, and 5 Symond's-Inn, Chancery-lane
Wingrove, D., 44 Commercial-road, Lambeth
Wolter, William, 54 Drury-lane
Wood, F., 2 Windmill-road, Kennington
Woolnough, C., 6 Bateman's-row, Shoreditch
Woolnough, C. 7, Upper James-st, Golden-sq
Woolnough, J. A., 4 Charles-st, Hackney-road
Worthington, T., 3 Mayfield-place, Kensington
Wright, John, 14, 15 & 16 Noel-street, Soho
Wright, Josh., 2 Newcastle-place, Clerkenwell
Zachnsdorf, Joseph, 90 Drury-lane

Bookbinders' Cloth Manufacturers.

Eadie, A. H., 53 Great Queen-st, Lincoln's Inn
Healey & Co., 9 Queenhithe
Houghton, John, Lamb's-passage, Chiswell-st.
Law, W. and Son, 37 Monkwell-st, Falcon-sq, and Suffolk-place, Snow's-fields, Bmndsy.
Ruding, Rogers, 51 Bunhill-row, St. Luke's
Wilson, James L., 13 New Ivy-street, Hoxton, Mansfield-st, Borough, and 128 St. John-street, West Smithfield

Bookbinders' Knife and Tool Makers.

Allen, James and George, 2 and 3 Coal-yard, Drury-lane
Allen, Thomas, 25 New-st, West Smithfield
Bookbinders' Material Dealers.

Eadie, Alex. H., 53 Great Queen-street, Lincoln's Inn
Harley, John, 5, Raquet-court, Fleet-street

Bookbinders' Press Manufacturers.

Hampson, W., 47 Old Bailey
Hill, John, 25 Gee-street, Goswell-road
Hopkinson & Cope, 14 New North-st, Finsbury
Mathews, Wm., 59 Coppice-row, Clerkenwell
Meager, George, 6 Great St. Andrew-street

Bookbinders' Tool Cutters.

Allen, T., 25 New-street, West Smithfield
Balle and Surrey, 9 Wine-office-court
Beard, F., 20 Exmouth-street, Clerkenwell
Carpenter, Wm., 70 Shoe-lane, Fleet-street
Eadie, Alex. Hart, 53 Great Queen-street
Edwards, Robert, 49, Old Bailey
Frances, John, 19 Phœnix-street, Soho
Francis, J. H., 51 Myddleton-st, Clerkenwell
Garton, Charles, 80 Newgate-street
Gooding and Bayman, 11 Lovell's-court, and 20, Paternoster-row
Hampson, W., 47 Old Bailey
Harley, John, 5 Raquet-court, Fleet-street
Hoare, Daniel W. M., 25a Hatton-garden

Hubbard & Dawe, 6 Red Lion-court, Fleet-st
Johns, W. C., 36 Hatton-garden
Knights, Henry H., 11 Shoe-lane, Fleet-street
Marchant, W., Cromwel-lane, Old Brompton
Morris & Son, 15 Cross-street, Hatton-garden
Morris, Joseph, 35 Ludgate-street
Royle, George, 20 Ivy-lane, Newgate-street
Staples, Thomas, 30 Castle-street, Holborn
Timbury, F., 104 Fetter-lane, Holborn; and 44 Paternoster-row

Book Clasp Makers.

Beavitt, Henry, 20 John-street, Tottenham-court-road
Biddle, John, 11 Queen-street, City
Bull, Charles, 5 New-court. Farringdon-street
Burtt, T., & Sons, 45 Northampton-street, Clerkenwell
Curtis, C., 48 Clerkenwell-close
Dace, W., 126 St. John-street, Clerkenwell
Dickens, Charles, 7 New-street, Cloth-fair
Downes, Robert, 53 Paternoster-row
Ford, James, 6 Monkwell-street, Falcon-square
Guy, T. J., 4 Harp-alley, Farringdon-street
Pike, Mrs. A., 8 Oxford Arms-passage, Warwick-lane
Powell, William, 10 Bolt-court, Fleet-street
Roue, G., 17 Dean-street, Fetter-lane
Tonkinson, J., 16, St. John-street, Clerkenwell

Book Edge Gilders and Marblers.

Bartholomew J. 21 Red Lion-st, Clerkenwell
Connery G. 3 Paul's-head-court, Fenchurch-st
Corfield J. W. 44 Kirby-street, Hatton-garden
Dollman T. F. 29 Charles-st. Hatton-garden
Gwynn John, 3 Litchfield-street, Soho
Hall James, 46 Barbican, City
Harley John, 5 Raquet-court, Fleet-street
Hobbs A. 3 Bell's-buildings, Fleet-street
Leighton A. & Son (*blockers*) 4 Lower Ashby-street, Clerkenwell

CARD AND CARDBOARD MAKERS, ETC. ETC.

Bancks (Bros.) A.&R.C. (playing) 20 Piccadilly
Bishop and Blundell (pasteboard) 1 Old Fish-street-hill, and 52 Little Britain
De la Rue, Thos. & Co. (play.) 109 Bunhill-row
Goodall, Chas., & Son, 12, Great College-street, Camden-town, and 30 Gt. Pulteney-street
Goodall, Jonat. C., 50 King-st. Camden-town
Heard, J. G., 145 Upper Whitecross-street
Norris, Joseph, & Co., 32 Bartholomew-close
Padbury, James, 5 Surrey-row, Blackfriars-rd.
Palser, Samuel, 10 Richard-st. Cornwall-road
Parrott, W., 9 Banner-street, Saint Luke's
Penn, T., & Co., 6 Bride-court, New Bridge-st.
Penny, Hy., 11 Old Bailey
Pope, Hy., 22 Budge-row
Reynolds, J., & Sons (playing, paste and drawing board) Vere-street, Clare-market
Roberts, Wm., 8 Turnagain-lane, Farringdon-st.
Rock, Brothers, & Payne (drawing, wholesale) 11 Wallbrook

Royston, Jas., & Co. (draw.) 9 Aldermanbury
Sheldrake, Hy. W., 8 Gt. Arthur-st. Goswell-st.
Taylor, Jas., 11 John's-row, St. Luke's
Taylor, Jno. (paste) 83 & 84 Old-st. St. Luke's
Treverton, Jno. H., 36 Hoxton-square, and
    Hoxton Old Town
Turnbull, J.L.&J. (playing, glossers, paste, &c.)
    Holywell-mount
Wheeler, H., sen. (paste) 14 Coppice-ro. Clerk.
Whiffin and Kirby, 486 Oxford-street
Whittaker, Robert (playing) Little Britain
Windsor, Jno., 23 Coppice-row
Woolley and Co. (playing, drawing, and paste)
    210 High Holborn

ENGRAVERS ON WOOD.

Adeney, T. S., 13 Millman-street, Bedford-row
Bennett, W., 16 Lavinia-grove, Caledonian-rd.
Bolton, T., 14 St. Augustin-rd. Camden-town
Bonner, G. F., 1 Bennett's-hill, Doctors'-com.
Brewer, W. H., 14 Red-lion-court, Fleet-street
Cleghorn, J., 4 Charlton-place, Islington
Cooper, Jas., 26 Great James-st. Bedford-row
Cunningham, J. 108 Dorset-street, Fleet-street
Davies, F. P., 162 Fleet-street
Delamotte, F., 7 Orange-street, Bloomsbury
Dodd, D. G., 53 Skinner-street, Snow-hill
Dorrington, G., 4 Ampton-st. Gray's-inn-road
Downes, E., 2 Walnut-tree-walk, Lambeth
Earle, W. E., 7, Regent-street, Lambeth-walk
Evans, G., 42 Acton-street, Gray's-inn-road
Fowler, T., 51 Exmouth-street, Clerkenwell
Gilks, Thomas, 170 Fleet-street
Gooding, Jos., 8 Elizabeth-terr. Liverpool-road
Greatbach, W., 2 Crescent-pl. Mornington-cres.
Greenaway, J., 4 Wine Office-court, Fleet-st.
Gyde, F., 7½ Red-lion-court, Fleet-street
Hart, R., 15 Gloucester-street, Bloomsbury
Hare & Co., 31 Essex-street, Strand
Hind, R., 13 Brewer-street, Goswell-road
Izod, T. G. & Co., 12A Gough-square
Jackson, M., 12 Cardington-st. Hampstead-rd.
Jenkins, P. F. L., 17 Eaton-street, Grosv.-sq.
Johnston, James, 36 Old Broad-street
Joyce, Thos., 6 Well-street, Cripplegate
Joyce, W., 11 Bolt-court, Fleet-street
Kelly, L., 15 Nicholas-square, Hackney-road
Knight, Jno., 7, Clerkenwell-close
Landells, Eben. Water-street, Strand, and 12
    Holford-square, Pentonville
Lee, Jas., 39 Princes-square, Kennington-road
Leighton, Hy., 40 Brewer-street, Golden-square
Loudan, R., 28 Ludgate-hill
Martin and Lundie, 100 Long-acre
Mason, A. J., 46 Argyle-square, New-road
Mason, H. C., 53 Exmouth-street, Clerkenwell
Measom, G. S., 74 Charrington-st. Oakley-sq.
Measom, W., 46 Liverpool-street, King's-cross
Nicholls, G. & J., 54 Paternoster-row
Pearson, G., 32 Stanhope-st. Hampstead-road
Quick, W. K., 42 St. John-square, Clerkenwell
Salmon, Henry, 2 Racquet-court, Fleet-st
Saunders, W. T., 24 Little Queen-st, Holborn
Seabrook, Thomas, 31 Bouverie-street
Sears, M. U., 5, Bride-court, Fleet-street

Sheeres, C. W., 14 Up. Barnsbury-st, Islington
Sheldrick, B., 11 Strahan-place, Ball's-pond
Slader, A. G., 126 Chancery-lane
Slader, S. V., 126 Chancery-lane
Smith, H. O. & C., 85 Hatton-garden
Smith, H. N., 69 Coleman-street West
Spon, F., Clarehall-row, Stepney-green
Starling, A., 36 Halliford-st, Islington
Swain and Armstong, 58 Fleet-street
Thomas, W., 17 Essex-street, Strand
Utting, R. B., 34 College-st. North, Camden-tn.
Wall, John P., 154 Strand
Whimper, E., 11 Lovell's-ct, Paternoster-row
Whimper, J., 20 Canterbury-pl, Lambeth-rd.
Whitaker, W. E., 262 Strand
Williams, E. M., 144 Fleet-street
Williams, T., 15 Wine-office-court, Fleet-st.
Withy, T., 8 Thanet-place, Temple-bar
Woods, H. N., 8 John-street, Adelphi
Wragg, G., 38 Ludgate-hill
Wragg, T. D., 17 Glasgow-terrace, Pimlico

EMBOSSERS.

Betts, B., 16 Gt. Pulteney-st, Golden-square
Braun & Wustlich, 2 Bury-ct, St. Mary Axe
Canton, Robert, 49 Watling-street, City
Davidson, S., 2 Claremont-terrace, Pentonville
Dove, E., 6 Fountain-place, City-road
Edmonds & Remnant, 8 to 12 Lovell's-court
Hands, W., 13 Tenter-street, Little Moorfields
Hardy, John, 5 Coburg-street, Clerkenwell
Hudson, G., 44 Goswell-street
Kronheim, J. M., & Co., 64 & 65 Shoe-lane
Layton, T. M., 3, Wilson-st, Drury-lane
Leighton, A., & Son, 3 & 4 Lower Ashby-st.
Newport, E., 13 Up. Ashby-st, Goswell-rd.
Pannell, R., 8 Brewer-st, Goswell-road
Parker, A., 303 Strand
Pelham, T. K., 86 Bridge-street, Southwark
Penny, John, 37 Union-st, Middlesex Hospital
Powell, E. & W. 10 Wilson-street, Finsbury
Purnell, G. 7 Hart-street, Cripplegate
Seagrave, J. 1 George-yd, Crown-st, Soho
Smith, L. D. 1 Little Knightrider-st, St. Paul's
Stupart, W. H. 40 Castle-street, Oxford-street
Sumfield & Jones, 6, King's Head-ct, Holborn
Summers, P. 12 Tabernacle-walk, Finsbury
Titterton, C. 89 Blackfriars-road
Todman, W. G. 42 Newgate-street

INK-MAKERS (PRINTING).

Baylis, H. F. & Co., Montague-st, Whitechapel
Blackwell & Farnell, 14 King-street, Chelsea
Brook, Jas. 21 Tottenham-rd, Kingsland
Clarke, Benj. 41 Kirby-street, Hatton-garden
Clunes, Wm. & Co. 274 Strand
Dane & Hemingway, 20 Bouverie-street
Field, George, & Co. 14 Red Lion-ct, Fleet-st
Gorringe, Richard, 1, Parkfield-st, Islington
Governor & Co. New North-road
Hodson, Harry, and Co. Dowgate-hill
Houssart, Richard V. 29, Dunston-street
Lawson, L. and Co. 1 Bouverie-street; J. R.
    Palmer, *Agent*
Morrell, Henry, 149, Fleet-street

Parsons, Fletcher, & Co. 22 Bread-st, City
Roper, Charles A., Danvers-street, Chelsea
Shackell & Edwards, 35 Coppice-row
Smith, Benjamin, 7 Wine-office-court
Stanbury, Geo. 20 Gt. New-st, Fetter-lane
Ward, Enoch W. & Co. 7 East Harding-st
Winstone, Benjamin, & Co. 100 Shoe-lane

Ink Makers, Writing, &c.

Amelang, L., 54 Red Lion-street, Clerkenwell
Anderson, And., George & Co., Plummers-row, Whitechapel
Arnold, P. & J., 135 Aldersgate-street
Baldwin, Henry, 13 Orange-street, Gravel-lane
Blackwood, John, & Co., Banbury-ct., Long Acre
Bousfield, Chas. 6 Whitefriars-street, Fleet-st
Brown, John, & Co., 96 Farringdon-street
Cleghorn, Robert, Weavers-lane, Tooley-street
Cooper, David, & Co., Shoe-lane
Finnemore, W. E., Euston-square
Franks, John W., 7 Printing-house-square
Fry, Joseph, 19 Cannon-street West
Glover, George, & Co., 19 Goodge-street, Tottenham-court-road
Hawthorne, James, 77 Charrington-street
Hill, R. & John, 2 Three Colt-st., Old Ford
Hoe, William, 18 Bishopsgate-street, Within
Hynam, John, Princes-square, Finsbury
Gerram, George T., 69 Hatton-garden
Jones, Stephen, & Brothers, Talbot-court, Gracechurch-street
Kent John, & Co. 21 Staple-st. Bermondsey
Letchford Robert & Co. Old Montague street
Mackley Thos. C. 7 New-inn-yard, Shoreditch
May Joseph, London-wall
Maynard John, 11 Bread-street-hill
Mordan Fras. 13 Frederick-place, Goswell-rd
Morrell Henry, 149 Fleet-street
Porteus Chas. 28 St. John's-street, Clerkenwell
Smith Clarke, Cross-street, Islington
Stephen Henry, 54 Stamford-street
Tate William B. 47 Seward-street
Taylor, Swan, & Co. 49 High-street, Borough
Temple William, Artillery-street, Bishopsgate
Truscott Henry, 16 Sussex-place, Old Kent-rd
Twelvetrees, Brothers, Holland-st., Blackfriars
Warren, Russell, 30 Strand
Watts G. F. 17 Strand
Willy William, 42 Princes-square, George-st
Wood, Wood, & Co. Neckinger-road

LITHOGRAPHERS.

See also ENGRAVERS ; *also* PRINTERS.

Marked *p*, are also printers ; *c*, copper-plate printers.

Abbott F. 17 River-street, Islington
Allen M. 18 Jewin-crescent, Cripplegate
Allen W. Thos. 31 Great Bush-lane,
Ambrose E. 1 Little Queen-street, Holborn
Aresti Joseph, 61 Greek-street, Soho
Ashbee & Dangerfield, 22 Bedford-st, Covent-garden, *p*
Banks J. H. 4 Little Queen-street, *p*

Basébé W. 2 Mayfield-place, Kensington, *c*
Basire James, 7 Princes-street, Holborn
Bedford Fras. 23 Rochester-road, Camden-rd.
Bewick W. E. 6 Oxford-court, Cannon-st. City
Black George B. 392 Strand
Bowler Robert E., 392 Strand
Bowles Jas. 274 Whitechapel-road, *c.p*
Brooks Vincent, 40 King-street, Covent-garden
Brown H. 67 Pearson-street, Kingsland-road
Buckle George, 15 London-wall, *c*
Burgess W. 25 Hart-street, Bloomsbury
Butler W. 30 King-street, Bloomsbury
Canton Robert, 49 Watling-street, *p*
Carter & Bromley, 23 Royal Exchange
Cartwright R. & F. W. 57 Chancery-lane, and 1 Warwick-place, Bedford-row
Cartwright R. jun. 2 Newman's-row, Lincoln's-inn
Cauldwell Jas. 30 Nichols-square, Hackney
Cawley, Drew & Reynalds, 90 Fore-street, City, and Little Moorfields, *p*
Chabot Chas. 9A Skinner-street, Snow-hill
Chambers & Sons, 55 Coleman-street
Chapé A. 99 Guilford-street, Russell-square, *p*
Cheffins C. F. 6 Castle-street, 9 & 11 Southampton-buildings, Holborn, and 24 Gt. George-street, Westminster
Clark Jno. 72 Gt. Bland-street, Dover-road, *c*
Coghlan Cornelius. 36 Basinghall-street
Collins H. H. & Co. 11 Gt. Winchester-street
Coon Martin, 15 Cheapside, City, *p*
Cooper Thomas, 162 Fleet-street
Cornish W. 63 Bartholomew-close
Cotterell F. 45 Nelson-square, Blackfriars-rd.
Culliford C. J. 22 Southampton-street, Strand
Davies B. R. 16 George-street, Euston-square
Davis, Chas. 31 Great Bush-lane, Cannon-st.
Davis Isaac, 25 Berwick-street, Soho
Day & Son, 17 Gate-street, Lincoln's-inn-fields
De Prez & Co. 3 Pancras-lane, Cheapside
Deulin Michel, 183 High Holborn
Deutsch & Co. 42 Upper Stamford-street
Dixon F. 13 Richmond-buildings, Soho, and 7 Poland-street, St. James's
Dodds Thomas Joseph, and Co. 4 Horseshoe-court, Ludgate-hill, *p*
Dolby Edwin T. 5 Stratford-place, Camden-tn.
Dower J. 6 Cumming-place, Pentonville-hill
Drew Fred. 1 Monkwell-street, Falcon-square
Dunkerly Henry, 5 Yardley-street, Clerkenwell
Farrow J. T. 32 Pudding-lane, Eastcheap, *p*
Ford and West, 54 Hatton-garden, Holborn
Francis William, 12 Gray's-inn-terrace, Gray's-inn-lane
Fuggle Charles, 10 St. John-square, Clerkenwell
Gardner John, and Co. 158 Fleet-street
Gavelle John, 35 Vere-street, Clare-market, *c*
George Benjamin, 47 Hatton-garden, Holborn
Giles John W. 9 Russell-terrace, Oakley-square
Gold G. 15 Gray's-inn-square, and 35 King-street, Westminster, *p*
Graf, Chas. Aldine-chambers, 13 Paternoster-row
Grant and Allen, 74 Newgate-street, and Bull Head-court
Groom R. S. & Co. 44 Paternoster-row, *p*

6

Hale John R. 6 Tavistock-row, Covent-garden, and 49A Lincoln's-inn-fields
Hall Henry J. 43 South Molton-street
Hancock Humphrey, 55 Aldermanbury, *p*
Hanhart M. and M. 64 Upper Charlotte-street, Fitzroy-square
Hardy C. and Co. 32 Castle-street, Holborn, *p*
Hardy Joseph, 190½ High Holborn
Hobday Alfred, 14 Red Cross-sq, Jewin-st, *p*
Houston Robt. 1 Skinner-street, Snow-hill
Howard G. 41 Luard-st, Caledonian-road, *p*
Huetson J. 8 Wine-office-court, Fleet-street
Hullmandel & Walton, 51 Gt. Marlborough-st
Hunt, Heine, and Co. 8 & 9 Weymouth-street, New Kent-road
Hunter R. J. 3 James-terrace, New North-rd
Hurst W. 48 Bedford-row, Holborn
Izod T. G. and Co. 12A Gough-square
James Peter & T. B. 97 Newgate-street, City, *p*
James George A. 113 Fleet-street, *c.p*
Jerrard Paul, 111 Fleet-street, City
Johnson and Bessent, 2 Tudor-place
Johnson John M. 10 Castle-street, Holborn, *p*
Johnson T. J. 3 East-street, Red Lion-square
Johnson, Grieve & Co, 100 Southwark-br-rd
Kellow Chas, 25A Hatton-garden, Holborn
King John, 63 Queen-street, Cheapside, *p*
Kirchhoff D. Grafton-st East, Tottenham-ct-rd
Lane John, 118 Chancery-lane
La Riviere A. 22 Paternoster-row, and 18 Clifton-street, Finsbury
Lascelles H. 12 Tavistock-pl. Tavistock-sq.
Laughton Wm. 6 Dyer's-buildings, Holborn
L'Enfant J. A. 18 Rathbone-place, *p*
Le Blond R. and Co. 24 Budge-rw. and 4 Walbrook, *p*
Lee George L. 245 High Holborn
Lee Lawrence, 498 Oxford-street
Leighton Brothers, 4 Red Lion-sq. Holborn
Lewis M. A. & Co. (*chr.*) 16 Camomile-st. *p*
Lingham S. 15 Cross-st. Hatton-garden, and 26 Caroline-place, Islington.
Louis Joseph, 1 St. Swithin's lane
Lovett, Wm. M. 17 and 18 Queen-st. City, *c.p*
Luntley J. and Co. 3 New Broad-st. ct. *p*
Lynch J. H. 29 Gloucester-pl. Camden tn.
M'Arthur Geo. 25½ and 26 Bouverie-street, *p*
M'Lean Thomas, 70 St. Martin's-lane, *p*
Maclure, Macdonald, and Macgregor, 37 Walbrook, Mansion-house
Macquarie J. 53 Clarendon-street, Somers-tn.
Madeley G. E. 3 Wellington-street, Strand
Maguire H. C. 98 Gt. Russell-st. Bloomsbury
Malby T. & Sons, 37 Parker-st. Drury-lane, *c.p*
Martin and Hood, 8 Gt. Newport-street
Martin and Lundie, 100 Long-acre
Merriman A. 15 Ashford-street, Hoxton
Merritt and Hatcher, 43 Cornhill
Metcalfe J. J. 3 Grocers'-hall-court, City, *p*
Metchim and Burt, 55 Parliament-street
Metchim William P. 20 Parliament-street
Mitchell R. 20 Mary-street, Hampstead-road
Moody Charles, 257 High Holborn
Morris Joseph, 35 Ludgate-street
Mourilyan and Casey, 4 Grane-court, Fleet-st

Murrell Wm. H. 24 Dowgate-hill, and 9 Philpot-lane, *p*
Murrill Edwin, 27 Noble-street, City
Netherclift and Durlacher, 18 Brewer-street Golden-square, *p*
Netherclift Joseph sen. 100 St. Martin's-lane
Newbery Robert, 43 Castle-street, Holborn
Newman W. R. and Son, 27 Widegate-st. *p*
Nicholson T. 4 Adelaide-terrace, Islington
Nicholson T. W. 8 St. Michael's-al. Cornhill
Nosworthy and Snell, 79 Coleman-street
Offor Edward, 28 Leadenhall-street
Page Wm. 36 Basinghall-street
Palmer and Cottrell, 34 Gt. Marlboro-street
Parmenter Samuel, 303 & 313 Strand
Pearson C. 22 Elder-street, Norton Folgate
Petter A. S. and Co. 4 New-street, Doctor's-co
Picken Thos. 13 Murray-street, Camden-town
Pocock T. W. 27 Coppice-row, Clerkenwell
Bownceby H. 43 Leman-street, Whitechapel
Read Mrs. M. and Co. 10 Johnson's-court, Fleet-street, *p*
Read T. and Co. 4 Agar-street, *c.p*
Reeves and Hoare, 15 Warwick-ct. Holb. *c.p*
Robertson J. 9 Hatton-garden, Holborn
Robinson Worsley, 113 Fenchurch-street
Ross G. 7 Seacoal-lane, Farringdon-street, *c*
Rymer and Co. 16 Red-lion-square
Sanderson and Co. 17 Little Britain
Sexton Fred. 23 Led-lion-square, Holborn
Shaw Henry, 13A, Serle's-place, Lincoln's-inn
Shephard Wm. J. 11 Bell-yd. Temple-bar, *c.p*
Shuttleworth John S. 3 Chapel-pl. Poultry, *p*
Silverlock H. 3 Wardrobe-terrace, Doctors' com. and Rutland-pl. Up. Thames-street
Simmons Geo. 3 Gt. Turnstile, Holborn
Skelton Robt. 2 Racquet-court, Fleet-street
Sleap Thomas, 3 Tower Royal, City
Smith Brothers and Co. 4 King-st. Cheapside
Sorrill J. 13 Featherstone-build. Holborn, *c*
Sparkhall W. 10 Duck-lane, Wardour-street
Standidge H. and Co. 36 Old Jewry, City
Stannard and Dixon, 7 Poland-st. Oxford-st.
Stannard and Rae, 8 Gray's-inn-place
Stanton H. 27 and 32 Noble-street, City
Straker A. M. and Co. 76 Basinghall-street, *p*
Straker Sam. 80 Bishopsgate-street within
Stutter Thos. 76 Church-st. Shoreditch, *c.p*
Such J. 29 Budge-row, Watling-street, *p*
Swinford Brothers, 276 Strand
Tasman H. 4 Grocers'-hall-court, Mansion-ho
Thomson Benj. R. and Edwd. M. and John M 6 Symonds'-inn, and 9 Chancery-lane
Tupper G. F. 4 Barge-yard, Bucklersbury
Turner Thomas, 8 Hatton-garden
Varty Edw. 15 and 27 Camomile-street, *p*
Warrington R. S. and Co. 27 Strand, *c.p*
Waterlow and Sons, 24 and 25 Birchin-la. 6½ to 68 Lond.-wall, and 49 Parliament-st. *c.p*
Waters J. and Co. 5 and 6 Sambrook-ct. *p*
Wedgwood J. V. 16 Walbrook, *p*
Wells and Haverson, 38 Gresham-street, and 1 Aldermanbury *c.p*
Wells Thos. and Co. 35 Basinghall-street, *p*
West Edwd. 17 Bull and Mouth-street, *c.p*

White G. 26 Gt. Russell-st. Bloomsbury, *p*
Whiteman H. J. and Co. 21 Gt. Queen-st. *c*
Whitmarsh J. G. 118 Bishopsgate-st. with. *c*
Williams, Mrs. A. 110 St. John-st. W. Smithf. *c*
Wood E. 19 Featherstone-street, City-rd. *p*

LITHOGRAPHIC PRESS MAKERS.

Barrett Stephen, 20½ Camomile-street, City
Hughes and Kimber, 102 to 107 Shoe-lane
Meager Geo. and Co. 6 Gt. S. Andrew-st.
     Seven Dials
Merritt and Hatcher, 43 Cornhill
Nosworthy and Snell, 79 Coleman-street
Shaker S. 80 Bishopsgate-street-within

LITHOGRAPHIC STONE IMPORTERS.

Ackermann and Co. 96 Strand
Hughes and Kimber, 102 Shoe-lane
Schwartz Fredk. A. and Co. 14 Earl-st. Blkfrs.
Straker S. 80 Bishopsgate-street-within
Verey H. St. Ann's-wharf, Earl-street, Blkfrs.

MAP ENGRAVERS.

Addison J. 47 Swinton-street, Gray's-inn-road
Becker F. P. & Sons, 11 Stationers'-hall-court
Cross J. & Son, 18 Holborn-hill
Davies B. R. 16 George-street, Euston-square
Dower J. 6 Cumming-place, New-road
Phillips C. H. 19 Gracechurch-street
Pulsford E. 7 Gt. William-st. Caledonian-rd.
Walker J. & C. 9 Castle-street, Holborn
Welland G. 32 Holford-sq. Bagnigge-wells-rd.
Welland J. 11 Pembroke-ter. Caledonian-road
Wright W. 6 Frederick-street, Gray's-inn-road
Wyld J. 457 West Strand and 2 Roy. Exchange

NEWSVENDERS AND AGENTS.

See also BOOKSELLERS; *also* STATIONERS.

Marked *s*, are stationers; *b*, booksellers;
w, wholesale.

News Exchange, 2 Black-horse-alley, Fleet-
     street; Thos. Spilling, *Secretary.*
Adams Henry, 9 Parliament-street
Adams Wm. Jas. 59 Fleet-street, and 2 Pley-
     dell-street, City
Adcock C. 14 Great James-street, Lisson-grove
Algar F. 11 Clement's-lane, Lombard-street
Allen C. J. 58 Old-street-road, Shoreditch
Allen Francis, 19 Saint Martin's-le-grand
Alley Geo. 89 Chiswell-street, Finsbury
Appleyard Henry, 1 Duke-street, Adelphi, and
     11 Fleet-lane, Farringdon-street, *b.w*
Attryde J. 8 Adam-street West, Bryanst.-sq.
Austin Miss C., 1 Queen's-head-row
Awberry Misses C. & E. 47 Lisle-st. Leices.-sq. *s*
Bagshaw R. 31 Brydges-st. Covent-garden
Bailey Edw. 5 York-place, Kennington-road
Bain Mrs. S. 2 Duke-street, Westminster
Barker Charles, 12 Birchin-lane, City
Barker Jas. 19 Throgmorton-street, *b*
Barker Wm. J. 187 Brick-lane, Spitalfields
Barlow Geo. 32 Jewin-street, Cripplegate
Barnes George, 7 Bower-place, Camberwell-rd.
Barrett E. 32 Bishopsgate-st. within, *b*

Bastin E. 32 Little Earl-street, Seven-dials, *b*
Bedford Chris. 46 Park-street, Mile-end
Bell, Wm. 13 Crown-street, Walbrook, *s*
Belle Gus. 14 Maiden-lane, Covent-garden
Bignell, F. W. 1 Bishop's-pl. Fulham-road, *b*
Bingham Charles E. 84 Mount-st. Gros.-sq. *b.s*
Bishop J. 1 Lillypot-lane, Noble-street, City
Black C. W. 19 Catherine-court, Tower-hill
Blagden Jno. 3 Marylebone-lane
Blake James, 103 Great Dover-street
Blockley Jas. 14 Great Marylebone-street, *s*
Born William A. 115 London-wall
Boullen John, 60 Wilson-street, Finsbury
Bouffler J. 5 Vernon-place, Bagnigge-wells-rd.
Bowering Fred. 211 Blackfriars-road, *s*
Bridge Geo. 2 Sherrard-street, Golden-square
Bromley P. 3 Great Ormond-street, Queen-sq.
Brooks Henry, 24 Old Cavendish-street
Brooks H. 12 Warwick-square, Newgate-street
Brooks, W. T. 7 Shepherd-street, May-fair
Brown and Standfast, 4 Little George-st. West.
Brown Mrs. M. & Co. 19 Warwick-sq. City
Brown Dl. 51 Holywell-street, Strand, *b*
Brown G. 6 Little Earl-street, Seven-dials
Brown Thos. 1 Avery-row, Bond-street
Brown Thos. 51 Green-street, Bethnal-green
Buckoke E. 17 Robert-street, Grosvenor-sq.
Bult B. E. 25 New Quebec-st. Pertman-sq. *b*
Burkett Chas. 43 Queen's-road, Bayswater
Bush Thomas, 15 Jewry-street, Aldgate
Butcher Wm. 44 Leader-street, Chelsea
Byfield, Hawksworth & Co. 21 Charing-cr. *s*
Callaway E. W. 16 Upper Lambeth-marsh
Carter Daniel, 257 High-street, Poplar, *b.s*
Carter T. 19 James-street, Oxford-street
Castle and Lamb, 7 Bull-head-ct. Newgate-st.
Clark John, 39 Curtain-road, Shoreditch
Clarke Edw. O. 29 King-street, Tower-hill
Clarke Robert (for.) 21 Finch-lane, Cornhill
Clayton Joseph & Son, 223 Piccadilly, and 265
     Strand, *w*
Cleaver Chas. 18 Commercial-road, Lambeth
Cleaver Mrs. H. 46 Piccadilly *b.s'*
Clemence John, 29 City-terrace, City-road
Clements Chas. 2 Winchester-st. Caledon.-rd.
Clifford, Wm. 5 Inner Temple-lane
Cole Eben. 16 St. Saviour's-churchyd. Boro.
Cole Mrs. Susan, 3 Crozier-street, Lambeth
Coles Jas. 39 Kingsgate-street, Holborn
Cook L. 1 Maiden-lane, Covent-garden
Cooke & Whitley, 1 Bouverie-street, Fleet-st.
Cooks Mrs. J. 28 St. Mary-axe
Cornish E. 11 & 12 Red Lion-street, Holb. *b*
Corns Sam. 64 William-street, Regent's-park
Cottrell Miss E. 8 Robert-street, Grosv.-sq. *b*
Cowie James and Son, 2 St. Ann's-lane, Saint
     Martin's-le-Grand, *b*
Cox John, 78 Drury-lane, *b*
Cruse Archelaus, 73 Little Britain
Dagg T. 25 Sussex-street, Tottenham-court-rd.
Dalley Mrs. E. 22 Queen-street, Seven-dials
Daniel Rich. 2 King-street Covent-garden, *b*
Dare Henry M. 55 Watling-street, City
Davies Thos. & Co. 1 Finch-lane, and 2 Birchin-
     lane, Cornhill

Davies Mrs. M. 50 Broad-street, Bloomsbury
Davison Mrs. H. 6 Nowell's-build. Liverp.-rd.
Dawson W. & Sons, 74 Cannon-street and Abchurch-yard, Abchurch-lane, *b.s*
Deeks Wm. 20 Market-street, Shepherd's-mar.
Deverell T. 33 Great Bush-lane, Cannon-street
Dodsworth J. 52 Cannon-st. St. George East, *s*
Douglass Thos. 16 Little Knight-Rider-st. *s*
Duncombe E. 28 Little St. Andrew-street
Eames E. 45 New Compton-street, Soho
Edmonds T. 2 Little Bell-alley, City, *s*
England Robert, 11 Little Grosvenor-street
Evans Frederick, 2½ Bell-yard, Temple-bar
Everett Wm. & Son, 17 Royal Exchange, *b*
Everett Charles, 75 Old Broad-street
Everett Rt. 15 Great Bath-street, Clerkenwell
Farmer J 1 Bloomsbury-terrace, Com.-rd. East
Farmer J. Jun. 3 Bloomsbury-terr. Com.-rd. E.
Farquharson, Rob. 10 Bloomsbury-street, *s*
Fielding R. 33 Old-street-road, Shoreditch
Fortin Philip, 97 Dean-street, Soho, *b*
French Thos. 26 Great Quebec-st. Dorset-sq.
Gilbert S. & T. 4 Copthall-buildings, *b.s*
Golding Geo. 31 Seething-lane, City *b*
Goldwin Mrs. A. 114 Fetter-lane, Fleet-street
Gordon James, 146 Leadenhall-street, *b.s*
Gravatt Robt. 11 King-street, Cheapside
Gregory J. 8 Bouverie-street, Paddington
Greville B. 62 Gt. Cambridge-st. Hackney-rd.
Grey Mrs. M. A. 62 St. George's-rd. Southw. *s*
Griffin Rich. 21 Brownlow-st. Drury-lane
Grindon Jno. 33 Felton-street, Hoxton
Grove J. 7 Regent-place, Westminster
Grove P. 2 Leathersellers'-builds. London-wall
Grubb, James, 105 Cornwall-road, Lambeth
Guthrie George 2 Old Jewry, City
Hall Edward, 74½ Mark-lane, and 223 Strand
Hammond M. 27 Lombard-street, City
Harris George, 9 Dean-street, Holborn
Harrison Edward, 146 Kingsland-road
Hatfield I. E. 78 Tottenham-court-road
Hathways Henry, 16 Royal Exchange
Hayes Charles, 67 Brook-street, West-square
Hayes W. G. 2 Lillypot-lane, City
Headen Mrs. E. 12 Park-side, Knightsbridge
Heward R. 5 Young-street, Kensington
Hibbard H. S. 1 Cobourg-street, Clerkenwell
Hill C. 4 Constitution-row, Gray's-inn-road
Hilton D. 8 Penton-street, Pentonville
Hinchliff J. 7 Globe-road, Mile-end
Hirst Jonathan, 15 Dean-street, Soho
Hoane Miss E. 192 Church-street, Shoreditch
Honeysett E. H. 137 High-st. Camden-town *s*
Horne John, 19 Leicester-square, *b*
Horsman Jas. 9 Brownlow-st. Holborn, *b*
Howes G. & Co. 7 Thavies-inn, Holborn
Humphrey R. 66 Theobald's-road, Holborn
Hyland Wm. 3 Arcade, Hungerford-market
Jaggers John, T. 55 Lambeth-walk
Jay Geo. 32 King-street, Camden-town
Jennings Mrs. E. 5 Crown-street, Finsbury
Joel Mrs. S. 42 Fore-st, Cripplegate, *s*
Johnson George B. 16 Beaufort-buildings
Jones Yarrell, & Cliffords, 6 Little Ryder-st, St. James's

Jones John, 73 Princes-st, Leicester-sq.
Jones John W. 39 Bury-street, St. James's
Jones Wm. 96 Bridport-place, New North-rd.
Jones W. B. 61 Lower Kennington-lane
Jopling W. Hy. 13 Wootton-st, Cornwall-rd.
Jordan George Warder, 169 Strand
Kemp Mrs. I. 27 Queen's-rd. West, Chelsea
Kemp W. 3 Albion-place, New Brompton
Kennedy Thomas, 31 Royal Exchange, and 34 Fetter-lane
Kerbey Charles, 118 Whitechapel-road
Kerby E. 5 Gt. Ryder-st, St. James's
Kerton Wm. 14 Ann's terrace, Camb.-heath
Kettle Miss E. M. 13 Little Queen-st, Holborn
Kilburn Mrs. Elizb. 14 New Compton-st
King Mrs. L. 32 and 33 Chancery-lane, *s*
King Wm. A. 22 Old Gravel-lane
Knight Miss E. 27 Water-lane, Blackfriars
Laking F. 26 Half Moon-street, Piccadilly
Laughton James, 60 Victoria-terr. Union rd
Lawless Mrs. Patience, 13 Philpot-lane
Lawrence William, 10 Gt. Trinity-lane
Layzell Joseph, 14 Hand-court, Holborn
Layzell, William, 36 Thayer-street
Leathwait J. 1 Pope's Head-alley, Cornhill
Lee Joseph, Billiter-sq. Fenchurch-street, *b.s*
Lester W. 59 Henry-street East, Regent's-pk
Line Joseph, 43 Margaret-st. Wilmington-sq
Lock W. 52 Upper North-pl. Gray's-inn-rd, *s*
Lofting Wm. 2 Webber-street, Blackfriars-rd
Macmichael J. 2 Pier-terrace, Chelsea, *b.s*
Maddox J. 10 Upp. Albany-street, Regent's-pk
Mallard Chas. 50 Palace-street, Pimlico
Mann Miss R. 3 Princes-street, Holborn
Markwell J. T. 46 Gt. Titchfield-street, *b*
Marlborough E. & Co. 4 Ave Maria-lane, *s*
Marshall R. 22 Porter-st. Newport-market, *s*
Mattocks Wm. 15 Crown-row, Mile-end, *s*
Maw Mrs. Minna, 20 Barne's-pl. Mile-end-rd
May Frederick, 42 Bury-street
Mayne Robert, 6 Star-street, Edgware-road
Miles Thomas, 1 York-place, Islington
Miller John, 1 Little College-street, Wesmnstr
Mitchell W. O. 39 Charing-cross, *s*
Morley Samuel, 103 Old-street, St. Luke's
Morley Z. 27 Park-terr. Regent's-park, *b.s*
Mosley & Keell, 16 Catherine-street
Mossop W. 13A Pollen-street, Hanover-square
Mudie T. & Sons, 15 Coventry-st. Haymkt., *s*
Myers R. G. 26 Swan-street, Minories
Nash & Teuten, 4 Savile-place, Regent-street
Nash H. 4 Upp. Weymouth-st. Portland-pl. *s*
Newcomb C. 5 Lillypot-la. Noble-st, City
Norvell Mrs. M. A. 47½ York-street, City-road
Nye Edwin, 78 Theobald's-road
Olley Miss E. 2 Dispensary-place, Boro
Onwhyn J. 1 Catherine-street, Strand, *w*
Osborne G. 46 Baldwin's-grdns. Leather lane
Owen Mrs. C. 8 Artillery-lane, Bishopsgate
Owen Horatio, 21 & 22 Noble-street, City, *s*
Paice Robert, 5 Millpond-street, Bermondsey
Parker J. P. 38 White Lion-street, Islington, *s*
Parkinson C. J. 51 Wilsted-st. Somers-town
Pausey Robert, 27 Exeter-street, Sloane-st. *b*
Pavey G. 47 Holywell-street, Strand, *w*

Payn John, 6 Trinity-street, Borough
Payne Chas. 11 Bridge-street, Westminster
Payne John, 19 Lower-street, Islington
Payne Wm. 82 Great Titchfield-street
Perks William, 111 St. Martin's-lane
Perschky J. 14 Union-street, Hackney-road
Phillips John, 13 Gerrard-street, Soho
Pike John, 3 Princes-terrace, Chelsea
Pilcher W. 71 Gray's-inn-lane, Holborn, s
Plummer Mrs. A. 46 Theobald's-road, s
Plummer G. 42 Spicer-street, Spitalfields, b
Ponten J. B., & Co. 66 Cannon-street
Porter Joseph, 9 Marylebone-lane
Potter George Aug. 53 Piccadilly, s
Pottle J. & Son, 14 & 15 Royal Exchange, b
Prowse Wm. 11 Mercer-street, Long-acre
Puddicombe Mrs. Bridge-house-pl. Newington
Puddicombe Thomas, 153 Waterloo-road
Purkess George, 60 Dean-street, Soho, w
Pyle George, 1 Huggin-lane, Gt. Trinity-lane
Rayden Wm. 26 Parker's-row, Bermondsey
Reeve J. 17½ Little Newport-street, Newport-market, and 79 Castle-street, Leicester-sq
Reeve R. Gray's-inn gateway, Holborn, s
Rendall Chas. 103 Brick-lane, St. Luke's, s
Reynolds W. 154 Princes-road, Kennington
Roberts Charles, 17 Brompton-row
Roberts Geo. 72 Brewer-street, Somers-town, s
Rogers Thomas, 9 Bridge-row, Pimlico
Rose Samuel, 138 Waterloo-road
Russell Mrs. E. 3A James-street, Oxford-street
Saker Mrs. A. E. 201 Whitechapel-road
Saunders Brothers, 106 London-wall, b.s
Sawyer, Mrs. Catherine & Sons, 7 St. Michael's-alley, Cornhill
Scales, W. 195 Shoreditch High-street
Scripps Thomas, 13 South Molton-street
Sergeant, G. 7 Christopher-ct. St. Martin's-le-Gr
Sharp, John, 47 Tabernacle-walk, Finsbury
Shaw & Nelson, 7 Brydges-st, Covent-garden
Sheard, Ch. 70 Compton-st, Clerkenwell, b
Sheffield, W. 59 Gt. Sutton-st, Clerkenwell
Sibley, Mrs. Frances, 92 Chancery-lane
Simmonds, Samuel, 32 Greek-street, Soho
Simpson, Charles, 57 Theobald's-road
Smith, Bros. 10 Kittisford-place, Hackney-rd.
Smith, W. H. & Son, 136 and 137 Strand, w
Smith, Henry, 3 Graham-street, Islington, b
Smith, Wm. 25 Silver-street, Golden-square
Smith, W. R. 71 Crawford-st, Portman-sq.
Spencer, Mrs. A. 97 Cromer-st, Brunswick-sq.
Spilling, Thomas, 58 St. John-street-road
Spong, Thos. Chapel-st. Tottenham-court-road
Squire, T. 22 Thornhill-place East, Caledonian-road, and 47 Chapel-st. Somers-town, s
Stacey, W. 34 Clipstone-st, Fitzroy-sq, s
Stanley, H. 4 Albion-place, Rotherhithe
Stansell, Ed. 46 Prebend-st, New North-road
Stevens, George, 33 Goswell-road
Stevens, Wm. 23 Trinity-sq., Tower-hill
Street, Brothers, 11 Serle-street
Stroud, John, 21 Brown-st, Bryanston-square
Such, Henry, 123 Union-street, Borough
Swale, J. 23 Cross-street, Blackfriars-road
Swallow, Frederick, 63 Pratt-st, Camden-town

Swale, Jas. 23 Cross-st, Blackfriars, Lambeth
Swift, Chas. Wm. 48, Broad-st, Lambeth
Tanner, E. 48 Boston-place, Dorset-square
Tatchell & Blunt, 12 Staining-lane, City
Taylor, Adolphus, 22, London-rd, Southwark
Terry, Peter, 6 Hatton-garden, b
Thomas, Davies, and Co. 1 Finch-lane, Corn-hill, and 2 Birchin-lane
Thomas, W. & Co. 19 to 21 Catherine-st, Strd.
Thomas, John, 8 Horseferry-rd, Westmr.
Thomas, Joseph, 2 Catherine-st, Strand, and 8 White Hart-street, Drury-lane, w
Thompson & Utting, 2 Palsgrave-pl, Strand
Thornhill, G. & Co. 27 Noble-st, Cheapside
Thridgould, J. 9 Sidney-st, Commercial-road East, b
Thridgould, T. H. 31 Oxford-street
Tidd, John Lister, 57 Goswell-road
Town, A. F. Suffolk-pl. Comm. rd. East
Tucker, Mrs. S. A. Nine Elms-lane
Turner, H. 2 Drummond-st, Euston sq, b
Turner, R. 10 Hertford-place, Haggerston
Verney, George, 1 Orford-place, Chelsea
Vickers, Geo. 28 and 29 Holywell-street, and Angel-court, 272 Strand, w
Vincent, Philip, 118 Blackfriars-road
Walker, George, 26 Maddox-st, Regent-st, s
Waller, Mrs. M. 9 Lillypot-lane, Noble-street
Walter, C. D. 36 Bell-yard, Temple-bar, 18 Temple-street, Whitefriars, & 31 Brydges-street, Covent-garden, s
Watling, Miss Elizabeth, 409 Strand
Weston, Wm. 135 Church-st, Shoreditch, s
Welbank, Rich. 21 Sloane-square, Chelsea, s
Wells, Mrs. H. 3 Leigh-street, Burton-cres. b
Whiteley, T. & Co. 191 Shadwell High-st, b.s
Whitehorn, Jas. 62 Mount-st, Grosvenor-sq.
Whiting, Mrs. S. 7 Hosier-la, W. Smithfld, b.s
Wickham and Cooper, 163 Strand
Wild, E. 44 Marshall-street, Golden-sq, s
Wild, Lancelot, 13 Catherine-st, Strand
Wilgoss, J. W. 38, High-st, Portland-town
Willshire, Raym. 13 Tyler-st, Regent-street
Wilson, Sam. 33 Stanhope-st. Regent's-park
Wilson, Mrs. S. 6 Lamb's Conduit-passage
Windsor, W. 99 Bethnal-green-road
Windust, E. W. 2 Cumberland-st, Chelsea
Windsor, Wm. 99 Bethnal-green-road
Wingfield, Rd. 9 Middle-row Knightsbridge
Winter, Mrs. Shepperton-terr, New North-rd
Wood, Jonathan, 67 St. John-st, Clerkenwell
Wood, James, 38 Hackney-road
Young, James P. 6 East-st, Walworth
Young, Mrs. M. 3 Seymour-row North, Bromp.

PARCHMENT AND VELLUM DEALERS AND MANUFACTURERS.

Collins G. 18 Cross-street North, Bermondsey
Cooper D., and Co. 5 to 7 Shoe-lane
Cripps and Starkey, 24 Skinner-street, City
Crook J. 117½ Bermondsey-st, and 20 Granger-terrace, Blue Anchor-road
Gibbs G. and Son, Richardson-street, Bermondsey, and 40 Princes-st, Blackfriars-rd
Hawker J. 37 Gray's-inn-lane

6 §

Hepburn W. and A. 7 St. Pancras-lane
Hulbert H. 3 Grange-walk, Bermondsey
Lever J. and J. 13½ Sise-lane, City, and Neat-
    street, Cobourg-street, Old Kent-road
Nice T. 1 Swan-lane, Rotherhithe
Redgrave and Co. Blue Anchor-rd, Bermondsey
Smith J. and Co. 52 Long-acre
Smith W. H. Gloster-row, Walworth
Sparkhall E. 142 Cheapside
Sparks C. 9 Salisbury-square, Fleet-street, and
    22 Cross-street South, St. George's-street,
    Bermondsey
Tomlin W. Canal-bridge, Old Kent-road
Tomlins W. Russell-place, Bermondsey
Warren H. Russell-place, Bermondsey
White and Crow, Southampton-court, Holborn

LONDON PRINTERS (LETTER-PRESS).

Abraham H. 35 St. Mary Axe
Adams and King, 30 Goswell-street
Adlard J. E. 22 Bartholomew-close
Aird D. and Tunstall, 340 Strand and 18½
    Exeter-street, Strand
Ambridge —, Elliot-row, Islington
Arliss H. M. 15 Gt. Queen-street, Holborn
Arnold E. 37 Tabernacle-walk
Ashfield W. T. 6 Church-street, Lambeth
Atkinson, J. P. Mount-row-house, City-road
Bagot and Co. 21 Cullum-street, Fenchurch-st
Bagster and Son, 14 King's-rd, Gray's-inn-lane
Ballard W. 18 Cannon-street
Bank Printing Office, Bank
Banks J. H. 4 Little Queen-street, Holborn
Banks G. J. & K. 6 & 14 Bermondsey-new-rd
Barclay G. Castle-street, Leicester-square
Barnes, 44 Southwark Bridge-road
Barrett R. 13 Mark-lane, Tower-street
Bartleet P. 2 Fountain-place, City-road
Batchelor D. 14 Crescent, Hackney-road
Bateman J. B. 1 Ivy-lane, Paternoster-row
Bateman R. 19 Cursitor-street, Chancery-lane
Bateman and Dennis, 95 Leadenhall-street
Batho and Co. Sherborne-lane, Lombard st.
Batten, Clapham-common
Batty J. H. 159 Fleet-street
Bealby R. F. 13 Arlington-st, St. John's-st-rd
Beetlestone G. 11 Ship-yard, Leadenhall mark.
Beeton S. O. 18 Bouverie-street, Fleet-street
Bell Henry, 118 St. John's-street-road
Benbow R. 93 Cornwall-road
Bewick, 46 Barbican
Bidmead W. H. 2 Brownlow-st, High Holborn
Billing & Son, 186 Bermondsey-street
Blades and East, Abchurch-lane, Lombard-st
Blanchard and Sons, 62 Millbank-st, Westmr.
Blenkinsop and Walsh, 19 Bucklersbury
Bonsor Jos. 134 Cullum-street, Fenchurch-st.
Boot A. Dockhead, Rotherhithe
Bowie, J. 7 Mark-lane, Tower-street
Bowles J. 274 Whitechapel
Bowles —, 73 Mark-lane, Tower-street
Bowry & Son, 8 King's-terr, Bagnigge-wells-rd
Boyd B. 2 York-pl, Upper-st, Islington
Bradbury and Evans, Bouverie-street, Fleet-st.
Brandon G. French Horn-yard

Brettell W. 24 Rupert-street, Leicester-square
Brickhill W. 6 Cumberland-row, Walworth-rd
Briscoe B. Three-herring-court, Redcross-st
Brown —, 17 Old Broad-street
Buck and Co. 8 Billiter-street
Burdett —, 151 St. John's-street, Euston-sq
Burns & Co. 86½ Connaught-terr. Edgware rd.
Burrell —, Featherstone-buildings
Burrell and Co., Wych-street
Burrell J. G. 2½ Houghton-st, Clare-market
Burt J. K. 90½ Holborn-hill
Carrington N. B. 2 Clifton-terr, West Bromp.
Catline W. J. 3 Terrace, Old Kent-road
Causton H. K. Nag's Head-court, Lombard-st
Chambers and Son, 55 Coleman-street, City
Chaplin Henry, 213 Bermondsey-street
Chapman J. 103 Star-street, Edgware-road
Chapman & Co. Shoe-lane, Fleet-street
Charles & Tiver, 38 Chancery-lane
Christie Geo. 1 Pudding-lane, Eastcheap
Clarke J. O. 38A New Bridge-street
Clarke, —, 17 Brunswick-street, Islington
Clay Rich. Bread-street-hill, City
Clayton J. 10 Crane-street, Fleet-street
Clements W. Nettleton-court, Nicholl-square
Clowes & Son, Stamford-street, Blackfriars, &
    14 Charing-cross
Collingridge W. H. 1 Long-lane, Aldersgate-st
Collis M. & W. 50 Bow-lane, Cheapside
Colyer, 17 Fenchurch-street
Cookes, Jas. 51 Fenchurch-street
Cooper, 12 Old-road, Stepney
Cooper G. 208 Brick-lane, Whitechapel
Corker Edm. L. 11 Queen-street, Cheapside
Couchman Edw. 10 Throgmorton-street, City
Court Mrs. E. A. 140 Brook-st, Holborn-hill
Coventry John, Church-street, Hackney
Cox W. H. 5 Gt. Queen-street
Cox & Wyman, 75 Gt. Queen-street, Holborn
Crockford J. 29 Princes-st, Little Queen-st
Crofts W. F. Dufour-place, Broad-street
Cross Mrs. H. 92 Leadenhall-street
Cross Geo. 85 Chancery-lane
Crozier & Mullen, Silver-street, Golden-square
Cunningham, 77 Three Colt-street, Limehouse
Cuthbert & Southey, 155 Fenchurch-street
Darby J., 2 Inverness-terrace, Bayswater
Darling & Son, 31 Leadenhall-street
Davidson Mrs. Old Boswell-court, Strand
Davidson G. H. Peter's-hill, Doctors'-commons
Davy & Son, 137 Long-acre
Dawson & Sons, 141½ Fenchurch-street
Dawson —, High-street, Poplar
Dao —, 29 Ebenezer-pl, corner Kennington-la
Dean T. & Son, 31 Ludgate-hill
Deane E., 11 Carey-street, Chancery-lane
Dunford C. High-street, Notting-hill
Eccles Mrs. A. 101 Fenchurch-street
Eglington Wm. 92 Goswell-street
Elliott Mrs. M. 14 Holywell-st, Strand
Elliott, W. H., 475 New Oxford-street
Ellis Wm. J. 2 Great Dover-road, Borough
Evans & Co. 7 Oakley-terrace, Old Kent-road
Farrow J. J. 32 Pudding-lane, Eastcheap
Field W., Storey's-gate, Westminster

Field and Williams, 105 Blackfriars-road
Fisher & Jackson, Angel-street, Aldersgate-st
Ford Wm. 28 Russell-court, Chancery-lane
Ford —, 52 Long-acre
Forsaith —, 118 Bethnal-green-road
Foster Jas., Primrose-street, Bishopsgate
Francis David, 21 Mile-end-road
Francis R. S., Catherine-street, Strand
Gadsby, George-yard, Bouverie-street
Galabin W. G. 91 Bartholomew-close
Gardiner, Prince's-street Cavendish-square
Gee and Adams, Middle-street, Cloth-fair
Gilbert, 52 Carey-street, Chancery-lane
Gilbert and Rivington, St. John's-square
Godfrey, 259 Whitechapel-road
Grammar C. 8 Princes-st, Little Queen-street
Green, 64 Blackman-street
Gregory J. King's Head-court, Shoe-lane
Grubb & Co. 102 York-st, Upper-st, Islington
Gunn Thomas, 196 Piccadilly
Haddon and Son, Castle-street, Finsbury
Haig and Co. New-buildings, Fetter-lane
Hall, Cambridge-terrace, Camden-town
Hansard, 29 Parker-street, Little Queen-street
Harrild T. Dudley-court, Falcon-square
Harris, 16 Great Titchfield-street, Oxford-street
Harrison and Son, 45 St. Martin's-lane, Or-
    chard-st, Wesminster, and Foreign-office,
    Fludyer-street
Hartnell, Langley-street, Long-acre
Harvey, 26 Little Charlotte-st, Blackfriars-rd
Hayman & Co. Whitefriars-street, Fleet-street
Hedgman C. 12 London-wall
Henderson and Co. High-st, Newington-butts
Hill G. Mount-place, Westminster-road
Hodgson, 1 Goughssquare, Fetter-lane
Hodson, 22 Portugal-street, Chancery-lane
Holmes, 4 Tooke's-court, Chancery-lane
Holstock, 43 Bridge-street, Southwark
Holyoake, 147 Fleet-street
Hopcroft, 42 Mincing-lane
Hoskins, 30 Rood-lane, Eastcheap
Howitt and Le Maitre, 2 Blackfriars-road
Howlett and Son, 10 Frith-street, Soho
Hunt and Co. Weymouth-pl, New Kent-road
Isham's, 4 Johnson's-court, Fleet-street
Jackson and Co. Serles-place, Chancery-lane
Jaques and Robinson, 30 Lower Sloane-street
Jaques and Son, Kenton-st, Brunswick-square
Johns Thomas C. Wine-office-court, Fleet-st
Johnson Robert 10 Brook-street, Holborn
Johnson W. S. 60 St. Martin's-lane
Jones and Beck, 81 Cheapside
Jones and Causton, 47 Eastcheap
Joyce, 96 St. John-street-road
Judd, Calthorpe-place
Kelly and Co. 20 Old Boswell-court, Strand
Kelly and Pritchett, Houndsditch
Kelly S. 10 Lambeth-hill, Doctors'-commons
Kennedy, 4 Queen--street, Cheapside
Kenny and Co. Heathcock-court, Strand
Kerr, Chichester-rents, Chancery-lane
King, Queen-street, Cheapside
Kingcombe, Pentonville-hill
Lane, 5 Lamb's-conduit-street

Lesty Wm. 65 Castle-street, Southwark
Levy and Robson, Gt. New-street, Fetter-lane
Lewis and Son, 21 Finch-lane
List Fred. 104 High-street, Shadwell
Little, 218 High-street, Islington
Lloyd Edw. Salisbury-square, Fleet-street
Lofts John, 262 Strand
London Printing Company, 97 St. John-street,
    Smithfield
Lovegrove, 25½ Gee-street, Goswell-street
Lowe C. H. Charles-street, Hatton-garden
Lowe, 182 High Holborn
Luntley & Co. New Broad-street-court
Mackintosh A. Great New-street
M'Gowan, Great Windmill-st, Leicester-sq
Mallett, Jos, Wardour-street
Mansell, 5 King-street
Marchant and Co. Ingram-ct, Fenchurch-st
Mason, M. 12 Ivy-lane, Paternoster-row
Mason Wm. 22 Clerkenwell-green
Masters J. 38 Aldersgate-street
Matthews Edward, 46 Berwick-street
McCorquodale and Co. Cardington-st, Euston-
    square and 79 Duke-street, Tooley-street
McKewan and Co. 47 Finsbury-circus
Meaden, High-street, Clapham-road
Metcalf T. E. 63 Snow-hill
Metchim and Burt, 55 Parliament-street
Miall and Co. Horse-shoe court, Ludgate-hill
Mills, 11 Crane-court, Fleet-street
Mitchener, Wm. 23 Red Lion-street
Mitchener E. A. 116 Great Russell-street
Mitchener E. A. Edward-street, Euston-square
Myers Wm. H. 202 Whitechapel-road
Napier, 26 Seymour-street, Euston-square
Needham Robert, 9 Ave Maria-lane
Newman & Co. Widegate-street, Bishopsgate
Newman E. Devonshire-street, Bishopsgate
Newton John, Silver-street Monkwell-street
Nichols J. Chandos-street, Covent-garden
Nichols Geo. Earl's-court, Leicester-square
Nicholls and Son, King-street, Westminster
Nicholls F. 45 Hoxton-square and 2 Milton-st,
    Cripplegate
Nicholls, 32 London-wall
Nisbet, 9 Union-street
Nissen and Parker, 68 Great Tower-street
Norman G. Maiden-lane, Strand
Novello J. A. 21 Dean-street, Soho
Oakey, Johnson, and Darkin, 121 Fleet-street
Odell and Co. 18 Prince's-st, Cavendish-square
Orr W. S. & Co. Salisbury-square
Ostell Wm. Hart-street, Bloomsbury
Painter William E. 342 Strand
Palmer & Co. 3 Savoy-street, Strand
Palmer & Co. 17 Brownlow-street, Holborn
Palmer and Son, 18 Paternoster-row
Parker George, 24 Tavistock-st, Covent-garden
Passmore Josh. 45 Borough-road
Paul C. 18 Great St. Andrew-street
Pearse W. C. 2 Queen-street, Cheapside
Peart H. D. 163 St. John-street, Clerkenwell
Peel J. W. 74 Charlotte-street, Blackfriars
Peirce George, 310 Strand
Perry Wm. J. 20½ Warwick-lane

Petter & Duff, New-street, Doctors'-commons
Petter & Galpin, Playhouse-yard, Blackfriars
Pettet, Greek-street, Soho
Pickburn, Rosoman-street, Clerkenwell
Pite H. Cheyne-walk, Chelsea
Pittman & Son, 20 Warwick-square
Plummer J. 29 Pudding-lane, City
Poplett J. J. 43 Beech-street, Barbican
Poulter & Co. 143 Strand
Pounceby H. Leman-street, Whitechapel
Powell W. T. 118 Brunswick-st, Hackney-rd
Prentics & Dale, 204 Upper Thames-street
Rawlings, 5 Brewer-street, Somers-town
Rayner & Hodges, 109 Fetter-lane
Redford and Son, 96 London-road, Southwark
Redford A. B. S. 24 Albion-place, Walworth
Reed & Pardon, Lovell's-court, Paternoster-rw
Reeves S. 41 North-street, Pentonville
Reynell & Wight, Pulteney-street, Soho
Reynolds G. W. M. 40 Parker-st, Gt. Queen-st
Richards Thomas, 37 Gt. Queen-st, Long-acre
Rickerby, Miss M. S. 73 Cannon-street
Rider J. & W. Bartholomew-close
Riley, Palestine-place, Cambridge-heath
Roberts J. 8 Cannon-street-road
Roberts J. H. 41 Tabernacle-walk
Roberts A. T. 2 Hackney-road
Robins Alfred, 7 Southampton-street, Strand
Robins J. & W., 57 Tooley-street
Roche H. T. and J. 25 Hoxton-square
Rogerson & Tuxford, 246 Strand
Rothwell & Son, 6 Cross-lane, St. Mary-at-hill
Roworth & Sons, Bell-yard
Ryles Ann, 3 Monmouth-street, Dudley-sq
Rymer, 7 New-road, Whitechapel
Savill & Edwards, 4 Maiden-lane, Strand
Scales William, 195 Shoreditch
Scaum G. Spur-inn-yard, Borough
Schultz & Co. Poland-street, Oxford-street
Scott T. Warwick-court, Holborn
Scott, Parker's-row, Rotherhithe
Sears, W. J. and J. Ivy-lane, Paternoster-row
Seyfang & Co. 57 Farringdon-street
Shaker Samuel, 80 Bishopsgate-street
Shakly, Red Cross-square
Shaw A. P. 11 Camomile-street
Shaw, 10 Devonshire-street
Shaw James, 41 Tooley-street
Shaw and Sons, Fetter-lane
Sheppard, Tufton-street, Westminster
Shepherd, Islington-green
Shoberl F. 51 Rupert-street, Haymarket
Shore T. H. 30 Old-street, City-road
Shorman John, Brewer-street, Golden-square
Silverlock H. Wardrobe-ter, Doctors'-comm
Simpkins H. 70½ Strand
Simpson, Brille-row, Somers-town
Simpson, 1 Prince's-street, Rotherhithe
Skelt B. 17 Swan-street, Minories
Skipper & East, 1 St. Dunstan's-hill
Small, 136 Union-street, Borough
Smith, Charles, Hart-street, Gt. Tower-street
Smith & Ebbs, 5 Postern-row, Tower-hill
Smith, Duke-street, Smithfield
Smith Wm. 74 Ebenezer-place, Kennington-la

Somerfield, 67 Marylebone-lane
Stevens & Co. Bell-yard, Temple-bar
Stratford, 2 Nassau-place, Commercial-road
Straker & Co. 7a Basinghall-street
Stutter, 76 Church-street, Shoreditch
Stuart, 38 Rupert-street, Haymarket
Such J. 29 Budge-row
Sullivan, 111 Chancery-lane
Sumfield T. King's Head-court
Sweeting A. Bartlett's-buildings
Symons W. M. 1 New-bridge-street, Vauxhall
Taylor A. 39 Coleman-street
Taylor & Francis, Red-lion-court, Fleet-street
Taylor & Greening, 5 Graystoke-pl, Fetter-la
Taylor J. E. 10 Little Queen-street
Taylor G. Little James-street, Gray's-inn-lane
Teape & Son, George-street, Tower-hill
Teulon J. 57 Cheapside
Thomas J. W. 26 Russell-court, Drury-lane
Thompson, 19 Great St. Helen's
Tirebuck J. & J. 40½ Monkwell-st, Cripplegate
Titherton, 13 Liverpool-street
Tomkins, 94 Finsbury-circus
Trapp J. 31 Budge-row
Triesse, 4 Beech-street
Trimen, 11 Portugal-street, Chancery-lane
Trounce, 6 Cursitor-street, Chancery-lane
Trounce, Somers-place West, New-road
Truscott Jas. 24 Nelson-square
Tucker & Co. Perry's-place, Oxford-street
Tupper, 4 George-yard, Bucklersbury
Tyler & Co. Bolt-court, Fleet-street
Unwin Jacob, 31 Bucklersbury
Vacher, Parliament-street, Westminster
Varty E. Camomile-street, Bishopsgate
Vinton & Son, Cardington-street, Euston-sq
Virtue & Co. Cottage-place, City-road
Vizetelly H. 15 Gough-square, Fleet-street
Walton & Mitchell, 24 Oxford-street
Ward, 8 Upper Dorset-place
Warr F. Red Lion-passage, Holborn
Warrington & Son, 27 Maiden-lane
Waterlow & Sons, London-wall
Watkins, Gravel-lane, & Nelson-square
Watson F. 110 Fetter-lane
Watson G. 5 Kirby-street, Hatton-garden
Watts, Crown-court, Temple-bar
Weight, Angel-place, High-street, Borough
Wells & Co, 38 Gresham-street
Wertheimer & Co. Finsbury-circus
Weston H. 40 Rathbone-place
Whiting C. Beaufort-buildings, Strand
Whittingham, 21 Took's-court, Chancery-lane
Whitwell S. 10 Northumberland-terrace, Bag-
   nigge-wells
Wicks Mrs. 27 Chichester-st, Gray's-inn-road
Wilcockson W. Rolls-buildings, Chancery-la
Willoughby, 72 Hatton garden
Willoughby & Co. Smithfield
Wilson & Ogilvy, 57 Skinner-st, Snow-hill
Wilson G. J. & E. 6 George-court, Piccadilly
Wood, 38 Gracechurch-street
Wood, 95 Goulburn-terrace, Barnsbury
Woodfall & Kinder, Old Bailey
Woolley & Cook, Bennett's pl, Doctors'-com

Wright W. A. Fulford's-rents
Yorwarth F. Eyre-street-hill
Yound H. 62 Tottenham-court-road

SEALING WAX.

Allen Geo. Marthas-buildgs, St. Luke's
Amelang, L. 54 Red Lion-street, Clerkenwell
Boatwright, Brown, & Co. Watling-street
Bousfield Chas. 6 Whitefriars-street
Brown John & Co. 96 Farringdon-street
Cooke John & Sons, 84 Cannon-street, City
Cowan John & Co. 8 Mansion-house-street
Craskell & Son, 1 Nelson-row, Trafalgar-sq.
Dodwell Mrs. E. 48 Ironmonger-row
Elliott J. E. Amelia-street, Walworth
Field John Charles and John, 12 Wigmore-st.
Fry Joseph, 19 Cannon-street
Goulston E. M. 34 Jane-st, Commercial-road
Goulston Jno. 4 Up. Fenton-st, Commercl.-rd.
Gracie Frederick, 62 Leonard-street
Harker Edmund E. 37, Fetter-lane
Harris Wm. D. & Co. 7 Earl-st, Blackfriars
Hinds, Joseph, 37 Ashford-st, Hoxton
Hoe Wm. 18 Bishopsgate-street Without
Hudswell John, 5 Three-crow-sq, Bow
Hyde George & Co. 61 Fleet-street
Jones S. & Brothers, Talbot-ct, Gracechurch-st
M'Rae James & Co. 7 Ave Maria-lane
Morrell Henry, 149 Fleet-st
Raven John, 46 Fish-street-hill
Rayner, Henry, sen. 16 Spencer-st. Goswell-rd.
Taylor Swan, & Co. 49, Borough High-st.
Temple Wm. 18 Artillery-pl. Bishopsgate-st
Watkins Thomas & Son, Cannon-st, City
Watson James, 6 Warner-place, Hackney-rd.
West James, 27 Lombard-street, City

STATIONERS, WHOLESALE AND MANUFACTURING.

See also PAPER MANUFACTURERS AND WAREHOUSES.

Marked thus *a*, are Account Book makers; *e*, are Envelope makers; *f*, are Fancy; *r*, are Rag merchants.

Stationers' Hall, Stationers'-hall-ct. Ludgate-hl

Addenbrooke Joseph, 2 Bartlett's-passage
Barandon Charles, 4 New London-street
Barry & Hayward, 18 and 19 Queenhithe, Up. Thames-street
Betty, Melville & Co. 174 Aldersgate-street
Bishop & Blundell, 1 Old Fish-street-hill, and 52 Little Britain
Bishop & Gissing, Cannon-street West
Blackwood J. 8 Lovell's-ct. Paternoster-row
Bonsor J. & Co. 132 Salisbury-square, Fleet-st
Boulter & Co. 143 Strand
Bowles & Gardiner, 49 Newgate-street
Brown & King, 239 Upper Thames-street
Bull & Vinen, 2 Regent-street, City-road, *f*
Bunney Henry and John, and Goodhall, 9 Pancras-lane, Cheapside, *a*
Camp James P. D. 27A Church-street, and 26 Wood-street, Spitalfields, *f*

Cawley, Drew and Reynalds, 90 Fore-street, and Little Moorfields
Chalfont Wm. 99 Gt. Tichfield-street, *a*
Clements John, 21 and 22 Little Pulteney-st
Cockayne H. 8 York-place, Walworth-road
Collier George, 15 Brownlow-street, Holborn
Collier George, 8 St. Dunstan's-ct. Fleet-st. *a*
Collins Wm. 8 Lovell's-ct. Paternoster-row
Cowan A. & Sons, Cannon-street West
Craggs Geo. F. 63 Basinghall-street, *f*
Creswick & Co. 5 John-street, Oxford-street
Cripps and Starkey, 24 Skinner-street
Crocker, Jonthn. & Co. 153 Up. Thames-st.
De La Rue and Co. 110 Bunhill-row
Dickinson John and Co. 65 Old Bailey, and 2 Irongate Wharf, 1 Praed-st, Paddington
Dixon, Marsden & Hale, 26 Budge-row
Dobbs, Kidd & Co. 134, Fleet-street
Dodds Thomas Joseph and Co. 4 Horseshoe-court, Ludgate-hill, *f.a*
Duggan C. S. 23 Alfred-pl, Nwngtn.-causeway
Dun and Duncan, 9 Fleet-st
Dyte and Son, 106 Strand
Evans and Co. 7 Oakley-terrace, Old Kent-rd.
Fisher Eden, 50 Lombard-street, *a*
Fitch W. 2 and 3 Old Fish-street-hill, Doctors' Commons
Foster Thos. 114 Union-street, Southwark
Fourdrinier, Hunt and Co. 12 Sherborne-lane
Fryer J. T. 23 Rupert-st, Goodman's-fields
Fuller B. and Co. 42 Brewer-st, Golden-sq.
Fuller H. and Co. 38 King-street, Cheapside
Gardner Edw. 45 Paddington-street
Gibbons and Roe, 17 Walbrook, City
Goodall C. & Son, 12 & 14 Gt. College-st. Camden-town, & 30 Gt. Pulteney-street
Grainger Arthur, 9 Holborn-bars, & 10 Fitzroy-terrace, New-road
Greenhill T. F. & Co. 26 Philpot-lane
Grimwade Chas. & Sam. 33 Cannon-street-w.
Grosvenor, Chater & Co. Cannon-street-west
Hammond R. J. 8½ Upper Queen's-buildings, Brompton, & 35 Edgw.-rd.
Harris J. E. & H. E. 21 Gt. Alie-street
Harris, Miller, & Co. 86, Queen-st. Cheapside
Harris Samuel, 83 Houndsditch
Harris Wm. 39 St. John-street, Clerkenwell
Harris Wm. Thos. 5 Queen-st. Cheapside *e*
Harwood John 26 Fenchurch-street, and 4 Rood-lane, *a*
Hatchett Chas. 34A Moorgate-street, City
Hawkings Jas. 5 Albion-pl. and Stamford-st. Blackfriars
Hawtin Wm. and Son, 28 Watling-street
Healey & Co. 9 Queenhithe, Up. Thames-st.
Herring, Dewick, & Hardy, 31 Walbrook
Heymanson Wm. 23 Coleman-street, City
Hodgkinson & Burnside, 50 Up. Thames-st.
Hodgkinson Sydney, 216A Up. Thames-st. *e*
Hodsdon Wm. 68 St. John-st. W. Smithfield
Hoe Wm. 18 Bishopsgate-street-without
Hogg John & Wm. 36 Friday-street, City
Holskamp Frederick, 1 Queenhithe
Hooper Stephen & Son, 45 Fleet-street
Hopkins J. 95 Lambeth Lower-marsh

Hopkins Thos. V. 42 & 43 Houndsditch, & 170 Fleet-street
Hudson Wm. & I. 26 Garlick-hill
Hunt, Heine & Co. 8 & 9 Weymouth-pl. New Kent-road
Hunt J. 34 & 35 Seacoal-la. Snow-hill, r
Imray James, 1 Circus, Minories, & 102 Min.
Jarvis Wm. 31 Norton-folgate, r
Job Alfred Mortimer, Cannon-street-west
Jones & Beck, 81 Cheapside, a
Jones Jas. 66 Lower Kennington-lane
Jones Mrs. P. 11 Red-lion-street, & 136 High-street, Wapping, r
Kirkman & Thrackray, 5 Old Fish-street
Levy John, 55 Houndsditch
Lewis M. A. & Co. 16 Camomile-street
Louis Chas. & Co. 6 Dowgate-hill, City
Lowe, Pewtress & Co. Gracechurch-street
Magnay & Bennets, 181 Upper Thames-street, & 11 College-hill
Magnus Samuel, 127 Fenchurch-street
Mansell Joseph, 9 & 10 Theobald's-rd. Blooms-bury, & 35 Red-lion-square
Marks H. 42 Gt. Alie-street, Goodman's-flds.
Marston E. 4 Cullum-street, City
Mason Robert, 3 Castle-street, Holborn
Matthews & Drew, 38 High Holborn
Mead & Powell, 101 Whitechapel High-street
Mead Henry, 63 Bishopsgate-street-without
Merrick John, 60 Watling-street, & 11 Cannon-street-west, City
Michel A. 32 London-st. Fitzroy-square, f
Millington & Hutton, 32 Budge-row, e
Morgan Charles & Co. Cannon-street-west, & Bull-wharf-lane, e.r
Morrell H. 149 Fleet-street, & 25 Gt. New-st.
Morrison William, 23 Fenchurch-street
Muggeridge, Sprague & Co. 61 Queen-street
Natowski Louis 111 London-wall
Newell Thos. F. 8 Cloak-lane, City
Newman, J. & Co. 48 Watling-street, City
Norris James, 207 Upper Thames-street
Norris J. T. 137 & 138 Aldersgate-street
Pamphilon and Brockwell, 64 Berwick-st. Soho
Paradise Benjamin, 40 Watling-street, City
Parkins and Gotto, 24 and 25 Oxford-st. and 58 Rathbone-place
Paxon Wm. 23 Skinner-street, Snow-hill
Pegg and Jackson, 20 Up. Ground-street, r
Penny Charles and Sons, 37 Bow-lane Cheap-side and 16 Cannon-street-west
Penny Henry, 11 Old Bailey, City, a
Perraton Jas. and Sam. 10 King-st. Snow-hill
Perryman Edward, 1 St. Swithin's-la.
Pewtress T. and Son, 67 Newington-causeway
Phelp Jas. 10 Change, East-road, City-road
Phipps John and Co. 176 Up. Thames-street
Phelps Geo. Hen. and A. London-wall, and 27 Martin's-la. Cannon-st.
Pinches T.R.&Co.27 Oxenden-st, Haymarket, e
Pollard George, 64 Watling-st. City, 9 Well-court, and 6 Charlotte-row, Walworth, e
Pope Henry, 22 Budge-row, and 36½ Percy-st. Bagnigge-wells-road
Pope John, 7 Dowgate-hill

Popkin Alfred E. 1 Old Fish-street
Poulter Thomas, 182 Upper Thames-street
Prince Geo. and John, 43 Watling-street
Pritchett T. 5 Windsor-pl. Old Kent-road, b
Pyke J. L. and S. 52 Great Prescot-street
Quaif William, 7 Coleman-street, City, a
Rands John, 21 Bread-street-hill
Raven John, 46 Fish-street-hill, and 3 Nag's-head-court, Gracechurch-street
Rhoads T. and Sons, 1 Vine-street, Minories
Richard John Edmund, 80 and 81 St. Martin's-lane, and 10 St. Martin's-court, e
Robinson & Todd, 79 Up. Thames-street
Rock Brothers & Payne, 11 Walbrook
Rodrigues Alfred, 73 Newgate-street
Row W. 28 Marlboro'-street, Regent-street
Royston & Brown, 40 & 41 O. Broad-st. City
Sanders H. & R. 7 & 8 Red-lion-ct. Fleet-st. f.e
Saunders John & Edward, 4 Cannon-street-west and 4 Budge-row, City
Saunders Thos. Harry, 10 Queenhithe & Maid-stone-wharf, Up. Thames-street
Schlesinger, Wells & Co. Albion-pl. Lond.-wall
Scroggie Wm. 1 Stone's-end, Borough
Shaw Edmund & Son, 124 Fenchurch-street
Shaw Mrs. Caroline E. 41 Tooley-street
Sheffield & Grimes, 77 Leadenhall-street and 75 St. George's-street a
Simmons J. & Co. 27 Artillery-lane, a
Simmons P. 34 St. Mary-axe
Smith John & Co. 52 Long-acre
Smith & Ebbs, 5 Postern-row, and 20 George-street, Tower-hill
Smith Thos. J. & Jos. 83 Queen-st. 14 Pan-cras-lane, City, and 30 Charterhouse-lane
Smith W. L. and Co. 32 James-st. Cov.-garden
Smith J. 42 Rathbone-place, Oxford-street, e
Somers and Isaacs, 67 Houndsditch
Spalding and Hodge, 145 to 147 Drury-lane
Spicer Brothers, 18½ and 19 New Bridge-st. Blackfriars
Stacy Robert S. 150 Shoreditch High-st. and 3 and 4 New-inn-yd. Shoreditch, f
Stanton Henry, 27 and 32 Noble-street, City
Sydenham D. 104 Gd. Junction-ter. Edgw.-rd.
Theobald Jas. and Co. 49 Watling-street, f.e
Thomas and Sons, 20 Cornhill
Thompson Jas. Berkley, 65 Long-acre
Thorp Chas. Barnham-street, Tooley-street
Tipper Benjamin, 11 Cloak-lane, City
Toovey and Wyatt, 75 to 77 Aldermanbury, a
Truscott J. 24 Nelson-sq. Blackfriars-rd. and 5 Suffolk-lane, Upper Thames-street
Tuck J. 160 Bishopsgate-street-without
Venables, Wilson, and Tyler, 17 Queenhithe, and Woking, Surrey
Ward B. 71 High-street, Boro
Weaklin F. Farringdon-street
Whitaker T. 10 Walbrook.
Wickwar Jno. 6 Poland-street, Oxford-street
Wiggins, Teape, Carter, and Barlow, 10 & 11 Aldgate, City.
Wightman S. 10 Regent-street, Westminster
Wilkinson, Poington, and Co. 3 Joiners'-hall-buildings, Up. Thames-street

Williams and Co. 3 and 4 Weymouth-pl. Old Kent-road
Williams, Cooper, and Co. 85 West Smithfield
Wills J. A. 18 Whiskin-st. Clerkenwell, *f. sta.*
Willis, Newgate-street.
Wilson T. and Sons, 103 to 105 Cheapside, *g.a*
Wilson W. 82 Hatton-garden, *e.a*
Wodderspoon J. 16 and 17 Portugal-street
Wood, Thos. 24 Milk-st. and Godfrey-ct. Ch.
Wrigley Jas. and Son, Cannon-street, Agent, Mr. Tibbetts

TYPE FOUNDERS.

Besley R. and Co. Fann-st. Aldersgate-street
Blunt E. 15 Mitchell-street, St. Luke's
Caslon H. W. and Co. 22 Chiswell-street
Chamberlain T. 32 Caroline-street, Lambeth

Chambers G. and Co. Gough-square
Constance F. John-street, Clerkenwell
Figgins, V. and J. 17 West Smithfield
Leighton Brothers (copper) 4 Led-lion-square
Marr Jas. and Co. 3 Upper Wellington-street
Miller and Richards, 22 Bartlett's-buildings
Morgan, S. 26 New-street, Smithfield
Orchard and Co. Farringdon-street, patent for copper-facing type (*see advertisement*)
Palmer H. W. 6 West-street, St..Ann's
Pavyer B. 31 Bartholomew-close
Pepper, Thos. 21 Richard-terrace, St. Luke's
Sharwood S. and T. 20 Aldersgate-street
Simmons J. and Co. 14 Newcastle-st. Farringdon-street
Sinclair and Sons, 48A Paternoster-row
Soult Chas. 10 Maidenhead-ct. Aldersgate-st.
Watts W. M. 12 Crown-court, Temple-bar

LIST OF MONTHLY PUBLICATIONS, &c.

Alison's Europe, Part
———— ——— Atlas
Appeal (The)
Archæologia Cambrensis
Army List
Artizan
Art-Journal
Athenæum, Part
Band of Hope Review
Banker's Magazine
Baptist Children's Magazine
——— Church, 1d
——— Magazine
——— Missionary Herald
——— Reporter and Tract Mag.
Bell's English Poets
Bentley's Miscellany
——— Monthly Volumes
Bible and the People
——— Class Magazine
Bibliotheca Sacra
Biographical Magazine
Blackwood's Magazine
Bond of Brotherhood
Botanical Magazine (Curtis's)
Boy's Own Magazine
British & Foreign Medico-Rev.
——— Controversialist
——— Mother's Magazine
——— Quarterly Review
——— Workman
Buds and Blossoms
Builder, Part
Bulwark (The)
Burn's Magazine for the Young
Cassell's Family Paper, Part
Chambers's Edinb. Journal, Part

Chemist
Chess-Player's Chronicle
Child's Companion
——— Missionary News
——— Own Magazine
Children's Friend
——— Jewish Advocate
——— Magazine, by Winks
——— Missionary Magazine
Christian Ladies' Magazine
——— Miscellany
——— Observer
——— Penny Magazine
——— Pioneer, ¼d
——— Reformer
——— Remembrancer, 6s
——— Spectator
——— Treasury
——— Witness
Christian's Companion
Church of England Magazine
——— ——— Quarterly Review
——— ——— Sunday Scholar
——— ——— S.S. Quarterly, 1s
——— the People
——— Missionary Gleaner
——— ——— Intelligencer
·——— ——— Juvenile, ½d.
——— ——— Record
Churchman's Compan. (Masters)
——— Magazine, 1s
——— Penny Magazine
City Mission Magazine
Civil Engineer and Architect's Journal
Colonial Church Chronicle
Copland's Dictionary of Medicine

Cottage Gardener, Part
Cottager's Monthly Visitor
Cumming's New Test. Readings
——— Old Test. Readings
——— Urgent Questions
Cyclopædia of Anatomy
Day Star
Dew-Drop
Dictionary Greek & Rom. Geog.
Dublin Medical Journal
——— Review
——— University Magazine
Early Days
Earthen Vessel
Ecclesiastic
Ecclesiologist
Eclectic Review
Edinburgh Medical Journal
——— Philosophical Journal
——— Review
Educational Expositor
Educational Gazette
Encyclopædia Britannica, Part
English Cyclopædia, Part
——— Journal of Education
Englishwoman's Domestic Magazine, 2d
Enquire Within
Evangelical Christendom
——— Magazine
Excelsior
Family Economist
——— Friend
——— Herald, Part
Farmer's Magazine
Female Missionary Intelligencer
Floricultural Cabinet (Harrison's)

Follet (Le)
Fraser's Magazine
Freemason's Monthly Review
Friendly Visitor
General Baptist Repository
Gentleman's Magazine
——————————— of Fashions
——————— Herald of Fashion
Gospel Herald
——————— Magazine
——————— Missionary, ½d.
——————— Standard
Governess
Harbinger (The)
Harry Coverdale's Courtship
Herald of Peace
Hogg's Instructor
Holland's Scrip. Expositor, No.
Home Companion, Part
—————— Friend, Part
—————— Thoughts
Homilist
Household Narrative
Household Words, Part
Illustrated Byron, Part
——————— London Magazine
Index to the Times
Intellectual Repository
Jardine'sAnnals of Natural Hist.
Jewish Herald
——————— Intelligence
Johnston's Chem. of Geolog.Life
Journal of Eng.AgriculturalSoc.
——————— Geological Society
——————— Photographic Society
——————— Sacred Literature
Juvenile (The)
——————— Missionary Herald, ½d.
Juvenile Missionary Mag. ½d.
Ladies' Cabinet of Fashion
——————— Companion
——————— Gazette of Fashion
Lamp of Love
Lancet, No.   to
Law Journal
—————— Magazine
—————— Review
Leisure Hour, Part
Leonard and Dennis
Library of Biblical Literature
Literary Gazette, Part
Local Preacher
London and Paris Fashions
——————— Journal, Part
——————— Quarterly Review
Martins of Cro-Martin

Masonic Mirror
Mechanics' Magazine Part
Medical Times & Gazette, Part
Methodist Magazine, 1s
——————————— abridged, 6d.
Midland Florist
Millennial Harbinger
Missionary Magazine, 1d.
——————— Register
Montgomery'sPoetical Wks.Vol.
Monthly Belle Assemblée
——————— Journ. of Med. Science
——————— Messenger
——————— Packet of Even. Read.
——————— Record Soc.Prop.Gosp.
Morris's British Birds, 1s.
——————— Game Birds
——————— Naturalist
——————— Nidification
Mother's Magazine
——————— Friend
Museum of Science and Art.Part
Musical Times
National Illustrated Library
——————— Miscellany
——————— Review
——————— Society's Paper
——————— Temperance Chronicle
Nautical Magazine
Navy List
New Monthly Magazine
—— Quarterly Review, 2s 6d
—— Sporting Magazine
—— Army List, by Hart
—— Navy List, 7s. 6d.
Newcomes, by Thackeray
Newton's Journal of Arts
North British Review
Notes and Queries, Part
—— on Scripture Lessons
O'Byrne's Monthly Navy List
Old (The) Church Porch
Olive Leaf
Orr's Circle of the Sciences, Part
Papers for Schoolmasters
Parlour Library
——————————— cloth
Penny Post
Pharmaceutical Journal
Philanthropist (The)
Philosophical Magazine
Phonographic Correspondent
——————— Reporter
Pictorial Bible, Part
——————— England, Part
——————— Pages

Popular Biblical Educator
——————— Educator, Fine
Practical Mechanics' Journal
— Sermons on CharactersO.Tes.
Presbyterian Messenger
Primitive Church
Prospective Review
Protestant Magazine
Pulpit (The), Part
Punch, Part
Quarterly Review
——————— Journal of Agriculture
——————— Prophecy
———-Jl. Microseopical Science
Ragged School Union
——————— Children's, ½d.
Railway Library
Rambler (The)
Repertory of Arts
Reynolds's Miscellany, Part
Rowe's Monthly Pulpit
Sailor's Magazine
School (The) and the Teacher
Servant's Magazine
Sharpe's London Magazine
ShortSermonsforFamilyReading
Sporting Magazine
——————— Review
Sportsman (The)
Stories & Lessons on Catechism
Sunday School Teacher's Mag.
——————— Penny (Whitfield)
——————— Scholar's Companion
Sunday at Home, Part
Tait's Edinburgh Magazine
Tales for Young Men and Women
Teacher's Offering
Thirlwall's(Bp.)Hist.Greece,Vol
Townsend's Costumes
Tract Magazine
Traveller's Library, No
——————————— Vol.
Turner's Florist, &c.
Union Magazine for Teachers
United Service Magazine
Veterinarian
Waverley Novels, 1s. 6d.
Wesleyan Methodist Penny Mag.
Westminster Review
Winslow's Psychological Journ.
World of Fashion
Youth's Magazine
——————— Instructor
Zion's Trumpet
Zoist
Zoologist

Booksellers, &c., whose names arrived too late for insertion in their proper places.

Braun, A. and Wustlich, 2, Bury-court, St. Mary Axe
Gibson, W. F., Longton, Nottingham
Harris, Ben. (binder and printer), Hilperton-road, Trowbridge, Wilts
Land, Jas. and Co. (late Cole and Land, wholesale stationers and booksellers), 18, George-street, Plymouth
Plaxton, James, 51, Longate, Hull
Trundle, J. S., Market Drayton

THE EVIDENCE OF PRACTICAL PRINTERS
IS AS FOLLOWS :—

74, 75, GREAT QUEEN STREET,
LINCOLN'S INN FIELDS,
September 12th, 1854.

GENTLEMEN,

We have now had your Copper-faced Type, to the extent of about 5,000 lbs. weight, in use for some twenty months or more, in printing " The Builder," " Eliza Cook's Journal," and in the Railway Library of Messrs. Routledge and Co., and other works in which large impressions have been required, and we are entirely satisfied with the result. In printing, the work is certainly delivered cleaner, and, no doubt, a considerable advantage is experienced where Stereotype Plates are required to be cast from the fount.

Very respectfully yours,
COX BROTHERS & WYMAN,

MESSRS. ORCHARD & CO. *Printers to the Hon. E. I. Company.*

THE BIBLE OFFICE, SHACKLEWELL,
April 24, 1855.

GENTLEMEN,

We feel great pleasure in saying, from our long experience of the use of our Type and Stereotype Plates faced with Copper by your process, that we consider their durability has been very considerably increased, and have found great value therefrom in preserving the sharpness and beauty of the type from the wear consequent on the Stereotyping process. We also consider it of great value to the trade, and can bear testimony to its advanced state of perfection, both as regards durability, texture, and evenness of surface, together with the valuable improvement of surfacing, or coating the copper with silver, thereby preventing all fear of corrosion. Yours faithfully,

MESSRS. ORCHARD & CO. EYRE & SPOTTISWOODE.

BOLT COURT, FLEET STREET,
September 12th, 1854.

GENTLEMEN,

I have much pleasure in expressing my opinion, that there is a great advantage in the use of Copper-faced Type, especially for works having a large circulation. I have had a fount of Copper-faced Type in use for upwards of twelve months. It has been found *to deliver the ink more freely* than ordinary type, and requires *much less ink.* It also wears much longer. I am, Gentlemen, yours very faithfully,

MESSRS. ORCHARD & CO. WILLIAM TYLER.

London Gazette Office.   HARRISON & SONS' PRINTING OFFICE,
45, ST. MARTIN'S-LANE,
April 21, 1855.

GENTLEMEN,

Having now had in use nearly three years Type Copper-faced by your process, we have great pleasure in saying, that we have found it to preserve the original sharpness and form of the letter, and works very clean, especially the smaller founts, nonpareil and pearl. We have used our Copper-faced founts both for Printing and Stereotyping.

Yours faithfully,

MESSRS. ORCHARD & CO. HARRISON & SONS.

PAUL'S WORK, EDINBURGH,
November 25, 1854.

GENTLEMEN,

Having now had considerable experience in your method of coating Types and Stereotype Plates with Copper, we have no hesitation in expressing our warmest approval of the same We are, &c.,

MESSRS. ORCHARD & CO. BALLANTYNE & CO.

STEAM PRINTING OFFICE,
5, GRAYSTOKE PLACE, FETTER LANE,
January 10th, 1854.

GENTLEMEN,

I have printed 538,000 impressions from a sheet of Copper-faced Stereo, and have had only to renew a small number of plates. I consider that Copper-faced Plates are better calculated to bear half a million copies taken from them than uncoppered to stand the working of a fifth of that number. You can refer any printer to me for a view of the plates.

I am, Gentlemen, yours obediently,
SAMUEL TAYLOR.

MESSRS. ORCHARD, WILLIS, & CO.

PATERNOSTER ROW,
June 29th, 1855.

GENTLEMEN,

Though we have not subjected your Copper-facing to any very severe pressure of long numbers, yet we are satisfied of its value, having used the same for twenty months; and we now uniformly have our new founts faced by your process.

We are, yours faithfully,

MESSRS. ORCHARD & Co.   REED & PARDON.

BEAUFORT BUILDINGS PRINTING OFFICE, STRAND,
September 12th, 1854.

GENTLEMEN,

After having used your Copper-facing on type and plates for more than eighteen months, I am fully prepared to state the following are among the many advantages of Copper-faced type:—The greater facility of stereotyping from Copper-faced type, and producing better-faced plates; the picking being greatly diminished. In composing, the greater facility of distinguishing the letters, *especially by night:* in printing, its working cleaner, and producing a better colour with less ink. Its durability is increased at least three or four-fold.

I am, Gentlemen, yours, &c.,

MESSRS. ORCHARD & Co.   CHARLES WHITING.

STEWART & MURRAY'S PRINTING OFFICE,
15, OLD BAILEY, LONDON,
September 12th, 1854.

GENTLEMEN,

Having now had sufficient time to test the character of your process of Copper-facing, we beg to state that we consider it not only of great efficiency in preserving the type, but also in giving off a cleaner and sharper impression in working. The practice you have lately adopted, of covering the Copper with a coating of Silver, must materially enhance the value of your principle, for, whilst the advantage of the durability of the Copper is obtained, the action of the ley upon it is entirely prevented by the application of the Silver.

We are, Gentlemen, yours, &c.,

MESSRS. ORCHARD & Co.   STEWART & MURRAY.

GENERAL STEAM PRINTING OFFICE,
BOUVERIE STREET, FLEET STREET,
August 19th, 1853.

DEAR SIRS,

Your system of Copper-facing Type has my entire approval. For Machine Printing its hardness is of essential advantage, effecting the delivery of ink to the paper with great facility and clearness, yielding a bright colour with less ink than is ordinarily required, and thereby decreasing the setting-off. To say nothing of its increased durability, I regard the *sharp beauty of the impression* obtainable from Copper-faced Type of *sufficient importance* to me for adopting its use. I am, your obedient Servant,

MESSRS. ORCHARD, WILLIS, & Co.   FREDERICK SALISBURY.

---

11 & 12, NORTHAMPTON SQUARE,
September 19th, 1854.

GENTLEMEN,

Having for some time past used your Copper-faced Metal for Colour Printing, I have great pleasure in bearing my testimony to its many advantages over Electrotype, which I formerly used, but have now abandoned, much preferring your process.

Yours obediently,

MESSRS. ORCHARD & Co.   GEORGE BAXTER.

4, RED LION SQUARE,
September 16th, 1854.

DEAR SIRS,

Your Copper and Silver-facing is an invaluable acquisition to Letter-press and Block Colour Printers. It enables the Stereotyper to obtain beautiful casts, without damaging the face of the letter, as formerly. We also consider it enhances the value of the type or plate at least *five times* that of ordinary type. We have given it a most severe trial by printing on cloth with a stout thread, and the durability of the letter is quite astonishing.

In colour printing it gives the power of producing effects to *a great number of impressions,* which cannot be done in stereotype without the aid of your process.

Respectfully yours,

MESSRS. ORCHARD & Co.   LEIGHTON BROTHERS.

GOUGH SQUARE,
July 3rd, 1855.

GENTLEMEN,

I have been for some time past in the habit of using Copper-faced Type, and my opinion is strongly in its favour. Two works with which I am connected are regularly printed from it—the " Illustrated Byron," and " The Illustrated Times ;" and as with both of these, and particularly the latter, the number printed is very large, I think they furnish satisfactory opportunities of testing its advantages.

MESSRS. ORCHARD & CO.

HENRY VIZETELLY.

LONDON JOURNAL OFFICE, 334, STRAND,
August 10th, 1853.

This is to certify that the Copper-faced Type, now in use for printing the " London Journal," has given me the greatest satisfaction; for the Type has not only maintained its original sharpness and beauty, but has been made at least THREE TIMES MORE DURABLE. I have had over **FIFTEEN MILLIONS** of impressions from this font, which was new in August, 1852.

G. STIFF, PROPRIETOR.

The Patentees have lately Copper-faced a THIRD *fount of Type for " The London Journal."*— *January*, 1855.

WORKS PRINTED FROM COPPER-FACED TYPE.

ENGLAND.

THE LONDON JOURNAL.

THE ILLUSTRATED TIMES.

THE FIELD.

THE BUILDER.

THE SUNDAY TIMES.

DIOGENES.

HOME NEWS FOR INDIA.

THE ENGLISH CYCLOPEDIA.

SUSSEX ADVERTISER.

NOTTINGHAM JOURNAL.

THE LEADER.

PUNCH, OR LONDON CHARIVARI.

AMERICA.

NEW YORK TRIBUNE.

NEW YORK HERALD.

NEW YORK SUN.

MORNING COURIER & ENQUIRER.

NEW YORK EXPRESS.

NEW YORK JOURNAL.

AMERICAN MESSENGER.

BOSTON JOURNAL.

BOSTON COMMONWEALTH.

BOSTON HERALD.

BOSTON TRANSCRIPT.

BOSTON POST.

FRANCE.

LA REVUE DES DEUX MONDES. GALIGNANI'S MESSENGER.

LES ROMANS POPULAIRES ILLUSTRÉS.

MESSRS. ORCHARD & CO. (the Patentees of the Copper-faced Type, &c.), beg to call your attention to the *present* condition of the Type used on " PUNCH," which was Copper-faced by them for that publication in December, 1852. Since that time between 40,000 and 50,000 copies have been printed *weekly*, under a cylinder machine ; in addition to which, *each* number, when worked off, was Stereotyped. This gives an aggregate of upwards of

6,000,000 Impressions Printed from the Type,

exclusive of the forms having been Stereotyped upwards of ONE HUNDRED AND TWENTY TIMES.

WHITEFRIARS, *July 30th*, 1853.

GENTLEMEN,

We have much pleasure in bearing testimony to the advantages derivable from the use of Copper-faced Type and Stereotype Plates, combining, as far as our experience enables us to judge, *preservation of surface, sharpness of impression, and increased facility and economy in working.* We remain, Gentlemen,

Your obedient Servants,

BRADBURY & EVANS.

MESSRS. ORCHARD, WILLIS, & CO.

July 2, 1855.

TAYLOR & GREENING, Printers, Graystoke Place, Fetter Lane, London.

Ralph's Registered Envelope Paper,

Registered 6 & 7 Vic. cap. 65, *July* 16, 1855,

AFFORDING

VE DISTINCT PAGES FOR CORRESPONDENCE,

EACH 5½ BY 8 INCHES.

IS REGISTERED PAPER is already prepared for use; having been first carefully
ased and afterwards pressed quite smooth for Writing, each sheet will form readily
its own Envelope,

SELF-SEALING AND PERFECTLY SECURE,

Price 11s. 6d. *per Ream.*

is Paper is admirably adapted for FOREIGN, INDIAN, and COLONIAL patronage,
The Weight being under a Quarter of an Ounce.

Ralph's Envelope Paper

AT REDUCED PRICES.

F. W. RALPH respectfully draws attention to this particular Paper, to which he has
ʋoted much attention; and begs to announce that he is enabled, by having Papers
ʋressly manufactured, to make a very

IMPORTANT REDUCTION IN PRICE.

Superfine Satin . . . . . . **5s. per Ream.**
(A very strong paper and thin.) (*The mere price of postage envelopes, less stamp.*)

Superfine Middle Satin . . . **8s. per Ream.**
(An excellent medium paper.)

Superfine Thick Cream Laid
(An improved quality.) }
Superfine Thick Blue Laid } **9s. 6d. per Ream.**
Superfine Thick Blue Wove }
Superfine Foreign

Ralph's Sermon Paper,

PECIALLY MANUFACTURED FOR THE PURPOSE,

SIZE OF PAGE, 5¾ BY 9 INCHES.

Price 5s. *per ream, or Ruled as required* 6s. *per ream.*

Sermon Cases, Black Roan, 2s.; Black Spanish Morocco, 3s. 6d. each.

F. W. RALPH,
MANUFACTURING STATIONER,
36, THROGMORTON STREET, LONDON.

BOHN'S LIBRARIES.

RECENT VOLUMES.

STANDARD LIBRARY.—3s. 6d. per volume.

113. **History of Russia from the earliest period to the present time,** compiled from the most authentic sources, including KARASMIN, TOOKE, and SEGUR, WALTER K. KELLY. In two vols. Vol. II, *with General Index, and fine portraits of Emperor Nicholas and Prince Mentschikoff.*

114. **Goethe's Wilhelm Meister's Apprenticeship,** a Novel, translated by R. BOYLAN. Complete in one vol.

BRITISH CLASSICS.—3s. 6d. per volume.

14. **Gibbon's Roman Empire;** complete and unabridged, with variorum Notes including, in addition to all the Author's own, those of Guizot, Wenck, Niebuhr, Hugo Neander, and other foreign scholars. Edited by an ENGLISH CHURCHMAN. In seven volumes, with *portrait and maps.* Vol 6.

16. **Addison's Works, with the Notes of Bishop Hurd.** New edition, which is added upwards of 100 UNPUBLISHED LETTERS. *Portrait and eight engraving on steel.* Vol. 4.

17. **Defoe's Works, edited by Sir Walter Scott.** Vol. IV, containing Roxana or the Fortunate Mistress; and Life and Adventures of Mother Ross.

18. **Burke's Works.** Vol. III, containing his Appeal from the New to the Old Whigs; the Nabob of Arcot's Debts; the Catholic Claims; etc.

CLASSICAL LIBRARY.—5s. per volume.

65. **Suetonius, Lives of the Twelve Cæsars, and other Works.** The translation of THOMSON, revised, with Notes, by T. FORESTER, Esq.

66. **Demosthenes' Orations on the Crown and on the Embassy.** By C. RANN KENNEDY, Esq.

67. **Pliny's Natural History,** translated, with copious Notes, by the late JOHN BOSTOCK M.D., and H. T. RILEY, Esq. Vol. II.

PHILOLOGICAL LIBRARY.—5s. per volume.

5. **Kant's Critique of Pure Reason,** translated by J. M. D. MEIKLEJOHN.

ILLUSTRATED LIBRARY.—5s. per volume.

32. **Nicolini's History of the Jesuits.** *Portraits of Loyala, Lainèz, Xavier, Borgia Aquaviva, Père la Chaise, Ricci, and Pope Ganganelli.*

33. **Robinson Crusoe,** with Illustrations by STOTHARD & HARVEY, 12 beautiful engravings on steel, and 74 on wood.

ANTIQUARIAN LIBRARY.—5s. per volume.

33. **Marco Polo's Travels,** the translation of Marsden, edited by T. WRIGHT.

34. **Florence of Worcester's Chronicle,** comprising Annals of English History the Reign of Edward 1, by THOS. FORESTER, Esq.

35. **Hand-Book of Proverbs,** comprising an entire republication of Ray's Collection English Proverbs, and a complete Alphabetical Index, in which are introduced large Additions, edited by HENRY G. BOHN.

SCIENTIFIC LIBRARY.—5s. per volume.

35. **Hand-Book of Domestic Medicine;** popularly arranged. By an EMINENT PHYSICIAN. 700 pages, with a complete Index.

36. **A Classified Synopsis of the Principal Painters of the Dutch & Flemish SCHOOLS.** By GEORGE STANLEY.

37. **Prout's Bridgewater Treatise on Chemistry, Meteorology, and the FUNCTION of DIGESTION.**

FRENCH MEMOIRS.—3s. 6d. per volume.

1. **Memoirs of Philip de Commines.** To which is added, The Scandalous Chronicle or Secret History of Louis XI. Edited by A. R. SCOBLE, Esq. In two vols. Vol. I *portrait of Charles the Bold.*

EXTRA VOLUMES.—3s. 6d. per volume.

6. **Cervantes' Exemplary Novels.** To which are added, El Buscapié, or, The Serpent La Tia Fingida, or, The Pretended Aunt. Translated from the Spanish by WALTER K. KELLY. Complete in one volume, *with portrait of Cervantes.*

7. **The Heptameron of Margaret, Queen of Navarre,** a Series of Tales in the manner of Boccacio, translated from the French, with a Memoir of the Author by W. K. KELLY, *and fine portrait.*

CHEAP SERIES.

46. **Irving's Wolfert's Roost, and other Tales,** complete in one vol. fcap 8vo. *bds* 1s.—Or, ON FINE PAPER, in post 8vo, *with portrait of the Author* (printed uniform with the copyright edition of Irving's Works), bds. 1s. 6d.

47. **Irving's Life of Washington,** AUTHORIZED EDITION (uniform with Bohn's edition of the complete Works). Vol. I, containing his Early Life, Expeditions into the Wilderness, and Campaigns on the Border. Post 8vo. *fine portrait,* bds. 2s. 6d.

HENRY G. BOHN, YORK STREET, COVENT GARDEN.